W9-AGZ-586

ITALIAN BAROQUE AND ROCOCO ARCHITECTURE

ITALIAN BAROQUE AND ROCOCO ARCHITECTURE

John Varriano

New York · Oxford
OXFORD UNIVERSITY PRESS
1986

Oxford University Press

Oxford   New York   Toronto
Delhi   Bombay   Calcutta   Madras   Karachi
Petaling Jaya   Singapore   Hong Kong   Tokyo
Nairobi   Dar es Salaam   Cape Town
Melbourne   Auckland

and associated companies in
Beirut   Berlin   Ibadan   Nicosia

Copyright © 1986 by Oxford University Press, Inc.

Published by Oxford University Press, Inc.,
200 Madison Avenue, New York, New York 10016

Oxford is a registered trademark of Oxford University Press

All rights reserved. No part of this publication may be reproduced,
stored in a retrieval system, or transmitted, in any form or by any means,
electronic, mechanical, photocopying, recording, or otherwise,
without the prior permission of Oxford University Press.

Library of Congress Cataloging in Publication Data
Varriano, John L.
    Italian baroque and rococo architecture.
    Bibliography: p.
    Includes index.
    1. Architecture, Baroque—Italy.
    2. Architecture, Rococo—Italy.
    3. Architecture—Italy. I. Title.
NA1116.V37   1986   720'.945   85–2902
ISBN 0–19–503547–X
ISBN 0–19–503548–8 (pbk.)

Printing: (last digit): 9 8 7 6 5 4 3

Printed in the United States of America
on acid free paper

To my mother and father

Acknowledgments

For various kindnesses, courtesies, and encouragements given at critical points along the way, I would like to thank Joseph Connors, William Durfee, Dorothy M. Habel, Hellmut Hager, T. Kaori Kitao, Thomas Kren, William MacDonald, Peter Murray, Mary Myers, Ursula F. Pace, Valentino Pace, John Pinto, Nan Plummer, Michael Stoughton, and my first teacher of Baroque architecture, Nathan Whitman. Special thanks must also go to Tod Marder whose careful reading of the entire manuscript led to improvements in a number of factual and interpretive passages. In addition, I would like to acknowledge the assistance given by the staff of the Bibliotheca Hertziana, Rome, Kevin Wilson, who drafted the ground plans, and those who had a share in printing my uneven photographic negatives—Elmont Abbot, Linda Callahan, Thomas Jacob, and Michael Zide. I am also sincerely grateful to the Samuel H. Kress Foundation which funded the printing of those photographs and the drawing of the ground plans, and to the trustees of Mount Holyoke College, whose repeated Faculty Grants assisted my research in a number of important ways. Finally, a personal *ringraziamento* must go to my wife, Wendy Watson, for her unflagging encouragement and assistance throughout all phases of the project. Her special flair for diverting the attention of suspicious or loquacious building custodians made visits to countless monuments more profitable and enjoyable than they otherwise would have been.

Contents

ITALIAN BAROQUE AND ROCOCO ARCHITECTURE

Turin
Milan
Crema
Venice
Bra
Genoa
Bologna
Florence
Rome
Caserta
Naples
Avellino
Lecce
Palermo
Catania
Siracuse
Ragusa Ibla
Noto

BAROQUE SITES
IN ITALY

1

Introduction

"Capricious and bizarre" were the words used by a popular seventeenth-century Roman guidebook to describe buildings that today we call Baroque. Later critics wrote of such buildings in even harsher terms. Francesco Borromini, one of the most progressive of Baroque architects, was accused of trying to "debauch mankind with his odd and chimerical beauties," and equally acerbic comments and unflattering assessments prevailed in the literature until the beginning of the twentieth century. Even then, expressions like "rough, rude, and uncouth" were still applied to structures of similar character. Undoubtedly, it was the self-assured, at times flamboyant way in which the design of many Baroque buildings violated the cherished canons of classical architecture that disturbed most critics. To those raised in other faiths, the predominant associations of Italian art with institutions of post-Reformation Catholicism could be just as offensive. Only in our own secular age, now as weary with modernist reduction as with premodern censures against flaunting accepted conventions, have students of architecture become sympathetically attentive to the imaginative solutions of the Italian Baroque.

The origin of the word Baroque is so steeped in confusion as to be itself the subject of a growing scholarly literature.[1] Only in the last century has it been freed from its traditional associations with speciousness and a lack of refinement. Like Gothic, which had long been synonymous with barbaric but which now usefully describes the art of the late Middle Ages, Baroque has become the most widely accepted designation for the period-style that prevailed in Europe from the end

3

of the Renaissance to the beginnings of the modern age—in Italy, roughly from 1600 to 1750.

Nonetheless, some scholars still feel uneasy about using the term. Historians of the visual arts, conscious of the lack of stylistic and expressive homogeneity in works of the period, find that no single label can describe adequately the diversity of artistic practice. Attempts to distinguish between the exuberant, genuine Baroque and a more restrained "Baroque Classicism" have met with skepticism, but in dismissing this oversimplification, critics ignore the consistency, if not the virtual independence of two coexisting expressive modes.[2] An alternative perhaps would be to call these two stylistic trends of seventeenth-century architecture "progressive" and "conservative." In each, there are strong classicizing elements, but in the former there is a greater determination to break decisively with the established methods of the Renaissance. Accordingly, the conservative trend emphasizes a greater sense of calm, idealized form, while the progressive tends toward a more individual, impassioned expression. Nowhere are these opposing tendencies more vividly juxtaposed than in the careers of the Roman architects Gianlorenzo Bernini and Francesco Borromini. If we call them both Baroque artists, it is as much for their having worked at the same time as for their essential similarity of style. Here, flexibility in the use of the term leads to a certain conceptual imprecision. The recent publication of Margaret Lyttleton's book *Baroque Architecture in Classical Antiquity* and Eugenio d'Ors' assertion earlier this century that the Baroque style was a recurrent phenomenon that has occurred twenty-two times since antiquity only adds to the confusion.[3]

What then is Baroque beyond its meaning as a periodic designation? The more progressive seventeenth- and early eighteenth-century buildings do share some features that differ, sometimes superficially, but at times radically from more conservative works: a fondness for complex, often centralized ground plans; an increasing tendency toward greater height, eventually establishing the dome rather than the high altar as the physical and spiritual focus; the love of curved wall planes, of projecting columns rather than flat pilasters, and of rhythmic bay arrangements; controlled illumination; a fusion of sculpture with architecture; a sensitivity to site and location; and a coextensive space that actively engages the sensory perceptions of the spectator.

It has been said that, above all, Baroque architecture is rhetorical, and there is little doubt that the primary intent of many buildings was to persuade.[4] Churches constructed in the post-Counter-Reformation era were intended to overpower all who entered with a dramatic spectacle that, in Bernini's own words "would reach out to Catholics in order to reaffirm their faith, to heretics to reunite them with the church, and to agnostics to enlighten them with the true faith."[5] Seldom has the rhetoric defending the goals of the church been so feverishly pitched. Paralleling Dryden's concept of heroic drama, Baroque architects believed that the most powerful and energetic works of art induce strong passions capable of transporting one's soul into a higher realm. If Renaissance architecture was to be contemplated on an intellectual level, Baroque architecture was to be experienced with the emotions and the senses. When Mary Shelley wrote "in the churches you hear the music of Heaven and the singing of angels," she had obviously come under this spell. The great patrons and builders of the period clearly understood the propaganda value of architectural grandiloquence: "Those who imagine," Louis XIV remarked, "that these [works of art] are merely matters of ceremony are gravely mistaken. The peoples over whom we reign, being unable to apprehend the basic reality of things, usually derive their opinions from what they can see with their eyes." Gregory the Great's dictum of a thousand years earlier that art served as the "books of the illiterate" had never been so resoundingly confirmed.

Needless to say, the love of material splendor for its own sake may have compromised the pious intentions of some rich and influential patrons. Was the prior of the Roman church of S. Carlo alle Quattro Fontane being disingenuous when he expressed the wish to have the church "made richer than Solomon's Temple, with a pavement of emeralds and precious stones, since exterior splendor expresses an interior love of God, and since nothing could be excessive when it came to God's House?" Nineteenth-century visitors from the Protestant countries may not have been completely wrong when they viewed, as they usually did, the most richly decorated Baroque churches in such a cynical light.[6]

Because of its successive phases of stylistic development, Italian Baroque architecture has usually been classified as Early, High, and Late. The Early phase corresponds to the period from about 1590 to 1625, High from about 1625 to 1680, and Late from about 1680 to 1750. Of these, the Late phase is the most problematic, for it encompasses a broader range of stylistic alternatives than the simple progressive/conservative or Classical/Baroque dialectic of the earlier stages. By the second quarter of the eighteenth century, three competing styles existed, and the split between them was, in some quarters at least, characterized by greater polemic. For its part, the conservative trend of the seventeenth century continued and became increasingly theoretical and rigid under the aegis of the Accademia di S. Luca, the long-inactive artists' academy in Rome which was to achieve international influence in the eighteenth century. The main opposition was the refined and ornamental style that came to be known as the Rococo, because of its original association with French *rocaille,* pebble or shell work. In Italy the Rococo was derived mostly from the earlier decorative vocabulary of Borromini, who, ironically, exerted little influence in his own day. A third style—which was almost exclusively limited to the provinces, and which, while powerful, usually betrays a provincial lack of sophistication—may be called the Ultra-Baroque because of its tendency toward dramatic self-representation.[7] These distinct styles, which all flourished at about the same time, are exemplified by Galilei's severe Lateran facade (104), Raguzzini's playful Piazza di S. Ignazio (99), and Dotti's theatrical Arco del Meloncello (159)—three buildings that show how difficult it is to draw general conclusions about early eighteenth-century style.

Architectural Practice and Theory

It was during the Renaissance that architects, painters and sculptors were first regarded as intellectuals rather than as mere craftsmen, even though few of them were actually versed in the liberal arts. The training of an architect had little in common with today's practice, and schools of architecture in the modern sense did not come into existence for another couple of centuries. There were professional standards however. In Milan, for example, the College of Architects and Engineers issued a set of rules in 1563 governing admission to the trade. A four-year apprenticeship was required of each applicant, who was also expected to be "an honorable person, born of good parents, who believed in God and regularly received the sacraments."[8] From the end of the sixteenth century, the Academy of St. Luke in Rome also served as a professional society, although its standards for admission, especially when it came to apprenticeships or professional experience, were not so strict. Ironically, while it was easier for women to join than men—just a simple majority vote rather than two-thirds of the membership was required—only one woman architect, Plautilla Bricci, achieved a reputation that survives to the present day. Throughout Italy, aspiring architects received their training on the job—either by working in an architect's studio or, as was more common earlier in the Baroque period, by rising through the ranks in the building trades. Domenico Fontana, Giacomo della Porta, and Baldassare Longhena, for example, followed the latter route, while Carlo Maderno, Carlo Fontana, and Filippo Juvarra began their careers as shop assistants of established architects. The Renaissance tradition of the amateur architect, especially one trained in another art like painting or sculpture, also continued into the seventeenth century: Pietro da Cortona, Gianlorenzo Bernini, and Guarino Guarini were among those who, in that less technological age, received no formal training.

In most parts of Italy, local architects satisfied local building needs, but in Rome, which had a surprising lack of indigenous artistic talent, the architectural and building trades tended to be dominated throughout the seventeenth century by family dynasties originating on the Lombard-Swiss border. One of the most illustrious of these was the line that began with Domenico Fontana, continued with his nephew Carlo Maderno and Maderno's great-nephew Francesco Borromini, and ended with their still more distant relative Carlo Fontana. From Viggiù the Longhi family sent architects to Rome for three generations. Martino the Elder, who came south in the late 1560s, was succeeded by his son Onorio and grandson Martino the Younger, who died in 1660. Other mobile Lombards like Lorenzo Binago and Giovanni Andrea Mazenta were just as active throughout the north of Italy in the early 1600s.

Professional training changed during the course of the seventeenth century as the Academy of St. Luke offered more courses of study and scheduled regular student competitions.[9] Indeed, by the end of the century, aspiring architects from all over Italy and even some from abroad were enrolling in the Academy. By 1700, traditional methods of training had been abandoned, for the most part. The new system was more democratic, but it unfortunately also encouraged a certain amount of stylistic conformity. In fact, the Academy of St. Luke became, especially in the 1720s and 1730s, the champion of what has been called "Late Baroque Classicism" or "Academic Classicism," a stepping stone between the conservative seventeenth-century currents of the Bernini circle and the appearance after 1750 of Neo-Classicism. Nor was such academic training confined to Rome. In Paris the Royal Academy of Architecture had existed since 1671, and in Italy, courses of instruction started to spring up in other cities as well. In 1729 the University of Turin became the first in Italy to sanction architecture, although only in 1762 were students there required to take courses before being admitted to the exams. Most Italian universities, however, like many professional societies, failed to distinguish between architects and engineers until much later.[10] The University of Rome, for example, did not have a chair in architecture until 1817, and its first occupant was a specialist in mechanics and hydraulics from the University of Bologna.

Outside academic debate, architectural theory was not so commonplace or important as it was in the earlier Renaissance or as it again became in the later Neo-Classical period. Between the publication of the architect Sebastiano Serlio's *Architettura e prospettiva* in 1566 and the posthumous publication of Borromini's *Opus Architectonicum* in 1725, no treatise with any significant influence appeared within Italy.[11] Serlio's volume is, in fact, little more than a well-executed pattern-book, bereft of theoretical formulation, while Borromini's work is but a detailed report of the construction of one of his commissions (the Oratory of S. Filippo Neri), partially ghost-written by his friend and patron Virgilio Spada. The first learned treatise of the Baroque period was written by Guarino Guarini, but only published in 1737, some fifty-four years after his death. The late publication of this and Borromini's folio is somewhat of a surprise since both men represented viewpoints that ran counter to the prevailing academic taste. Yet like Borromini's *Opus,* Guarini's *Architettura civile* was still fundamentally an architectural autobiography. Its arguments are long and often intricate, but it can hardly be called either comprehensive or primarily theoretical in its outlook. It was not until 1768, when Francesco Milizia's *Lives of the Celebrated Architects* was published that a rigorous theoretical tract was available in post-Renaissance Italy. Its polemic by then was strongly anti-Baroque with a bias toward the functional classicism that was typical of the day.

Looking back, Giacomo della Porta's nonchalance in failing to appear for a lecture on theory that he was scheduled to give at the Academy of St. Luke seems to typify the untheoretical attitude of architects of the Baroque period. In fact, no intellectual discourses at all are recorded at the academy—the logical place for them to take place—until the notorious debates on painting between Pietro da Cortona and Andrea Sacchi in the mid-1630s. Despite Cortona's efforts to schedule such debates regularly, his exchanges with Sacchi were isolated events. This was a time when creative practice took precedence over abstract formulations.

Architectural shop-practice in the seventeenth and early eighteenth centuries is a subject that has yet to be fully explored.[12] Some contracts between patrons and master masons have been preserved, but few records exist that document the relationship between architect and employer or architect and construction crew. A letter sent in 1568 by Cardinal Alessandro Farnese, patron of the Gesù, to his architect Vignola is exceptional both in its carefully detailed instructions and in the very fact of its survival. Despite active archival research in recent decades, few similar documents have come to light, and only occasionally do we know why one architect, or one design, was selected over another. Apparently most architects furnished a master mason with drawings and made only infrequent appearances at the site, while an assistant supervised the actual construction. Even the largest projects do not seem to have required the architect's full-time presence on the job. While Carlo Maderno was actively engaged in the completion of the basilica of St. Peter's, he still found time to take on new commissions elsewhere. Bernini may even have run a sort of mail-order business, if the attribution to him of several buildings in remote places can be trusted. Some patrons, however, were more demanding and required direct supervision of their projects; relatives of Innocent X, for example, sharply criticized Borromini in 1657 for not spending more time at the site of the family church of S. Agnese in Piazza Navona.

Fortunately, many architectural drawings still survive that provide some idea of how buildings were conceived and constructed. A rare glimpse of a building under construction is given in Nicola Michetti's drawing of Ss. Apostoli in Rome in 1708 (1). At the lower left of this sketch, a man who may be the architect discusses the building with his companions, while several workers hoist stone and put it in place. The drawing is especially informative in that it shows the kind of winching tools used and the method of constructing arches and vaults.[13] It is interesting that none of the masons are consulting drawings or models. No large-scale working drawings—the equivalent of modern blueprints—have ever been found, and it is doubtful that they were used at the time. Most of the drawings that survive are of three basic types: (1) the *primo pensiero,* or first idea (a rough sketch, often

1. Nicola Michetti, drawing of Ss. Apostoli under construction, 1708.

in plan); (2) a more finished drawing, intended for a patron, sometimes with alternate designs for sections on pasted-down flaps and, after the late 1600s, often executed in colored washes; and (3) for the mason, a small, precisely measured drawing, usually of particular details. Models were occasionally made for the patron or the builders, but this practice seems to have been less common than in previous centuries, no doubt because of the increased use of drawings. On rare occasions, full-scale wooden models were actually hoisted into place as a preview of the final design.[14] This was done, for example, with Bernini's proposed towers of St. Peter's, but the expense of such ventures obviously limited their use. Besides drawings, Borromini also made small wax models of his major commissions which doubtless helped him to think of his designs in more sculptural terms. About two dozen of these models are listed in the inventory of his personal effects at the time of his death, but none survive today. The practice of sculpting models from soft materials probably was not so widespread among architects as it was among sculptors.[15]

An architect's professional success frequently depended as much on his ability to make social contacts as it did on his talents as a designer. A strong alliance with a rich or influential patron—a papal nephew, for example—could help keep an architect in the limelight and generate further commissions. Countrymen of the pope were looked upon with particular favor, and their rise to fame could be meteoric. But the fall from grace could be equally spectacular when such a benefactor died. After the death of Urban VIII, only Bernini's insuperable genius saved him from the obscurity that descended upon Filippo Raguzzini after Benedict XIII died in 1730. Yet for Alessandro Galilei and Ferdinando Fuga, the election that year of their Florentine countryman Clement XII was a great stroke of luck. In letters written some years later, Luigi Vanvitelli lamented that it was difficult to keep a steady practice going in Rome where merit and ability counted for little and political favoritism was widespread.[16] It also was an advantage for an architect to belong to a religious order. Lorenzo Binago and Guarino Guarini, as members of the newly founded Barnabite and Theatine orders, respectively, received commissions for several churches sponsored by those organizations. Conversely, in more than one instance an architect of real ability failed to find regular work because of his idiosyncrasies—the irascible and anti-social Martino Longhi the Younger comes immediately to mind—or because geographic or economic circumstances prevented him from finding a sympathetic patron. This presumably is what happened to the talented Andrea Nono from the small town of Crema, who built very little.

Then as now, patrons considered the cost of construction carefully. Architects who could do the job cheaply but stylishly had a decided advantage, and it was here that the temperamental, misanthropic Borromini excelled. For the Spanish Trinitarians in Rome he built the church of S. Carlino (28) so inexpensively that they publicly boasted of its low cost as well as of their satisfaction with its "artistic merit, fantasy, and excellence." The Piedmontese architect Bernardo Vittone also enjoyed a reputation for working cheaply, and this led to some three dozen church commissions, more than any of his contemporaries. The secret of both Borromini's and Vittone's success lay at least partially in their ability to work creatively with stucco, a much cheaper material than the marble traditionally used to face buildings. If the cost of building S. Carlino is compared with that of Bernini's S. Andrea al Quirinale, a roughly contemporary marble-clad church of about the same size, the advantage of hiring the "difficult" Borromini over the "gracious" Bernini becomes immediately apparent. S. Carlino cost just 12,000 *scudi,* while S. Andrea in the end cost nearly five times as much.

The use of stucco in the eighteenth century has been viewed as instrumental in the development of the Rococo style.[17] This is true for at least two reasons: the material lends itself to delicate surface handling much more readily than marble, and its low cost made it possible to ornament the sort of small-scale domestic building with which the Rococo is often associated. In the virtual absence of structural innovation in the seventeenth and eighteenth centuries, the notion of covering brick walls with ornamental stuccoes was a significant advance. Stucco had been used for architectural embellishment in antiquity but its application had never before been so widespread. Moreover, the material could be painted, and eighteenth-century architects like Vittone and Raguzzini frequently applied to their buildings the lovely pale pastel colors that so appealed to Rococo taste.[18]

Climate and the intrinsic properties of local building materials were not irrelevant to architectural practice either. On the average, Sicily receives 1,000 more hours of sunshine each year than Turin. That the more intense, protracted light of the south may have encouraged architects there to construct more boldly projecting columnar facades than their counterparts in the north finds support in the orientation of many of Sicily's most dramatic Baroque facades. Is it merely a coincidence that so many north Italian exteriors seem underplayed by comparison? In a similar vein, the soft, easily carved local stone of Lecce in the heel of Italy lent itself to very different surface effects than the bright but brittle travertine of Rome, the hard grey *pietra serena* of Florence, or the sparkling white Istrian marble of Venice. Architects in each of these places learned to take advantage of the intrinsic quality of these materials and seldom sought anomalous effects.

Historical Factors

Italy as we know it today is, of course, a nineteenth-century creation. Before its unification as a political state in 1870, the peninsula consisted of a shifting assortment of republics, duchies, principalities, foreign domains, and the Papal States. Consequently, it is not easy to generalize about the political, economic, social, and religious conditions that prevailed during the seventeenth and eighteenth centuries.

Circumstances in the Venetian Republic were naturally bound to be different from those in the Spanish possession of Naples, and Rome under the temporal and spiritual rule of the popes had little in common with Turin under the House of Savoy. The peculiar but pertinent aspects of individual provinces will be discussed in the appropriate sections of the text, but some general remarks can be made here on the complex of factors which shaped the heterogeneous character of Baroque architecture in Italy as a whole.

The one unifying element in Italian life, apart from language, was the Catholic Church. Its influence on architecture cannot be overstated, for from the Middle Ages to modern times, the grandest buildings in Italy, and indeed most of Europe, were built to serve ecclesiastical purposes. Although the temporal power of the papacy extended only to Perugia, Ancona, Bologna, and Ferrara, its spiritual powers were far-reaching. From Rome, recalcitrant sovereigns could be excommunicated, public worship prohibited, and ecclesiastical burial denied. In 1606, Pope Paul V issued just such an interdict against Venice in response to what His Holiness considered to be challenges to papal authority that were tolerated by that city. Paul came to regret his censure, however, when Venice's ally France threatened to step into the fray that resulted. Such a move by the papacy was as rare as it was severe, but up to the time of its conquest by Napoleon in 1809, Rome commanded the respect of every Italian province, if not most of Europe. Naturally the papacy was no military match for the great nation-states of seventeenth-century Europe, but the Enlightenment had not yet deposed faith in the name of reason either. Reverence for the church, of course, produced various revenues, which often funded new churches and public monuments that generated esteem among religious pilgrims and other visitors to the Holy City. Exactly how much money came to the Vatican's treasuries is not known, but it has been estimated that about 20 percent of its income was from outside the Papal States.[19]

Italy during this period was in a state of steady economic decline.[20] The textile industry, long the backbone of the economy of northern and central Italy, suffered huge losses to competition from England, France, and Holland. In Milan, to cite an extreme example, there were at the beginning of the seventeenth century sixty to seventy firms that produced about 15,000 woolen cloths a year; by 1709 only one firm existed and the output had fallen to about 100 cloths per year. The textile industries of Venice, Florence, and Genoa experienced similar if less severe reversals, and while certain advances did occur in agriculture and other parts of the economy, the seventeenth century was not a prosperous one for the Italian peninsula. Between 1630 and 1657, two major epidemics of plague swept over the land, killing almost a third of the population. Soaring wages and inflation followed in the wake of these tragic events at a time when Italian industry could least afford them in the face of foreign competition. As a result, few private fortunes were made, and the principal patrons of architecture were the church and those who derived income from the church.

In Rome, where trade and industry were negligible, the effects of the economic downturn were only indirect.[21] The Holy City did, however, enjoy certain economic advantages over other Italian cities. As the center of Catholic Christendom, it attracted thousands of religious pilgrims—as many as five times the permanent population during a Holy Year. In 1600, 540,000 pilgrims from all of Europe flocked to the Holy City. Even eighteenth-century Venice, a key attraction on the popular Grand Tour, could not rival such numbers, and by then Rome too had become a focal point on the secular tour. Meeting the spiritual and physical needs of these visitors provided Romans with occupations ranging from booksellers to restaurant chefs. The construction industry in Rome so prospered that by the late sixteenth century it had become the largest employer in the city.[22] In the seventeenth century the construction or refurbishing of churches, palaces, fountains, and other buildings not only played a major role in Rome's economic life but strongly enhanced its status as the artistic capital of Europe.

Local citizens occasionally used colorful graffiti, known as pasquinades, to protest the expenditure of more funds on architecture than on social welfare—as they did during the construction of the Piazza of St. Peter's—failing to grasp what John Maynard Keynes would later point out: in trying times, the construction of even the most useless buildings can contribute to the general welfare by providing work and generating income.[23]

The Vatican also supplemented its regular revenues from taxation and other sources by making appeals to public credit. *Luoghi di monte* (bonds) were floated all over Italy and even abroad, trading on the name of the papacy as security. Some 380 tons of silver, more than eight times the entire cost of the basilica of St. Peter's, were raised in this way during the second half of the sixteenth century alone.[24] In the same period, Sixtus V (1585–1590) instituted the lucrative practice of selling offices that previously either had not existed or simply had been given away. Later, in the eighteenth century, Clement XII (1730–1740) helped defray the expenses of his largest architectural projects—the Trevi Fountain and the facade of the Lateran—by holding public lotteries. Relative to other Italian cities, Rome was in the fortunate position of having the administrative know-how and the prestige to find public support for many of its endeavors.

Even Roman secular architecture was more closely tied to the financial well-being of the church than might be imagined. Until Innocent XI (1676–1689) waged a successful battle against papal nepotism, the great fortunes of Rome were invariably linked to the clergy and the most impressive residential buildings usually belonged to families who had had the good fortune of having a relative ascend to the papacy. Each family from that of Paul V (1605–1621) through Clement X (1670–1676) commissioned at least one private building that bespoke their prestigious new status; the Barberini and Chigi palaces (22 and 61) stand as evidence of that practice. And while there were some limits to spending—as the profligate family of Urban VIII discovered in the fiscal scandal that ensued after the pontiff's death—little distinction was made between a pope's personal funds and those of the Vatican treasury. Other aristocratic families, for the most part, refrained from aping their spiritual betters.

The relationship between architecture and religion was a changing one during the sixteenth through the eighteenth centuries. Our survey begins in the last third of the sixteenth century, when the church was in the midst of the Counter-Reformation, the movement aimed at remedying some of the abuses challenged by Protestants earlier in the century. The chief agent of this stern internal reform was the Council of Trent, which in the last of several lengthy sessions held from 1545 until 1563, formulated decrees regarding the visual arts. The decrees were more directly concerned with narrative painting than with architecture, but to the extent that they addressed the building of churches, they, like a few independent tracts that appeared around the same time, were primarily guided by practical concerns and by the desire to make sure that no traces of pagan antiquity lingered on in the design of new buildings.[25]

Of equal importance for late Renaissance and early Baroque architecture was the impetus for new sacred construction resulting from the Counter-Reformation's emphasis on the establishment of new religious orders. Between 1524 and 1575, the Barnabite, Jesuit, Oratorian, and Theatine orders came into being, and as their influence spread, more and more new churches were built. A somewhat later wave of new construction accompanied the canonizations of some of the leaders of the recent Catholic revival: Charles Borromeo in 1610, and Ignatius Loyola, Francis Xavier, Phillip Neri, and Theresa of Avila in 1622. By 1725, there were 323 churches in Rome serving a population of fewer than 150,000 people.[26]

The notion that the most vigorous and fully developed works of Baroque art can be viewed as the product of the Counter-Reformation was rightly refuted many years ago. The major figures of Baroque architecture—Bernini, Borromini, Cortona, and Guarini—in fact represent a later phase of religious and cultural sensibility, and their mature works reflect the renewed self-confidence of a church that had successfully withstood the challenge of a century of reform. Strict and rigorous adherence to religious doctrine had given way by the middle of the seventeenth century to more fervent and mystical attitudes toward the faith, and concrete forms and images were considered the best means of stirring the passions of the soul.[27] In religious architecture this meant the manipulation of natural building materials to produce a phantasmic effect on the beholder. And it is here that the seeming paradox of the Baroque is encountered, described by Leibniz as "the spiritualization of the material." The modern dichotomies between the senses and the intellect, the mystical and the physical, the spiritual and the material, had yet to come into conflict.

To John Evelyn, an Englishman visiting Rome in 1645, Italian religious practice seemed "unimaginably superstitious." The celebration of the mass was, indeed, deliberately cloaked in mystery. The tone is reflected in the Bishop of Tortona's book published in 1672, entitled *Mysteries and Mystical Senses of Each Part of the Mass*. A major point of disagreement with Luther had, of course, been the Catholic Church's refusal to allow a vernacular bible to the laity. It was not until 1769–1781, during the Enlightenment, that an officially sanctioned bible was published in Italian.[28] For Italians of the seventeenth and early eighteenth centuries—most of whom could neither read nor write anyway—religious devotion was founded on faith alone and buttressed by an Augustinian dependence upon divine grace and mercy.[29] The Baroque church edifice, ornate as it may seem to modern viewers, served with perfection the spiritual needs of its early congregations.

By the time of the papacy of Urban VIII (1623–1644), a grand,

worldly atmosphere began to permeate Rome for the first time since
the High Renaissance. A renewed aesthetic appreciation of the fine
arts gradually led to the creation of works of religious art whose didactic content was often matched if not overshadowed by the delectation
they offered to the eye. For a pontiff like Alexander VII (1655–1667),
the artistic embellishment of Rome was a matter of the utmost importance. He energetically sponsored the construction or renewal of scores
of churches and squares, and taking advantage of the talents of the
most gifted architects available, he realized his ambition of turning *his*
city—*Roma Alessandrina*—into one of the most modern and stylish
capitals of Europe. The utility of these monuments was often of less
importance than the impression they gave of his magnanimity and
good taste as a patron. Alexander further publicized the works he sponsored by featuring them on the many widely circulated medals he commissioned during his reign.[30]

Times changed again in the last quarter of the century, when Innocent XI (1676–1689), Alexander VIII (1689–1691), and Innocent
XII (1691–1700) occupied the papal throne. Pressed to commit ever
larger sums of money to the prolonged religious war against Moslem
aggression in eastern Europe, they all but abandoned significant architectural patronage in Rome. The buildings they did commission
tended to be utilitarian—orphanages, hospitals, and granaries—which
are more interesting for what they tell us about changing papal prior-
ities regarding social and religious welfare than they are for their aesthetic merit. The papacy's withdrawal from more glamorous patronage
lasted for half a century.

It was not until the second quarter of the eighteenth century, during the pontificates of Benedict XIII (1724–1730) and Clement XII
(1730–1740) that papal patronage found renewed vigor and Rome
again became a major center of architectural and urbanistic activity.
From this period sprang forth the Spanish Steps (103), the Trevi
Fountain (108), and the facades of three of the city's most important
and venerable basilicas, the Lateran (104), S. Maria Maggiore (106),
and S. Croce in Gerusalemme (105). Curiously, such ambitious
undertakings came at a time of continuing impoverishment for the
papal treasury, but owing perhaps to the death of Louis XIV in 1715
and the comparatively peaceful times which followed in Europe, the
Vatican was somewhat freer to indulge in its traditional pursuit of the
artistic embellishment of the Holy City.

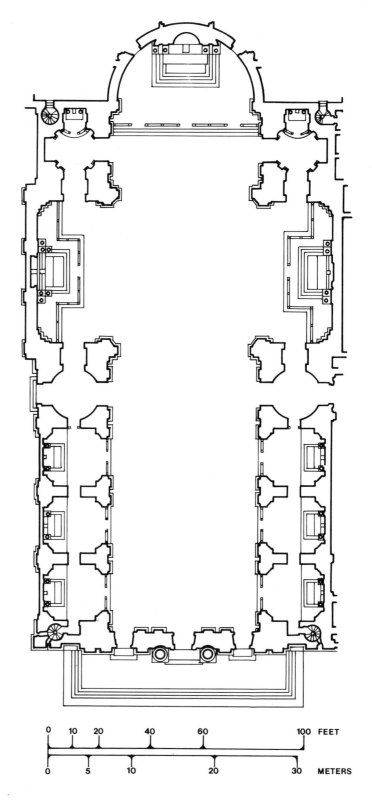

2. Giacomo da Vignola,
Il Gesù,
Rome, plan.

0 10 20   40   60   100 FEET

0   5   10   20   30 METERS

2

Precursors of the
Roman Baroque:
Vignola to Carlo Maderno

The great church of Il Gesù occupies a pivotal position between the Renaissance and the Baroque. Built as the Mother Church of the Jesuit Order between 1568 and 1575, the Gesù looks back to prototypes in the Renaissance and ahead to countless Baroque derivations. Nonetheless, its somber, restrained appearance is wholly in keeping with the asceticism of its own age. More than the periods which immediately preceded or followed it, the late sixteenth century was an age that preferred sobriety and orthodox conformity to lively invention in church architecture.

The Gesù was the first of many Counter-Reformation churches built in Rome, and throughout, it reflects the practicality and decorum so strongly urged in the final decrees of the Council of Trent. The plan (2) differs sharply from the centrally planned circumfluent schemes so common in the Renaissance and so ingeniously adapted in two earlier Roman churches designed by its architect, Giacomo Barozzi da Vignola (1507–1573).[1]

Vignola used the longitudinal basilican plan in the church at the request of his patron, Cardinal Alessandro Farnese, who wrote to his architect stressing the desirability of such a capacious and acoustically effective space. While possessing a strong sense of the practical, the designers of most churches of the time also recognized the symbolic value of architectural form, and the centrally planned church came to be regarded as iconographically inappropriate for Christian worship. Several tracts of the late sixteenth century argued that the traditional Latin Cross plan was the most suitable to express a church's symbolic

3. Leon Battista Alberti, S. Andrea, Mantua, interior.

dedication to Christ. Most prominent among these was Saint Charles Borromeo's influential guide for sacred architecture published in 1577, the *Instructiones Fabricae et Supellectilis Ecclesiasticae,* which left no doubt that the circular form should be studiously avoided in the design of major churches.[2] With Il Gesù, the Latin Cross became the standard plan for such buildings for years to come.

Much has been written about the architectural sources of Vignola's plan. While it did not evolve independently of a few of the recent developments in Roman sacred architecture, its major prototype probably was the great Renaissance church of S. Andrea in Mantua (3), begun in 1472 by Leon Battista Alberti. A comparison of the two buildings is illuminating: a compact plan, achieved by dispensing with the traditional side aisles and reducing the number of secondary chapels, is common to both. Vignola also followed Alberti by covering the nave with a monumental barrel vault that creates the impression of cavernous space (4). He achieved a comparatively greater sense of spatial unification, however, by broadening the nave and making .the transepts shallower. The side chapels in Il Gesù are also lower and com-

20

pete less with the main space, which is brighter and better fenestrated than its somewhat gloomy predecessor. Piers framing the side chapels are narrower and the pilasters ornamenting them are paired, quickening the tempo of the nave elevation. The overall impression of the Jesuit church is of a simple and sprightly functional structure that relies less on antique models than Alberti's more self-consciously artful creation. Originally the Gesù interior was whitewashed, in keeping with the austerity of Counter-Reformation taste, but by the end of the seventeenth century, a change in sensibility called for the rich decorative overlay now seen there.

The facade was the last part of the building to be built, and unlike the interior, it is not the work of Vignola. In June 1571, Cardinal Farnese elected to replace Vignola's project, known to us from Cartaro's engraving (5), with a subtly but significantly different one by Michel-

4. Giacomo da Vignola, Il Gesù, Rome, interior.

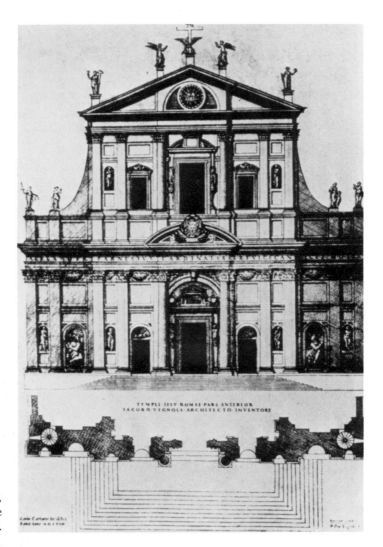

5. Giacomo da Vignola, project for the facade of Il Gesù, Rome.

angelo's disciple Giacomo della Porta (6). In concept, the two designs are similar. Both have a two-story elevation faced with Corinthian pilasters, and both relate exterior to interior by revealing the unequal heights of the higher nave and lower side chapels within. Renaissance architects had long been challenged by the problem of creating a harmonious facade to mask the irregular profile of longitudinally planned churches. The definitive solution of connecting the upper and lower stories with curved struts or scrolls appeared in both Vignola's and Della Porta's proposals. The inspiration ultimately derived from Alberti's facade of S. Maria Novella in Florence (1456), but two Roman

22

6. Giacomo della Porta, Il Gesù, Rome, facade.

7. Ottaviano Mascarino,
S. Maria in Traspontina,
Rome, facade.

churches of the mid-sixteenth century—S. Spirito in Sassia and S. Caterina dei Funari—were probably influential in the actual genesis of the design. Once this type of facade appeared at Il Gesù, it quickly became a standard feature of all longitudinal churches built in Rome.

The differences between Vignola's and Della Porta's designs are significant. In Vignola's unexecuted plan, the wall planes step forward from the sides toward the center, whereas in Della Porta's facade all horizontal movement is eliminated, and the vertical linkage between the pilasters of both tiers is emphasized instead. The disposition of pilas-

24

ters in Vignola's project is also more diffuse and less well related to the interior elevation than Della Porta's neatly paired, more evenly spaced system. On the other hand, Vignola's stepped arrangement, in avoiding the flatness of Della Porta's executed facade, would have yielded a more coherent and satisfying solution. Yet Della Porta's handling of the classical order is the more dynamic and forceful, though it does not achieve the full vigor of Michelangelo, his mentor. Judging from the many subsequent derivations of each design, neither emerged the clear winner. By the mid-seventeenth century, however, the exclusive influence of either Della Porta's or Vignola's design was no longer apparent; elements from both commonly appeared together, incorporated in later styles.[3]

Il Gesù was completed at a time when progressive development was not one of the ideals of Roman architecture. Architects who were active during the reign of Pope Sixtus V (1585–1590), a time of greatly renewed building activity in Rome, were seldom inclined to question accepted practices.[4] The bland facade of S. Maria in Traspontina (7) built by Ottaviano Mascarino in 1581–87 is a typical example of the timidity and lack of inventiveness for which the Sixtine style in architecture is noted. Like many Roman facades of the period, it relates generically to the Gesù without displaying any awareness of the nuances and subtleties of either Della Porta's or Vignola's design.

Other building projects sponsored by Sixtus V show a similar lack of creative imagination and occasional lapses of good taste as well. Visitors to the Vatican can only wonder at the insensitive placement of Sixtus' Library on the mid-axis of Bramante's magnificent Belvedere Courtyard. Equally anomalous and almost absurdly mundane was Sixtus' unrealized idea of transforming the Colosseum into a wool-spinning factory and the Baths of Diocletian into a public laundry. The bland repetitiveness of the Gesù-like churches was also matched by Sixtus' major nonreligious commission, the papal palace at S. Giovanni in Laterano (8). Domenico Fontana's two monotonous facades are so faithfully derived from Antonio da Sangallo's Palazzo Farnese (9), begun a half-century earlier, that they even failed to take account of Michelangelo's ingenious later revision of the upper story. The dull, unordered exterior of the Lateran Palace is a telling example of the unadventurous attitude of the generation and its lack of interest in architectural innovation.

When Sixtus did deviate from established norms, the results were unfortunate. Domenico Fontana's papal chapel in S. Maria Maggiore

8. Domenico Fontana, Lateran Palace, Rome, exterior.

9. Sangallo and
Michelangelo,
Farnese Palace,
Rome, exterior.

(begun in 1585) has been hailed as the most garish and vulgar of all the papal commissions (10). Joined by an undistinguished team of assistants, Fontana blithely ignored the Counter-Reformation admonition against vain display and undignified ornament. Every inch of the chapel, whose plan is a Greek Cross, is covered with frescoes, free-standing and relief sculpture, and richly inlaid marbles plundered from ancient buildings. Only the didactic nature of the narrative compositions kept the project from being seen as a mere display of papal ostentation.

Despite his failings as a patron of architecture, Sixtus made notable contributions to Rome's urban development. During his pontificate, a comprehensive town planning scheme (11) was carried out, which

10. Domenico Fontana, Sixtine Chapel, S. Maria Maggiore, Rome, interior.

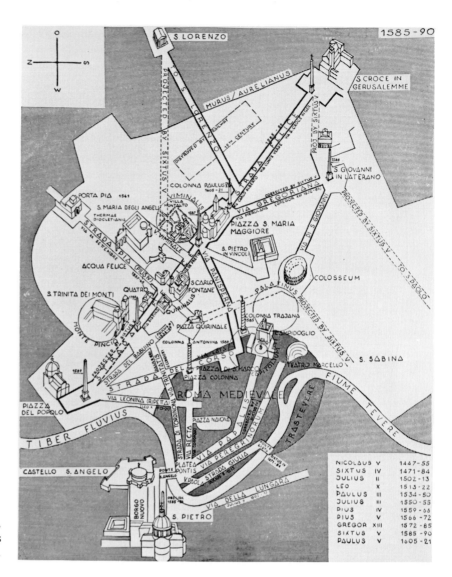

11. Rome,
Sixtus V's
town planning.

created a series of long straight avenues extending from the densely populated center to the outlying rural areas of the city.[5] The primary purpose of the new streets was to connect the seven major basilicas that have always been the objects of religious pilgrimages. Focal points on each axis were marked by strategically placed Egyptian obelisks prominently surmounted by crucifixes. Like most ventures at that time, Sixtus' urbanism was based on practical and symbolic considerations rather than on aesthetics. Although his axial concept of town planning had few parallels in Rome until the neo-imperial schemes of Mussolini, it remains Sixtus' most positive contribution to the city and one of the most important and influential developments in the history of European urbanism.

28

Of the seven popes that followed Sixtus, only two—Clement VIII and Paul V—held office long enough to change the course of Roman architecture through their patronage. Yet with few exceptions, neither Clement (1592–1605) nor Paul (1605–1621) supported innovative architectural solutions to any greater extent than Sixtus had, despite the coincidence of their pontificates with one of Rome's biggest building booms.

A handful of buildings and one or two architects do stand out however. In the early 1590s construction began on two longtitudinal churches in Rome that departed somewhat from the usual Gesù prototype. One of these was S. Salvatore in Lauro (1592–1598) (12), rebuilt by Ottaviano Mascarino after a fire in 1591.[6] The main innovation at S. Salvatore was the use of free-standing columns instead of the paired pilasters that lined the Gesù interior. Although the broken entablature and ribbed vault may have been added later, the introduction

12. Ottaviano Mascarino, S. Salvatore in Lauro, Rome, interior.

13. Grimaldi and Della Porta, S. Andrea della Valle, Rome, interior.

of columns in the nave lends a bolder and more vigorous architectonic flavor to the traditional cruciform plan. The stimulus for Mascarino's interest in columnar architecture is not known, but he was raised and trained in Bologna and his work may reflect the classical structuralism that was more prevalent in northern Italy. Yet it is also true that he would have had to look no farther than Michelangelo's church of S. Maria degli Angeli in Rome to find similar expressions of architectural bravura.

Less sensuously robust, but just as significant is the contemporary Roman church of S. Andrea della Valle (13). S. Andrea was begun in 1591 as the Mother Church of the newly founded Theatine Order, and the history of its construction is as complicated as that of S. Salvatore.[7] Its original architects, Padre Francesco Grimaldi and Giacomo Della Porta, attempted a revision of Il Gesù with an eye toward achieving a less ponderous and more engaging interior. Using a ground plan similar to that of the Jesuit church, they altered the proportions of the interior, increasing the height of the elevation by about one fourth. The architects also emphasized vertical continuities, opposing the natural flow of horizontal movement through the use of bundled pilasters that thrust upward into the entablature to meet the ribs of the vault. The tempo of movement down the nave is thereby quickened and the entire architectural system is unified and tightened. The lazy horizontal sprawl of Il Gesù with its paired pilasters becomes a tense equilibrium of horizontals and verticals, and what at Il Gesù are flat areas of wall surface, ripple and vibrate at S. Andrea della Valle. Without violating tradition, S. Andrea achieved a certain animation and individuality that usually was so lacking in other works of its period.

The interior of S. Andrea was not completed until 1625 when on Palm Sunday its first mass was celebrated. Carlo Maderno, who directed the final seventeen years of construction, was an architect of considerable ability who carried late sixteenth-century architecture into a more Baroque phase. His career, like his life, was rooted in tradition.[8] He was born in 1556 in the North Italian town of Capolago (now Switzerland) and went to Rome at about the age of twenty to work for his uncle Domenico Fontana, the favorite architect of Sixtus V. When Fontana moved to Naples in 1594, four years after the death of Sixtus, Maderno immediately established himself as an independent master.

The most prominent of Maderno's early works is the facade of S. Susanna (14), built in 1597–1603. A basilican interior dating to the Middle Ages posed the familiar problem of requiring a unified frontispiece to mask the irregular profile of its tall nave and low side chapels. Maderno, like nearly all of his contemporaries, was irresistibly drawn to the example of Il Gesù. The facade's basic composition—a two-story pedimented elevation with scrolls connecting the narrower upper story to its wider counterpart below—was obviously derived from the Jesuit church completed twenty-two years earlier. Yet Maderno, impressed by Vignola's unexecuted design with its sequential movement of stepped planes, based his smaller and more compact facade on that vigorous planar arrangement. The principal innovation of S. Susanna, however, was not its revival of the rejected project, but its original use of the classical order. The three bays of the lower story are now force-fully enframed by an order that expresses the energetically projecting wall masses behind it. Marking the terminal bays are pilasters that give way to engaged columns in the intermediate bays and to free-standing columns in the central bay. Even the upper-story pilasters project more assertively than was customary. The result is roughly comparable to the lively effect achieved in Mascarino's nave of S. Salvatore in Lauro, where another traditional elevation was also given new life through the more robust use of the classical order. Both compositions are pro-phetic of the coming Baroque and one of its basic themes, the full emergence of the column from the wall that had for so long enclosed it. This more sculptural use of the classical order is complemented by carved sculptural relief on Maderno's facade, another element that looks ahead to the High Baroque. Despite its deceptively traditional appearance, S. Susanna surpasses all Roman prototypes in imagination and visual presence.

The facade of S. Susanna was completed in 1603. In the same year Maderno received the most important commission of his career, the appointment to succeed the recently deceased Giacomo della Porta as Architect of St. Peter's. His first two years on the job were uneventful, but with the election of Paul V in 1605, there emerged a pontiff who, in the spirit of a new and more self-confident age, claimed for himself the challenge, the expense, and the glory of completing the great ba-silica begun by Julius II a century earlier. Students of Renaissance ar-chitecture will recall the grandiose intention of Bramante's original centralized plan, the unsuccessful efforts of his immediate successors to transform it, and its sensibly simplified restoration by Michelangelo. Such was the enormity of the scale that even Michelangelo could not complete it after eighteen years on the job, and it finally fell to Gia-como della Porta to raise the great dome to its present majestic height. When Maderno entered the scene, remains of the original fourth-century Constantinian basilica still stood on the site, and the entrance arm and facade had not yet been begun.

The decrepit remains of the Early Christian edifice soon were or-dered demolished by Paul V, who then called for a competition to de-termine how the new building was to be completed. Maderno, who supervised the demolition, and eight other architects submitted propo-sals ranging from respectful imitations of Michelangelo's outdated pro-ject to fanciful transformations of everything that had ever been con-sidered. The only functional requirements were a loggia in the facade

14. Carlo Maderno, S. Susanna, Rome, facade.

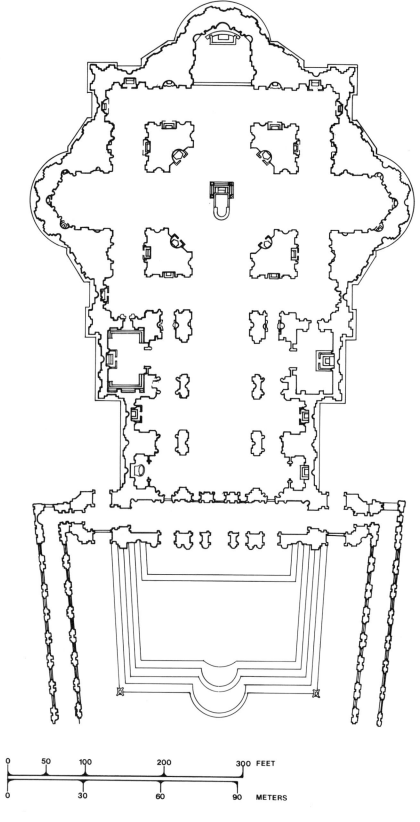

15. Carlo Maderno and others, St. Peter's, Rome, plan.

0	50	100	200	300 FEET

0	30	60	90 METERS

16. Carlo Maderno, St. Peter's, Rome, nave.

for papal benedictions and the addition of a sacristy and choir in the interior. The main question, of course, was whether to complete the basilica as a centralized building, as Bramante and Michelangelo had intended, or to transform it into a longitudinal plan by adding a nave. As late as October 1606 the *Congregazione della Fabbrica,* the governing body at St. Peter's, reportedly favored the central scheme despite the criticism recently leveled against such plans by pious theologians like Cardinal Borromeo and others. Aesthetic considerations aside, two factors may have fostered serious consideration of such a plan—the attitude toward symbolic propriety was now less dogmatic than it had been a few decades earlier, and, as the shrine and final resting place of St. Peter, the basilica was uniquely entitled to the central plan which in Christian usage had originated as a martyrium.

Nevertheless, the recommendations of the *Congregazione* were overruled by Paul V who, after wavering for some time, approved in June 1608 a design by Carlo Maderno that called for a three-bay nave to be attached to the existing structure (15). Paul's decision irrevocably

35

changed the character of the organic, symmetrical space that had been the nucleus of the church in the minds of its High Renaissance founders. In designing the nave (16), Maderno naturally was constrained by the need to blend his own creations harmoniously with the scale and articulation of the sixteenth-century structure. He was so successful that the transition between old and new is scarcely detectable. His nave, constructed between 1609 and 1615, forms part of a cohesive whole based on the original Bramantesque elevation of piers faced with paired pilasters supporting a barrel-vaulted roof. Only the design of the side aisles, with their sequence of oval cupolas and handsome transverse arches, reveals the independent personality of the architect.

Construction of the facade (17) actually preceded that of the nave by two years. Here, too, Maderno had to contend with an existing, practically inviolable design of the Renaissance—Michelangelo's

17. Carlo Maderno, St. Peter's, Rome, facade.

18. Carlo Maderno,
project for facade of
St. Peter's, Rome.

stately march of giant pilasters around the flanks of the building. Continuing the giant order across the facade precluded a design of the familiar two-story Gesù type, but Maderno did manage to apply some of the more salient features of S. Susanna to the greater scale of St. Peter's. The stepped arrangement of wall planes, the progressive projection of the order, and the centralizing emphasis of the pediment over the main entrance are all reminiscent of the lower story of the earlier facade. For the attic above, Maderno had little choice but to continue the fanciful treatment of the side elevations. One element that had not appeared previously at St. Peter's was the secondary order of low, free-standing columns set into the three principal doorways. This motif originates on the facades of Michelangelo's Capitoline Palaces, where it also helps to adjust the scale of the giant order to more human proportions. Maderno's adoption of the secondary order not only scales down the facade's immense size, but also adds a modest syncopation to the overall rhythm of the elevation.

The facade of St. Peter's had nearly been completed when the pope decided to modify Maderno's design by raising bell towers at either end. After the front had been extended by two bays to provide the substructures, underground springs were discovered at the site, and the foundations were found to be incapable of supporting the towers' tremendous weight. The towers, visible in Greuter's engraving of 1613 (18), were not built, but the substructures remained in place. These

37

extra bays are responsible for the impression that the facade is perhaps too wide for its height, too monotonous for its width, and is not organically related to the church behind it. Maderno's new nave also obscured the dome from view in the entrance square, another reason his efforts at St. Peter's have been judged as something less than a success. Twenty-five years later Gianlorenzo Bernini set himself the task of rectifying some of these shortcomings; an account of his travails will be taken up in a later chapter.

In 1623 Maderno designed a facade for the church of S. Andrea della Valle whose interior he had helped complete after the deaths of its original architects. The facade had risen just a few feet off the ground when the patron, Cardinal Montalto, died and work was halted in 1627. From an engraving of Maderno's design (19), we see that he returned once again to the theme of Il Gesù. This time, however, he tried to reconcile the alternative schemes of Vignola and Della Porta. While the lower story faithfully follows Vignola's three stepped planes, the upper story foregoes the stepped arrangement in favor of Della Porta's flatter but more dynamic vertical linkage. On both stories the classical orders are grouped in pairs with all but the outer members of the lower story expressed as engaged columns. Despite certain discrepancies between the upper and lower elevations, the projected facade had more animation than any of its Roman forebears. Unexpectedly, Maderno's design disregards the usual period practice of concentrating the animation around the entrance bay. With eight sets of paired half-columns and an equitable distribution of sculpture in the side bays, the pictorial effect is more diffuse than in a facade like that of S. Susanna. Maderno's design ultimately remained on paper, but the masonry that he raised between 1623 and 1627 determined to a considerable extent the character of the facade that Carlo Rainaldi built several decades later.

So far we have spoken of Maderno only as a designer of ecclesiastical architecture, but slightly more than half his commissions were for secular works. However, of his nearly three dozen domestic commissions, Maderno was responsible for the definitive design of only a few. Many were works he inherited from three of Rome's most prolific builders—Domenico Fontana (departed for Naples in 1594), Francesco da Volterra (died ca. 1594–1595), and Giacomo della Porta (died 1602)—which seldom allowed him free creative rein. Other commissions were altered by other architects after his death in 1629.

The Palazzo Mattei di Giove (1598–ca. 1617) is an exception. It

19. Carlo Maderno, facade project for S. Andrea della Valle, Rome.

20. Carlo Maderno,
Palazzo Mattei,
Rome, courtyard.

was the only palace designed and constructed exclusively by Maderno, and it provides a rare opportunity to examine an unaltered work of the architect. The spare and conventional facade on Via Caetani is modelled on familiar sixteenth-century patterns that recall the Palazzo Farnese, but the courtyard (20) is a masterpiece of Madernesque invention. The classical order appears on the short sides of the oblong court, and, like the Palazzo Farnese (as it then existed), two of the three stories open onto arched loggias. But unlike the Farnese or the Colosseum, from which the arched order ultimately derives, the Palazzo Mattei foreswears the engaged column in favor of the flat pilaster. The sense of plasticity is lost, but is more than compensated for by the loggia's striking interplay of mass and void and by the lavish use of ancient statuary, which is set into every available space. It is now the sculptural program and not the classical order that activates the wall surface and gives it its delightfully antiquarian charm. In this respect the Mattei courtyard looks back to Mannerist prototypes of the mid-sixteenth century like Pirro Ligorio's Casino of Pius IV in the Vatican, but Maderno organized the ornament in the more logical and cohesive manner characteristic of the Baroque. The sumptuous sculptual display of the courtyard contrasts sharply with the expressionless facade and gives the building a strongly introspective character.

One of the partially completed buildings that Maderno inherited from Giacomo della Porta in 1602 was the Villa Aldobrandini in Frascati, some ten miles southeast of Rome. The villa itself was all but complete, and Maderno could do little but continue the work of his predecessor, but he did have a freer hand in designing the adjacent fountain complex (21). A water theatre was a common feature of contemporary villa design, and like the residence itself, was intended for

21. Carlo Maderno, Villa Aldobrandini, Frascati, water theatre.

informal relaxation as an escape from hectic city life.[9] Maderno's theatre consists of a hemi-cycle with straight wings set on axis between the villa and the spring-fed cascade. Five fountains set into the niches of the hemi-cycle create the variegated patterns and sounds of splashing water. As in the courtyard of the Palazzo Mattei, Maderno ornamented the walls with a full complement of free-standing and relief sculpture, but here it is related even more harmoniously to the architectural framework. The sequence of herms and pilasters framing the niches adds a pictorial overlay to the basic rhythm of the wall elevation and an easy transition between the media of architecture and sculpture. The Aldobrandini fountain remains in the tradition of Mannerist works like Ligorio's organ fountain at the Villa d'Este in Tivoli, but in discipline and restraint is more in keeping with the compositional modes of the Early Baroque.

The Palazzo Barberini was the most important secular commission that Maderno ever received. Unfortunately it came late in his career and he died before he could determine all aspects of its final appearance. Soon after Maffeo Barberini became Pope Urban VIII in 1623, his family began to plan a suitably palatial residence for themselves just a few blocks from the pontifical palace on the Quirinal hill. Maderno's first design called for a traditional block-like palace with an enclosed courtyard, but for several reasons, among which was the difficulty of constructing such an edifice on a steeply sloping site, he subsequently proposed a more unusual, winged plan without an interior courtyard. Construction began a few months before Maderno's death in 1629 and was essentially complete by 1633 (22). Maderno's successors were his young assistant Francesco Borromini and another inexperienced young architect, Gianlorenzo Bernini, and it has long been debated which of the three men was responsible for the details of the final design. Particularly problematic is the role Maderno played in what may have been a collaboration among several architects, the patron Taddeo Barberini, and even a few interested observers.[10]

Although the U-shaped plan of the Palazzo Barberini is unusual among Italian city palaces, it was a common feature of suburban villas of the Renaissance. Maderno's plan may even be based on the most famous of such buildings, the Villa Farnesina in Rome, built by Baldassare Peruzzi ca. 1510. Like the Farnesina, the Palazzo Barberini's facade consists of superimposed arched loggias. Instead of being relegated to the rear, or garden facade as was customary, the loggias are placed more prominently on the main facade, facing the street.

22. Carlo Maderno and others, Palazzo Barberini, Rome, exterior.

The openness and relative informality of this solution reflects the more extroverted atttitude that characterized Roman architecture during the Barberini papacy. Certainly the decorations inside the palace—Pietro da Cortona's grandiose fresco of the Apotheosis of Urban VIII, in particular—proclaim the new self-confidence of the Pope himself if not the entire age. Later in the century, other popes built palaces for their families that were equally grand, but none were ever again so bold or so exuberant.

Maderno's major contribution to Roman architecture was to gradually transform the bland conformist thinking of his predecessors into a more energetic, more pictorial, and more disciplined mode of expression. That this transformation was gradual and even rather tentative, becomes obvious when compared to the work of some of his immediate successors.

43

3

Francesco Borromini

"Maderno's modest innovations . . . were like a boulder slowly detaching itself from the mountainside; in a matter of stylistic minutes there was an avalanche."[1] Francesco Borromini was without question at the center of that architectural upheaval. Distantly related to Maderno and Domenico Fontana, Borromini travelled the familiar route of architects from northern Italy, where he was born in Bissone in 1599, to Rome, where he arrived in 1619. He began his career as a stone-carver and draughtsman in Maderno's shop and was employed during the 1620s at the Palazzo Barberini, S. Andrea della Valle, and St. Peter's. Often during this period he found himself working side by side with the precocious Bernini, who was the avowed favorite of Urban VIII and the papal circle. It was fortunate for Borromini that Bernini was more occupied with sculpture than architecture early in his career, and their actual competition for commissions was kept to a minimum.

Borromini was notoriously difficult and ill-tempered.[2] He dressed eccentrically, was given to fits of hypochondria and melancholy, and was possessed by an irrational jealousy of Bernini above all of his other contemporaries. His bouts with depression finally became so unbearable that in 1667 he ended his life by impaling himself on a sword. It is remarkable that his career prospered as much as it did in light of his irksome personal traits, but eccentric behavior was often viewed as the stamp of genius in this saturnine age. Critics have occasionally been tempted to interpret his architecture as a dramatic expression of intense inner turmoil, but Borromini's work is not to be understood by

45

23. Borromini, S. Carlo alle Quattro Fontane, Rome, courtyard.

subjectivism alone. So great in fact were his intellectual gifts that numerous structural and iconographical complexities of his buildings still puzzle us today.

Borromini's first important independent commission came in 1634 when he was charged with designing a monastery for the Spanish Discalced Trinitarians at the intersection of the Via del Quirinale and the Via delle Quattro Fontane. This modest building so captivated its patrons with its unconventional banded wallwork on the exterior and the ingenious treatment of its tiny courtyard (23), that in 1638 he was asked to build an entirely new church next door. The church was dedicated to the newly canonized Saint Charles Borromeo and named for its site at the corner of the Four Fountains, S. Carlo (or S. Carlino) alle Quattro Fontane.[3] It is ironic, perhaps, that a building dedicated to the author of the Counter-Reformation *Instructiones Fabricae* em-

24. Borromini, S. Carlo alle Quattro Fontane, Rome, plan.

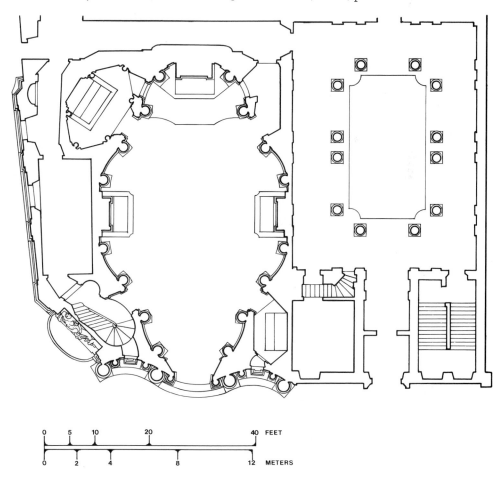

0   5   10   20   40 FEET

0   2   4   8   12   METERS

ployed a centralized rather than a longitudinal ground plan. While Borromeo did allow "lesser" churches to be constructed on alternate plans, times too had changed, and in the more permissive atmosphere of Rome under Urban VIII, religious architecture acquired a completely different character. The vast propagandistic churches built by didactic orders like the Jesuits, Theatines, and Oratorians gave way in the mid-1630s to smaller, cleverer, centrally planned buildings, whose creative ingenuity was as much admired as their practical and polemic effectiveness.

Borromini saw his church from the beginning as a centralized building. He took great pains in preparing the plan (24) which, typically for him, established the basis of all that came later. The plan's irregular shape might seem irrational and capricious, but ironically the genesis of his designs was typically more rational and mathematically precise than that of more "conventional" buildings. The controlling geometry of both plan and elevation is inspired by the simple geometrical unit of the equilateral triangle, an appropriate symbol for the Trinitarian patrons.[4] Borromini's passion for geometry was matched by his love for the flamboyant, anti-classical monuments of late antiquity. In S. Carlo, the continuously undulating, elastic wall recalls a similar wall at Hadrian's Villa at Tivoli, a building already well known in the seventeenth century. The rather startling curvature of the church's ground plan is just a prelude, however, to the more elaborate effects of the interior space.

The interior elevation of S. Carlo (25 and 26) is composed of three superimposed units. In the lower story, sixteen giant columns support an unbroken entablature that rephrases the undulating shape of the plan. But the fluidity of movement is interrupted by the uneven placement of the columns—the spaces between them are wider at the altar and entrance bays than they are at the wall bays—and by the irregular treatment of the bays themselves. An examination of the lower elevation reveals more than one possible rhythmic sequence, for the bays, being clustered in groups of three, have a tendency to overlap and to switch allegiance to neighboring clusters. By exploiting the ambivalence inherent in any sequence of triadic compositions, Borromini purposely created an unstable arrangement that engages the viewer in a constantly shifting set of perceptual experiences.

The second level of the elevation comes as a surprise, given the circumfluent nature of the plan below. The stately march of columns gives way to an alternating set of pendentives and illustionistically

25. Borromini, S. Carlo alle Quattro Fontane, Rome, interior.

foreshortened coffered half-domes suggestive of a simple Greek-Cross structure. An obvious contradiction in terms, this level can only be interpreted as a deliberate effort to mystify the unprepared spectator. Nothing is inevitable in Borromini's architecture, and the appearance of the pendentives—devices that traditionally serve as a transition between a square plan and a round dome—proves his fondness for startling and sometimes whimsical tectonic effects.

49

26. Borromini,
S. Carlo alle
Quattro Fontane,
engraving of interior.

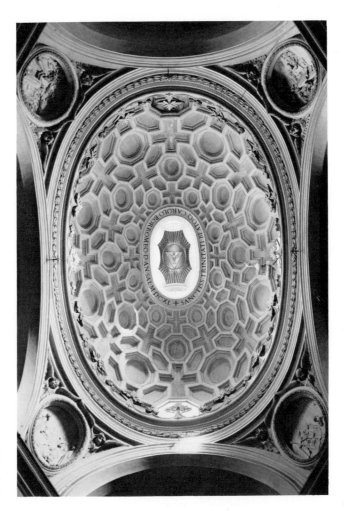

27. Borromini,
S. Carlo alle
Quattro Fontane,
Rome, cupola.

The simple oval dome of the third level (27) gracefully resolves the tension of the lower sections, while subtly reinforcing the principal liturgical axis that leads from the entrance to the high altar. Yet even here, simplicity of shape is counteracted by complexity of surface. The dome is richly coffered in an intricate design of deeply cut polygons and crosses that diminish in size, giving the illusion that the vault is higher than it actually is. The pattern, not surprisingly, is derived from antique prototypes and, according to some, its vocabulary further alludes to Trinitarian symbolism.[5] In both upper zones there is scarcely an inch of unworked surface. All areas not given over to structural members are densely overlaid with geometric or figurative relief. Borromini's intention was to keep the eye constantly engaged and in motion, but he stopped short of overwhelming the viewer by restricting the color scheme to a single, pale hue. This monochromatic tone unifies the interior and cools some of the heat generated by the architectural conflagrations.

Light also plays a role in S. Carlo, acting like a luminous fluid that dissolves the rigidity of solid forms. The interior is illuminated by subtle rays and indirect reflection. Most ingenious is the fenestration at the base of the vault. Windows in the drum illuminate most Italian domes, but Borromini's windows pierce the vault itself, and are concealed behind a crested ornamental band. The stylized vegetal forms of this band waver and are dematerialized by the flow of light which, when brilliant enough, gives the illusion that the entire vault is floating above a transparent ring. In an early chronicle of the church, the interior was likened to a beatific vision, an apt description for this otherworldly building.

The interior was completed in 1641, and the patrons were immensely satisfied with the results. Construction came to a halt, however, because funds ran short, and more than two decades (and most of Borromini's career) went by before the facade (28) could be started, in 1665. It has been suggested, on the basis of surviving drawings, that Borromini followed a design he had made many years earlier, but the sequence of his projects is far from clear and the date of the facade's conception remains unknown. The completion of the work, which was almost finished when Borromini died in 1667, was directed by his nephew Bernardo who, more than likely, was responsible for the clumsy appearance of the uppermost section.

The facade harmonizes remarkably well with the interior. It too rises on an undulating plan, but now the relationship between stories is closer and more subtle. The elevation consists of two stories of equal width and similar design—each organized around four giant free-standing columns and three pairs of smaller columns like those on the facade of St. Peter's by Maderno and the nearby front of S. Andrea al Quirinale by Bernini (53). This interlocking framework creates major and minor horizontal divisions that offset the facade's rather tall and narrow proportions. The balance of this basic arrangement is, however, disrupted by the inconsistent treatment of the two principal entablatures: while the lower one repeats the concave–convex–concave sequence of the interior, its counterpart above is uniformly concave in all three bays. This is just the beginning. The thematic variation that Borromini limited to horizontal progressions inside the church is now

28. Borromini,
S. Carlo alle
Quattro Fontane,
Rome, facade.

applied to vertical progressions too. Reversing and occasionally transforming his motifs, he created a work whose painterly exuberance can
only be understood after patient study. Beginning with the outer bays,
there is in the lower story a semi-circular niche above an oval window,
while in the upper story, niches and windows appear in reverse order.
In vocabulary and syntax, the central bays are even more unorthodox,
casually disregarding the traditional independence of architectural and
sculptural elements. What, for instance, is the classical pedigree of the
fanciful sentry-box window of the upper story, or of the central niche
with its aedicular canopy formed by the wings of cherubim who frame
the statue of S. Carlo?

When an inventory of Borromini's possessions was made after his
death, a wax model of the facade was found along with other models
of the entire building. His use of these small wax models might reveal
the extent to which he conceived of architectural works as pliant
sculptural entities. Creative fantasy is rampant in S. Carlo, but the
polyphonic phrasing of the full composition is organized into an extraordinarily cohesive whole. That S. Carlo was built by a man who
had begun his career only a decade earlier as Carlo Maderno's assistant, is striking evidence that progressive attitudes were again thriving
in Roman architecture.

Seventeenth-century opinion was sharply divided over the merits of
this kind of architecture. The papacy and better-established religious
orders generally shunned Borromini; Titi's famous guidebook to Rome
proclaimed his work "bizarre," and the classical polemicist and biographer Bellori called him "a complete ignoramus, the corrupter of
architecture, the shame of our century." The patrons of S. Carlo, on
the other hand, boasted that "nothing similar with regard to artistic
merit, fantasy, excellence, and singularity can be found anywhere in
the world." Indeed they perfectly described the experience of the
modern viewer when they wrote that "Everything is arranged in such
a manner that one part supplements the other and the spectator is
stimulated to let his eye wander about ceaselessly." The fluidity of
Borromini's space and the restless exuberance of his tectonic and sculptural forms set the standards by which all Baroque architecture can be
judged.

Just after the interior of S. Carlo was completed in 1641, Borromini
was commissioned to build the church of S. Ivo alla Sapienza in Rome.
His patron was the Roman Archiginnasio (later the University of
Rome) with which he had been loosely affiliated for almost a decade.

29. Borromini, S. Ivo alla Sapienza, Rome, exterior.

The institution occupied a large palace near the Piazza Navona that had been built in the second half of the sixteenth century by Ligorio and Della Porta. From the beginning, a centrally planned church was intended for the east wing, but this had yet to be begun. Borromini was free to design a plan of his own choosing, provided it fit the limited site and used the existing courtyard elevation as its principal facade (29). Not surprisingly, the geometry of his plan (30) was

55

30. Borromini,
S. Ivo alla Sapienza,
Rome, plan.

radically different from the regular circle envisioned by his predecessors. Inspired, contemporary sources tell us, by Urban VIII's family emblem, the bee, Borromini transformed this biomorphic shape into geometric patterns again based on the triangle.[6] Two equilateral triangles are inversely superimposed to form a six-pointed star whose apexes extend in an alternating series of semi-circular and polygonal recesses. This complex shape is known as a star-hexagon, and while its geometry is self-generating, prototypes for it are known in antiquity and the Middle Ages.[7]

Unlike S. Carlo, every effort seems to have been made at S. Ivo to resolve the complexities of the plan in designing the elevation (31). Eighteen giant pilasters carrying an unbroken entablature circumscribe the lower story. The progression is orderly and uniform with each of the six recesses subdivided into three bays whose central mem-

56

ber defines its function: altar, entrance, or gallery. Two minor bays now separate each major bay, clarifying the allegiance of each and eliminating the possibility of ambiguous overlappings of triadic clusters, which was used so effectively at S. Carlo. Variations and responses between the major bays do exist, but the visual alignment of all parts is firmly fixed. As a result, the lower story imparts a steady unvarying rhythm to the whole.

31. Borromini, S. Ivo alla Sapienza, Rome, interior.

Less frenetic too, is the view up into the vaulting (32) where no superfluous structural members, as at S. Carlo, disrupt the spatial flow. Perfect harmony is achieved between upper and lower elevations: as the drumless dome rises, the star-hexagon of its plan gradually becomes less pronounced until all complexity is resolved in the circular rim of the lantern. Light floods the interior both from the lantern and through six large windows at the base of the dome. The luminosity of this area reinforces the upward-thrusting motion of both the pilasters and the ribs of the vault. With few horizontal deflections, these elements accentuate the vertical axis, proclaiming a shift of visual and spiritual emphasis from the high altar to the dome. As the penitent attitude of late sixteenth-century worship gave way in the seventeenth century to the ideal of the transcendent, ecstatic religious experience, sacred architecture began to change too. These changes were not just stylistic; in subtle ways they suggested a new path to salvation.

Photographs taken before 1970 show accents of color that were added to the interior during a misguided restoration in the nineteenth-century. This garish painted decoration has recently been covered with whitewash, and the interior now approximates its original appearance. The stucco ornamentation of the vault is again discreet, textural, and monochromatic. Portions of this stucco relief represent the coat of arms of Alexander VII, the last of the three popes who sponsored the construction. Other motifs can be interpreted as more conventional theological symbols: the crowns, palm fronds, and lilies over the round-headed windows represent Christian virtue, martyrdom, and immortality.[8] The dove on the vault of the lantern should be understood, in the architect's own words, as coming from heaven, "with its rays making tongues of fire signifying the coming of the Holy Spirit which brings the true Wisdom." The iconographical message is perhaps best reflected in the inscription of Alexander's dedicatory medal of 1660: *Omnis Sapientia a Domino* (All Wisdom is from the Lord). This motto, like others in the building itself, diminishes the importance of secular learning within the university and reminds modern viewers of the institution's pre-Enlightenment origins.

The exterior of S. Ivo hardly prepares one for what lies inside. In many respects, the two could not be more unlike. Inside, the intricacy of the ground plan and lower elevation gives way in upward ascent to the unity of the circular lantern, while outside, the lantern is the most complex and flamboyant element in an ensemble based on the simple,

32. Borromini, S. Ivo alla Sapienza, Rome, cupola.

33. (*Above*) Borromini,
S. Ivo alla Sapienza,
Rome, lantern.
(*Below*)
Temple of Venus,
Baalbek.

arcaded hemi-cycle of the ground story. One suspects that Borromini may deliberately have ridiculed the tasteful design of his predecessors by saving his most idiosyncratic creation for the most visible part of the building.

In the view from the courtyard (29)—our principal view of the church—we first encounter Borromini's hand in the conservatively de-signed attic whose inscription introduces the visitor to the *Aedes Sapientiae,* or House of Wisdom. Above the attic, a tall hexafoil drum reverses the curvature while repeating the pilaster order of the hemi-cycle below. This drum, which has no structural counterpart inside the church, recalls the encased domes that are a more common sight in northern Italy than in Rome (131). On the next level, a conical ring of steps derived from the dome of the Pantheon is buttressed by mer-lons copied from Michelangelo's Porta Pia. These are the first signs of the eclectic attitude that underlies the form and iconography of the lantern. This fantastic creation (33), a singular tour-de-force on the Roman skyline, has long been considered the quintessential example of Borromini's "heretical" genius.[9] Of the lantern's two parts, the lower seems like a pastiche of Michelangelo's drum of St. Peter's and Hellenistic peristyles like that of the Venus Temple at Baalbek (33). The historical mix may be unsettling to some, but the formal combi-nation of these disparate elements is perfectly realized. The upper part of the lantern, with its distinctive flame-topped spiral, has stimulated more iconographical debate than any monument in Rome. The Tower of Babel, a *pharos* or lighthouse, the emblematic personification of Philosophy, and even Dante's vision of Mount Purgatory are some of the allusions that have been suggested. The most recent interpretation sees the lantern as combining references to the papal tiara and to the flaming crown that symbolizes Charity—the principal virtue of S. Ivo, and the chief attribute of Wisdom.[10] Borromini, like his great con-temporaries Rembrandt and Velasquez, was not intolerant of am-biguity, and the fullest understanding of the monument may need to take the possibility of multiple meanings and associations into account.

In their preoccupation with literary allusions, critics have tended to ignore or downplay the obvious natural associations of the spiral form.[11] The inventory of Borromini's estate listed two large conch shells—known in the seventeenth century as *corone papali* or papal crowns. For an architect who believed that architecture was ultimately based on nature, and who presumably had adopted the Barberini bee as the conceptual basis of the church's ground plan, it would not have

34. Borromini, S. Andrea della Fratte, Rome, dome and campanile.

been uncharacteristic to combine the spiral shell, which had its own associations with the papal tiara, with other more emblematic references.

The contrast between exterior and interior at S. Ivo underscores the duality of many Baroque churches: the rhetorical, propagandistic role of the public exterior, and the more intimate, spiritually stirring role of the interior, where the faithful gather to worship. Seen in this light, the spectacle of S. Ivo's exterior provides a perfect Baroque counterpoint to Sixtus V's obelisks. As the crucific tops the orb at the lantern's summit, so we are reminded that all confusion is resolved under the sign of worldwide religious ordination.

Consecrated in 1660, S. Ivo was Borromini's most accomplished and compelling work. By combining intricate geometry with picturesque literary allusions, he deftly infused Christian content into a scheme that delights the eye with its artifice while challenging the mind with complex metaphors. Never again was he given the opportunity to create so striking a visual and intellectual ensemble.

At S. Andrea della Fratte, whose transept and choir he helped complete between 1653 and 1665, Borromini was severely constrained by the Gesù-type plan that had been under construction since 1605. There was little he could do to transform the bland interior, but on the exterior, his campanile and dome (34) are among his most vividly pictorial and self-indulgent creations. The encased dome is transformed by the four piers that buttress it into a square with undulating sides. As at S. Carlo, these curving planes are stabilized by immured columns of the composite order and are capped by a heavy entablature. Borromini designed a lantern to crown the dome, but unfortunately it was never built. From surviving drawings, it is evident that he planned this lantern in accordance with the main theme of curve and countercurve. It is also likely that he intended to cover the rough brick surfaces with stucco facing.

The adjacent bell-tower is even more whimsical. Rising at the intersection of the left transept and tribune, it is typically Borrominesque in its playful superimposition of heterogeneous ingredients. The lowest story, which fronts on the narrow Via Capo le Case, is indistinguishable from the main flank of the church, but the story above is a classically ordered block whose treatment is related to that of the dome and its intended lantern. Surmounting this tall pedestal is an open *tholos* which serves as the belfry. The particular combination of ele-

35. La Conocchia,
Capua Vetere.

ments—a circular colonnade on a high base—again reflects Borromini's passion for antique monuments like the late Roman Tomb of the Julii at St. Remy or the one known as the Conocchia at Capua Vetere (35). Like the dome of S. Ivo, the pictorial quality of this composition also increases with height. In the upper sections, the tectonic members are entirely replaced by the sculptural forms of herms, flaming vases, scrolls, and a spiky crown. On Rome's harmonious skyline, the flamboyance of S. Andrea is a distinctive signature of both the church and its architect.

Secular architecture during the seventeenth century tended to be less inventive than its sacred counterpart. Although secular commissions were no less numerous, the worldly Catholicism that sponsored imaginatively designed churches seldom condoned an extravagant private architecture, and it was rare to find a domestic building with as much flair as that of the churches we have just discussed. With the clergy and the Roman aristocracy indissolubly linked, there were few patrons for such enterprises, and the major buildings were put up by families directly connected to the papacy. During his career, Borromini worked for more than a dozen private Roman patrons, but their commissions usually engaged him in collaborative efforts, as at the Palazzo Barberini, or allowed him little room for self-expression.

One minor but interesting exception to the sobriety of Roman residential architecture is the *prospettiva,* or perspective colonnade of the Palazzo Spada, constructed in 1652–1653 for Cardinal Bernardino Spada (36). Traditionally, this curious structure was considered an autograph work by Borromini, but recent research has proved that it was designed in collaboration with an Augustinian priest and mathematician named Giovanni Maria da Bitonto.[12] The corridor, which connects two small courtyards, is only about nine meters long, but by ingeniously slanting the walls, floor, and vault, its designers implied a space more than four times that length. The basic structure of the *prospettiva* is similar to the main entrance hall of the nearby Palazzo Farnese, built nearly a century earlier, but the illusionistic concept was probably suggested by an ancient monument from the Via Appia which had recently been reconstructed in a publication by the architect G. B. Montano.[13] The corridor serves no function but that of a witty *trompe l'oeil.* Its success, like that of the great illusionistic ceiling paintings of the Roman Baroque—Guercino's *Aurora* and Pozzo's false dome in S. Ignazio, for example—depends on the viewer's ability to recognize and unmask the deception. A contemporary author, Sforza Pallavicino, described wit as "a marvelous observation condensed into a brief sentence." The modest, epigrammatic quality of the Spada perspective can charm even those who have little interest in the more imposing structures of Baroque Rome.

Somewhat grander in scale are two of Borromini's buildings that serve a jointly religious and residential function. The Oratory and Casa (or monastic dependency) of the Congregation of St. Phillip Neri stands next to the Oratorian Mother Church of S. Maria in Vallicella (1575–1606).[14] Borromini entered the picture in 1637 when he replaced Paolo Maruscelli, a lesser architect who for thirteen years had directed the work with little visible result. During his tenure, Borromini designed and by 1640 had completed the chapel of the Ora-

36. Borromini with Giovanni Maria da Bitonto, Palazzo Spada, Rome, perspective colonnade.

tory, and continued to work on the monastic complex despite constant friction with the administration that led to his dismissal ten years later. The Oratory (37), whose informal services were never meant to compete with those held in the adjoining church, is simple in design, much like the monastery of S. Carlo. It is a wall architecture whose primary ornament consists of a linear network of flat pilasters and banded reliefs, and its spatial and tectonic restraint suggests that both the architect and the patrons desired a chapel that would complement rather than dominate the ritual it contained.

37. Borromini, Oratory of St. Phillip Neri, Rome, interior.

38. Borromini, Oratory of St. Phillip Neri, Rome, exterior.

The exterior (38) is more artful. Since the facade masks both the chapel and the monastic complex, Borromini wisely planned the front to be independent of all that lay behind it. The five bays of the central section, in fact, screen just two of the Oratory's five bays, and five of the eight bays of a library on the upper story. A greater effort was made to blend the new front with that of the adjacent church. Using brick to contrast with the Vallicella's travertine facing, Borromini maintained comparable door and pilaster heights on the lower story. Above, the facade is replete with subtle unorthodoxy. All of the Counter-Reformation starch is taken out of the sixteenth-century design: its flat front is given a slight bend, its correct Corinthian capitals are parodied by the lower order of pilasters, and its crisp pediments are fancifully transformed. In the reversed curvature and illusionistic half-dome of its central bay, one is reminded of S. Carlo alle Quattro Fontane which was under construction at the same time.

No Borromini composition would be complete without some reference to Roman antiquity. Although he certainly had not seen the building, one is again reminded of the little Venus Temple at Baalbek (33) whose split pediments are so prophetic of the Oratory's upper story window frames. Other windows attributed to the architect at the Palazzo Barberini (22) seem to have been similarly inspired. The curious "pediment" which crowns the facade lends a note of ecclesiastical dignity to the otherwise nonsectarian elevation. Its pedigree probably lies not in the classical tradition, but in the late medieval tradition of elaborately framed altarpieces and other luxury objects.

The Collegio di Propaganda Fide, a training school for young missionaries that lay off the Piazza di Spagna, presented Borromini with a similar challenge. Here the architect was asked to consolidate and amplify a complex of buildings that already contained a chapel by Bernini. From 1654 until his death in 1667, Borromini rebuilt the chapel, added new residential quarters, and constructed the major facade on the Via di Propaganda. This facade (39 and 40) responds to the narrow street on which it fronts by using the giant order and a heavy cornice (the attic story was added in the eighteenth century). Unlike the exterior of the Oratory, which can be viewed from a greater distance, the Collegio's facade has no crowning pediment to suggest its churchly character. More startling is Borromini's indifference to the traditional rules governing the use of the classical order. His giant pilasters are conceived with a lack of restraint that rivals that of the

39. Borromini, Collegio di Propaganda Fide, Rome, exterior.

most Mannerist architects of the sixteenth century. Rejecting the full repertory of the five orders, he adopted, perhaps from Michelangelo, a "capital" consisting of a block with five parallel grooves. Just as unorthodox is the entablature which has no architrave or frieze. The greatest caprice, however, was reserved for the window and door surrounds, whose idiosyncratic shapes are developments of a favorite Borrominesque type. As is typical of this architect, the central bay becomes the thematic basis for variations carried out in the other six bays of the *piano nobile,* or main floor.[15]

A comparison between the facades of the Oratory and the Propaganda Fide reveals the significant changes that Borromini's style underwent during the intervening years. The delicately worked wall surface of the earlier building has now given way to a bolder, more forceful projection of orders and relief. They are roughly the same size, but the Propaganda Fide with its giant order appears grander in scale. Anti-classical murmurs have become more pronounced, and architectural convictions are strengthened: It is as if a lyrical song had been turned into an operatic aria.

70

40. Borromini, Collegio di Propaganda Fide, Rome, detail of exterior.

41. Borromini, Collegio di Propaganda Fide, Rome, interior.

Dramatic self-realization also characterizes the chapel that Borromini built in the interior (41). He demolished Bernini's small oval chapel, and constructed a new one on an oblong plan similar to that of the Oratory.[16] The chapel was dedicated to the Re Magi, or Three Wise Men. Like the Oratory, the chapel runs parallel with the street, and the entrance is to the left of the main portal. Its interior is also organized with the giant order, but the surrounding wall is articulated with an alternating sequence of niche and altar recesses that eliminates all flat wall surfaces.[17] Better illumination is provided and vertical unification is increased by employing the entablature *en ressaut* above the cherub-capped pilasters. The crisply projecting order leads one's eye to an emphatic system of banded ornament in the vault. Although it shares few motifs with the facade of the complex, the chapel is just as lively in spirit.

The changes in Borromini's style parallel the developments of Baroque architecture in general, yet certain fundamental qualities of his work neither change or are shared by other members of his generation in Rome. Geometry, of course, is a concern of all architects, but Borromini's use of intricate triangulated systems was a departure from his fellow architects' reliance on the circle and other simple modular schemes.[18] Attempts have been made to relate this schematism to his interest in Gothic architecture, a style all but ignored at the time. There are more obvious relationships between his work and monuments of late Roman antiquity, although one suspects that some "ancient" forms were figments of his own imagination, independent of specific prototypes which, like Baalbek, could hardly have been known to him. Antiquity may have provided Borromini with a storehouse of ideas, but he owed at least as much to the liberating influence of Michelangelo and sixteenth-century Mannerist architecture. In the artistically permissive atmosphere of the Post-Tridentine seventeenth century, Borromini never strayed from the libertarian path. His vocabulary remained rooted in the classical tradition, but his grammar and syntax often took unexpected, anti-classical turns. As with Mannerist architecture, the full effect was reserved for those whose knowledge of the traditional rules made transgressions all the more delectable. Whether motivated by wit, polemic, or self-expression, Borromini's genius lay in his uncanny ability to create the most emotional and original forms through scientific and historical means. His originality can be appreciated even more fully by comparing his work with what his chief rivals, Bernini and Pietro da Cortona, were doing at the same time.

4

Gianlorenzo Bernini

By any account, Gianlorenzo Bernini was the most successful Italian artist of the seventeenth century. His fame has always been based primarily on the brilliance of his sculpture, but he was extraordinarily gifted as a painter and architect as well. Like Michelangelo before him, Bernini seemed the very personification of his age. While Michelangelo was a restless introvert plagued by self-doubt and anxiety over the perplexing religious and political controversies of the sixteenth century, Bernini was a gracious courtier who unhesitatingly accepted the more worldly and affirmative attitudes of the seventeenth century. Neither one embraced a monolithic concept of style. For Bernini this was largely the result of his different attitudes toward the various media. While his sculpture was unrivalled for its dramatic Baroque character, his architecture steadfastly adheres to the traditional values of ancient and Renaissance Classicism. Remarkable as it may seem, Bernini, the dominant and most progressive sculptor of his generation, was simultaneously its most conservative major architect.[1] The competition he faced in architecture was also stronger; in sculpture, he had few serious rivals to challenge his supremacy.

The son of a sculptor, Bernini was born in Naples in 1598 and moved with his family to Rome around 1606. He received his sculptural training in his father Pietro's shop, but his knowledge of architecture came from working alongside Borromini in the mid-1620s, while both assisted Carlo Maderno at the Palazzo Barberini and St. Peter's. Temperamentally, Bernini was no less passionate than Borromini, but his charm and versatile talent made him the favorite of eight successive

42. Bernini,
S. Bibiana,
Rome, facade.

popes, particularly Urban VIII (1623–1644), whose friendship was a
decisive advantage at the beginning of his career. Except for a visit to
France in 1665, Bernini remained in Rome until his death in 1680,
outliving all of his serious rivals by at least a decade.

Bernini received his first independent architectural commission in
1624, years before such an opportunity came to his contemporary,
Borromini. During a routine renovation of the fifth-century church of
S. Bibiana, workers had unearthed the saint's remains, a discovery which
inspired Urban to commission Bernini to carve a statue over the high

76

altar and construct a new facade (42). This modest new front is hardly breathtaking, but it did offer an original approach to the old problem of screening the irregular profile of a longitudinal church. Unlike the standard Gesù facade, it is contained within a square whose regular outline is broken only by the tall aedicular bay of the upper story. A few earlier Roman facades had attempted similar solutions, but none had given such strong emphasis to the central bay. Bernini no doubt used an arcaded loggia on the lower story to illuminate the narthex behind, but by tripling the Ionic pilasters around the central doorway, he gave emphasis to that otherwise undistinguished area. The upper story is not so well integrated; the low, balustraded side bays and tall pedimented central bay clash at the juncture of their respective pilasters.[2] Too close in scale to be as harmonious or sensible as Maderno's double order on the facade of St. Peter's, their arrangement also fails to correspond to the bay directly below. The contrast between the arcuation and trabeation of the two stories is rather ungraceful, tending, in fact, to exacerbate the already disjunctive appearance of the total composition. In spite of these shortcomings, S. Bibiana's facade, which was completed in 1626, harbingers two of the guiding principles of Bernini's mature architecture: the use of tripartite schemes with a climactic center and framing sides, and the preference for austere facades with flat pilasters, over the more sensuous columnar designs favored by many of his contemporaries.

In 1624 Bernini also received an independent assignment at St. Peter's for the design of a new baldachin in the crossing above the high altar and the tomb of the First Apostle. Combining architecture and sculpture, this monument (43) also joined two previously separate iconographical types: the ciborium, a permanent structure consisting of a dome on columns placed over a high altar, and an earlier baldachin in St. Peter's—a temporary structure consisting of a tasselled cloth canopy on a wooden framework supported by four angels.[3] To support the fabulous superstructure, Bernini designed spiral columns inspired by those still in the basilica that survived from the high altar of Old St. Peter's and which, according to legend, had been brought by Constantine from the Temple of Solomon in Jerusalem. The entire monument, which is about 90 feet high, was cast in bronze, a material whose dark burnished tones freed him somewhat from the need to accommodate his design to the staid architecture of the crossing. Yet removed as it is from its immediate formal context, there is no question that Bernini conceived the monument as the iconographic

43. Bernini, baldachin in St. Peter's, Rome.

44. St. Peter's, Rome, facade with Bernini's tower as it appeared in 1641–46.

focus of an extensive sculptural program that he was concurrently planning for the four great piers of the crossing. Borromini, who worked as Bernini's assistant during these years, was probably the author of the ornate scrolls at the top of the baldachin, but Bernini's own sensibility is easily recognized in the profusion of figurative imagery—vine tendrils, emblematic Barberini bees, papal medals, and other devices—that cover the monument from top to bottom.

Carlo Maderno died in 1629, and it came as no surprise that Bernini was appointed Architect of St. Peter's in his place. This position kept him fully occupied for several decades, and not until after 1650 did he undertake outside architectural commissions of consequence. At St. Peter's, where he was already working on several sculptural projects, Bernini also directed three interrelated architectural commissions: the renovation of the church facade, the creation of an open piazza in front of the basilica, and the raising of the Scala Regia, a flight of steps leading from the piazza to the papal palace.

The first of these efforts called for the renovation of the facade. Rather optimistically, Bernini proposed the construction of towers similar to those already planned by Maderno during the pontificate of Paul V (18), and in 1637 Urban gave his approval. He began the south tower (44) first, evidently ignoring reports that warned of un-

79

45. Bernini, St. Peter's Square, Rome, engraving.

stable ground beneath Maderno's foundations. The structure was
nearly complete by the summer of 1641 when, to everyone's dismay,
cracks began to appear in the substructure. Bernini was said to be so
mortified by Urban's reprimand that he took to his bed for several
days. Work on both towers was quickly abandoned. After the death of
his papal protector in 1644, the fiscal scandal which ensued made Bernini even more vulnerable to attack from rivals and from the new
pope, Innocent X, who viewed with suspicion all members of the Barberini circle. In 1646 an outside committee of architects convinced the
pope to demolish what had been built of the towers, and the facade
was restored to its old, ungainly appearance. Bernini made subsequent
proposals which would have lightened the towers' weight and isolated
them from the facade proper, but these were never taken seriously and
today the facade remains almost exactly as Maderno left it.

Bernini's other contributions to St. Peter's were more successful.
With the election of Alexander VII in 1655, he gained favor with a
pope who was to support his architectural career enthusiastically. One
of Alexander's first commissions called for a great colonnaded piazza
to contain the crowds that gathered in front of the basilica for pontifi-

80

cal blessings and other special occasions.[4] Two requirements made this a special challenge. The pope had to remain visible to as many people as possible from the two locations where public appearances were made—the benediction loggia of the facade and his apartment on the top floor of the palace to the right of the basilica—and the enclosing colonnade had to stand clear of nearby buildings and be wide enough to serve as a processional passageway to St. Peter's. After considering several alternatives, Bernini chose a composite plan consisting of a small trapezoid juxtaposed with a large, transversely positioned oval (45). This arrangement not only met the ceremonial criteria, but the low, converging side walls of the trapezoid (the so-called Piazza Retta) even served optically to make the facade appear narrower and higher and thus more visually pleasing. Bernini, moreover, was not unmindful of the symbolic advantages of the plan. In 1658 he wrote a memorandum comparing the colonnade to the maternal arms of the church which "reach out with open arms to embrace Catholics to reaffirm their belief, heretics to reunite them with the Church, and agnostics to enlighten them with the true faith." Originally he intended to close the far end of the piazza with a third colonnaded arm, thus restricting access to the square to two narrow, off-axis entrances. This third arm was never built, but if it had been, early visitors to St. Peter's would have experienced an exhilarating and dramatic entrance from the narrow access streets into the open expanse of the piazza, an approach in the tradition of such "surprise" Roman spaces as the Piazza del Pantheon or the Piazza Navona. Today one enters from the Via della Conciliazione, a broad boulevard planned by Mussolini in 1936 but only completed in 1950. Like the streets laid out by Sixtus V, the boulevard holds few surprises for approaching visitors, but does, from a distance, permit St. Peter's majestic dome to emerge from behind the facade. Closer to the church the height of Maderno's nave blocks this sight.

For the elevation, Bernini experimented with several designs before finally choosing a simple trabeated scheme (46) whose classical poise recalls the stately colonnades of ancient Rome.[5] Single Tuscan columns stand four deep, creating the required processional corridor between them, while suggesting—rather than fully defining—the parameter of the piazza. Both colonnade and piazza invite further exploration. An obelisk raised by Domenico Fontana in 1586 stood on axis with the basilica, and Bernini followed Michelangelo's example of the Capitoline Hill by creating a second cross-axis through this same focal

46. Bernini, St. Peter's Square, Rome, elevation.

point. The geometry of the transverse oval leads one's eye across the main axis where it is arrested by the accentuated central bay of each hemicycle and by the two fountains aligned with them.[6] Viewing the piazza while walking inside the colonnade is equally engaging (47). Four rows of columns converge, overlap, and separate, creating a dynamic scenography whose cumulative effect transcends the classically taciturn style of the component parts. Here lies the magic of Bernini's design: through the most simple and decorous means, he created a festive public space charged with excitement. The music of the fountains and the movement of throngs of people complement the architecture and provide the perfect setting for the spectacle of a papal appearance.

Despite occasional criticism from the populace and outspoken foreign visitors about the propriety of spending vast sums of money on architecture rather than on social welfare—a less familiar cry then

47. Bernini, St. Peter's Square, Rome, view from colonnade.

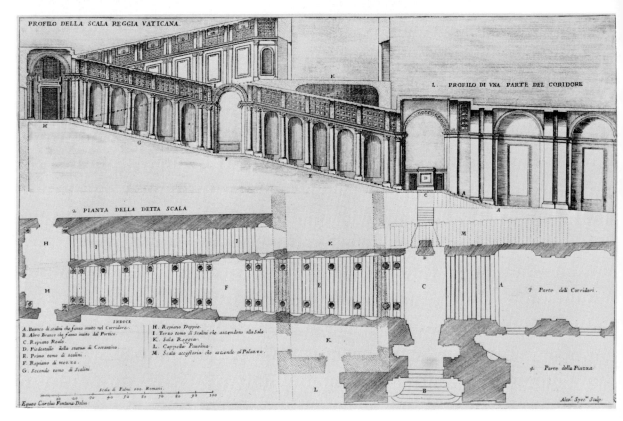

48. Bernini, Scala Regia, Vatican, section and plan.

than now—Alexander VII charged Bernini with his third Vatican
project in 1663, three years before the ruinously costly colonnade was
completed.[7] The Scala Regia (48 and 49) is a grand ceremonial stairway leading from the narthex of the basilica and north colonnade into
the Vatican palace.[8] Without changing the pre-existing landings or a
return flight that abutted the Sistine Chapel, Bernini expanded the
lower stairway and erected rows of columns along its sides. Because the
walls of his new corridor converged slightly, he varied the distance of
the columns from the wall and progressively reduced their diameter
to offset the structure's irregularity and persuade viewers that they
were experiencing the natural effects of perspectival diminution. The
controlled illumination of the landings, the rich sculptural effect of the
papal coat-of-arms, and Bernini's own statue of the rapturous Constantine placed at the juncture of the narthex and colonnade combine to
produce a unified impression of Baroque splendor.

In concept and articulation, the Scala Regia recalls the Borrominesque perspective corridor at the Palazzo Spada, built ten years earlier
(35). In each, a seemingly natural perspective was achieved through

84

49. Bernini, Scala Regia, Vatican, elevation.

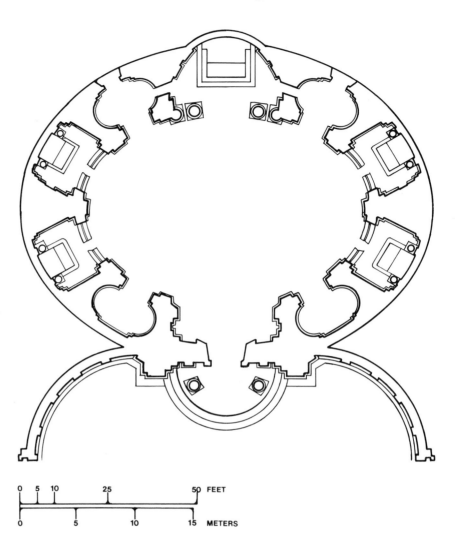

50. Bernini,
S. Andrea al Quirinale,
Rome, plan.

0 5 10   25   50 FEET

0   5   10   15 METERS

ingenious illusionistic contrivance. Yet, the formal similarities of the two corridors belie differences in the motivaton of their design. The Spada perspective is a witty and functionless *trompe l'oeil* intended perhaps as a parody of Sangallo's vestibule at the nearby Palazzo Farnese. Bernini's goal was exactly the opposite: He made every effort to construct a handsome but functional corridor in an anomalous space with a minimum of recognizable artifice. That he may have enjoyed the challenge is suggested by his contemporary biographer Baldinucci, who quotes the artist as having said "the highest merit lay not in making beautiful and commodious buildings, but in being able to make do with little, to make beautiful things out of the inadequate and ill-adapted, to make use of a defect in such a way that if it had not existed one would have to invent it."[9]

86

During the reign of Alexander VII (1655–1667) Bernini also accepted important architectural commissions outside the Vatican. Between 1658 and 1662, when he was already in his sixties, he began three small centralized churches in Rome and the outlying towns of Ariccia and Castel Gandolfo. The first and most ingeniously planned of these was S. Andrea al Quirinale, just down the street from Borromini's S. Carlo alle Quattro Fontane and directly opposite the pontifical palace on the Quirinal.[10] S. Andrea was built for the Jesuit novitiate with financial assistance from members of the Pamphili family, descendants of the late Pope Innocent X. The Jesuits were unusually fortunate in having an architect so sympathetic to their cause that he refused payment for his services, and patrons so generous that they sold some of the family silver to meet the church's spiralling costs.[11]

The site, unfortunately, was rather shallow and constricted, and the papacy imposed the further condition that the elevation be kept low so that the view from the adjacent Quirinal Palace would not be obstructed. Bernini, in typical fashion, was inspired by such limitations to new heights of imagination. Because the available space was somewhat wider than it was deep, he again chose a transverse oval for his ground plan (50). Formally, this was a logical solution, but it was less desirable liturgically since the geometric axis of such a plan runs perpendicular to the ritual axis. Bernini was attentive to the problems of orientation and he manipulated both plan and elevation to reinforce optically the primary liturgical axis leading from the entrance to the high altar. In most oval or circular churches, including ones of Bernini's own design, there are an odd number (usually three) of chapels or other recesses on either side of the high altar. Such an arrangement invariably juxtaposes the central bays of each side and establishes a visually responsive cross-axis between them. At S. Andrea, Bernini lessened the emphasis on the cross-axis by creating an even number of openings (four) on each side. Solid piers rather than open chapels face one another at the two central positions, thus drawing one's attention away from rather than toward the lateral axis.

The interior elevation (51 and 52) employs other equally effective devices to help accentuate the area around the high altar. Flanked by lower apertures, the altar bay is the only one in the church that is framed by free-standing columns and topped with a pediment. The idea of the columnar screen was probably derived from the Pantheon or another ancient temple reproduced in a sixteenth-century treatise by

51. Bernini, S. Andrea al Quirinale, Rome, interior.

Serlio.[12] The illumination of the high altar further emphasizes its importance among the church's chapels and recesses. A lantern hidden in the vault above the altar fills the chancel with a golden light that makes other areas seem gloomy by comparison. The most arresting element, of course, is Antonio Raggi's statue of St. Andrew breaking through the pediment. Often in his ensemble compositions, Bernini leaves classical reserve behind when called upon to set the stage for an exciting piece of narrative sculpture. The unabashedly Baroque pediment intensifies the emotionalism of St. Andrew's miraculous ascension, while providing both a formal accent for the high altar and an iconographical link between Guglielmo Cortese's altar painting of Andrew's Crucifixion and the celestial reward so brilliantly represented in the dome above. Here and elsewhere, Bernini's integration of tectonic, sculptural, and illuminative devices is based on a hierarchical system that emphasizes rather than lessens the importance of the individual parts.[13] In this system, sculpture that tells a story is the dominant element to which architecture defers.

52. Bernini, S. Andrea al Quirinale, Rome, cupola.

53. Bernini, S. Andrea al Quirinale, Rome, facade.

The lower story is clad with a rich revetment of colored marbles that suggest the influence of Raphael's luxurious interior of the Chigi Chapel in S. Maria del Popolo, where Bernini had carved two important sculptures a few years earlier. The rose tones of the marble-clad lower story are superseded by the even richer textural effect of gilt stucco in the dome above (52). Since pendentives were unnecessary in an oval church and the use of a drum might have blocked the panoramic view from the neighboring Quirinal Palace, Bernini raised a modest oval vault directly above the main cornice. The base of the dome is pierced by squarish windows topped by putti and sculptures of the apostolic fishermen. These illuminate the interior and accent the gilded dome. By Italian standards of the period, the dome is low, but Bernini partially offset that impression by springing vertical ribs above the pilaster order of the lower story and covering the vault with illusionistically foreshortened coffering. The combination of ribs and coffers in the same dome, of course, denies the traditional structural function of each. In Classical times, coffering was used to lessen the weight of a heavy concrete vault, whereas in the Middle Ages ribs were adopted as a means of concentrating the thrust of a thinner masonry vault. Pietro da Cortona combined the two systems for the first time at Ss. Martina e Luca (66), begun in 1635, and thereafter Bernini used it in all of his vaults.[14] Increased verticality was characteristic of most Baroque churches, but at S. Andrea al Quirinale, Bernini achieved the elevated effect through ornamental rather than structural means.

The exterior (53) is no less clever. The facade proper is composed of a single, pedimented bay whose stark simplicity contrasts sharply with the complex pictorialism of Borromini's neighboring and nearly contemporary facade of S. Carlo alle Quattro Fontane. On no other street in Rome does one find such a ready comparison of opposing artistic viewpoints. Bernini's composition is again hierarchical with the giant aedicular bay providing the framework to which all other structural elements defer. The vocabulary is traditional and recalls that of a few earlier Roman churches which were based on Palladian models in Venice.[15] In turn, the low semi-circular entrance porch may be thought of as a three-dimensional extension of the same Palladian prototype, of Maderno's secondary order at St. Peter's, or even as a reduction of Cortona's rounded portico at S. Maria della Pace (68). Regardless of its genetic background, the porch bears a strong familial resemblance to the columnar screen inside the church. While the latter is slightly concave and separates clergy and laity, the convex porch performs the opposite function, reaching out to welcome the congregation. In place of the interior statue of St. Andrew and its framing pediment, outside one finds the Pamphili coat-of-arms mounted between scrolls.

Contrasting elements abound throughout the exterior elevation. The curvature of the church's oval body is reversed by the concave, low walls that frame the facade. The parenthetical, tripartite composition was a favorite of Bernini's and in using the low quadrant walls he also created a forecourt that serves as a transition from the street.[16] The scheme is further related to the contemporary Piazza of St. Peter's in that Bernini planned but never executed a fully enclosing "third arm" for each. A drawing for S. Andrea dated 1658 reveals his original intention of enclosing the forecourt with a straight wall running parallel to the adjacent building fronts.[17] Like the unexecuted arm at St. Peter's, this wall was to have two off-axis entrances restricting the path of approach to a sharply oblique angle. In architecture as in sculpture, Bernini was concerned with the way his work was perceived and experienced by the spectator. For example, he once wrote that a centralized building required a deep entrance "because experience shows that people, upon entering a room, take a few steps forward and unless allowance is made, they will not be able to embrace the shape in its entirety." Here as elsewhere, he preferred that a diagonal view precede the more climactic frontal view. Unfortunately, Bernini seldom realized such a rigidly controlled scheme, and at S. Andrea the absence of the front wall has plainly diminished the effect he originally intended.

Since the exactly contemporary church of S. Tommaso di Villanova in Castel Gandolfo (1658–1661) presented few of the challenges of S. Andrea, it tested his imagination somewhat less. Castel Gandolfo, a well-situated hilltown some thirty miles south of Rome, is the site of the papal summer residence, which has been its main attraction since the time of Urban VIII. When Alexander VII decided to build a new church near the pontifical palace, Bernini was his natural choice as architect. The plan, which took the shape of a traditional Greek Cross, was rather like that of Sangallo's Renaissance church of S. Maria delle Carceri in Prato (1485) or Raphael's S. Eligio degli Orefici in Rome (1516). Other architects might have found the simple plan (54) conventional and outmoded, but Bernini so admired the art of Raphael and the High Renaissance that he felt no need to fundamentally transform the prototype.[18] The elevation (55) is also traditional in its volumetric reduction of the cross arms into a square crossing which, through the use of pendentives, supports a circular cupola. As might be expected, the overall proportions of S. Tommaso are somewhat taller than those favored in the Renaissance, and the church's seventeenth-century origin is also reflected in the controlled use of ornamental overlay. Unlike the austere interiors of most Renaissance churches, that of S. Tommaso is handsome and well-ornamented with paintings and sculpture. The colored marbles of the altars, the altar paintings, and the gilded stuccoes of the vault create a sumptuous atmosphere that proclaims an entirely new aesthetic. As in all of Bernini's centralized

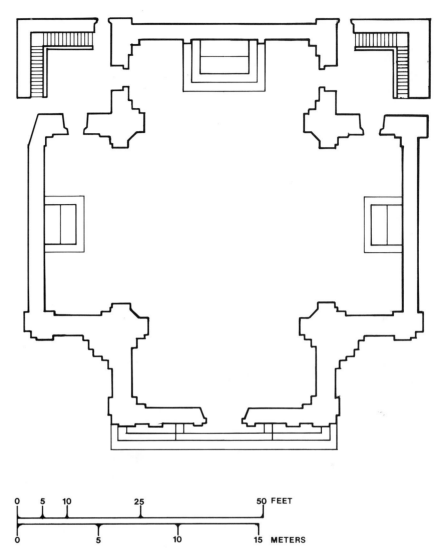

54. Bernini,
S. Tommaso di Villanova,
Castel Gandolfo, plan.

churches, most of the ornament is concentrated in the dome, which sits on a low drum pierced by eight windows. Above each window are putti and stucco medallions that reproduce some of the paintings hung in St. Peter's to commemorate St. Thomas' canonization in 1658. The remaining surface of the vault is overlaid with ribs and coffers similar to those at S. Andrea al Quirinale.

The exterior (56) is far less pictorial. Here Bernini was even more subtle in altering the sober style of his Renaissance prototypes. The structural arrangement of the interior is clearly expressed but made all the more satisfying by the insistent flatness of the outside wall planes.

93

55. Bernini, S. Tommaso di Villanova, Castel Gandolfo, interior.

56. Bernini,
S. Tommaso di Villanova,
Castel Gandolfo,
exterior.

By this time, most Roman architects had been captivated by the vitality of the engaged or free-standing column, but Bernini remained steadfast in his use of the pilaster. Moreover, at S. Tommaso the pilasters are of the Tuscan Order, the most chaste and ascetic of all. With its ornament limited to the customary papal coat of arms in the main pediment, the facade's Baroque character is revealed only by such minor features as the broken entablature, the rounded, deeply projecting door pediment, the intricate treatment of the corners, and the steep profile of the dome.

Castel Gandolfo is unique among Bernini's late churches in not being

95

57. Bernini, S. Maria dell'Assunzione, Ariccia, exterior.

flanked by separate stabilizing wings, but this may have been dictated by restrictions of the site. Nevertheless, he did manage to emphasize the building's orientation by capitalizing on the frontality inherent in the Greek Cross plan. The site sloped steeply to the rear, lending natural drama to the entrance arm, but Bernini further stressed the primacy of this facade by making it the only one to carry a classical order of pilasters and a crowning pediment.

This flat front, uncompromised by Baroque conventions of rhythm or massing, is further stabilized by the treatment of the side arms. Only those walls visible from the front are adorned with pilasters; all others are marked with simple wall strips. Because of the sloping site and the corner vestries, the side and rear elevations are taller, wider, and fenestrated more liberally than the front elevation. All of these elements lessen the inherent conflict between the formal advantages of the centralized plan and the functional demands of a non-centralized liturgy.[19] As is often true of Bernini's architecture, the ideal and the practical were reconciled in a brilliant synthesis.

In 1662 Alexander favored Bernini with the commission for another centrally planned church in the town of Ariccia, a sleepy hamlet not

96

far from Castel Gandolfo that had been purchased by the papal family
just a few years earlier. The new church, dedicated to S. Maria dell'
Assunzione (57), was located on one side of a wide piazza directly
opposite the family castle. Here, as at Castel Gandolfo, Bernini was
motivated by a revivalist spirit. Turning his attention from the Renaissance to Roman antiquity, he adapted no less venerable a monument
than the Pantheon (58). His interest in the Pantheon was hardly dis-
passionate, and he claimed that it was his favorite building; during the
decade 1657–1667 he was involved in the renovation of its interior
and the reconstruction of the disorderly accumulation of post-antique
buildings that had grown around it.[20]

Bernini followed the basic plan of his prototype but reshaped so
many individual features that the character of the Assunzione is entirely new. Chief among his exterior revisions was the substitution of
a three-bay arcaded portico, resembling that of S. Bibiana, for the
Pantheon's octastyle colonnade. By further substituting Tuscan pilasters for Corinthian columns, he made the porch appear more solid and
integrally related to the building behind it. As we have seen, Bernini
was greatly concerned with the urban context of his buildings, and
this was the area in which the Pantheon, hemmed in as it was by
shops, houses, and vendors' stands, was the least satisfactory. At Ariccia Bernini remedied this deficiency by setting the rotunda between
straight wings. Unhindered by spatial limitations, he was able to con-

58. Pantheon,
Rome, exterior.

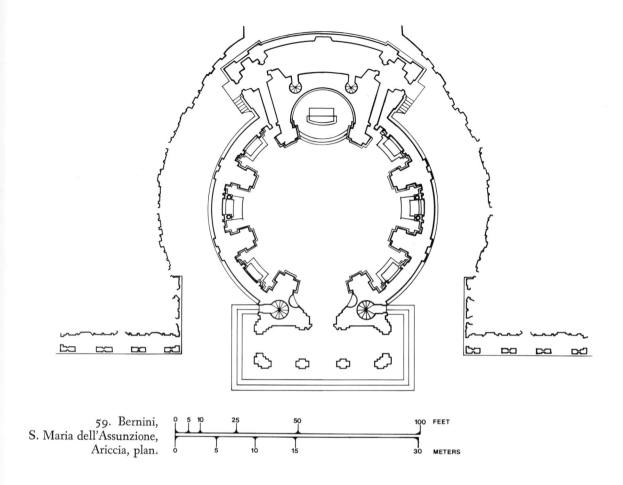

59. Bernini,
S. Maria dell'Assunzione,
Ariccia, plan.

struct full buildings instead of low screen walls as at S. Andrea al Quirinale. A building with similar wings appears in Montano's *Varii tempietti antichi,* a fanciful book of ancient reconstructions published in 1624, but Bernini in his final design superseded all previous models. Deferential without being obsequious, the wings are beautifully related in height, width, and articulation to the church that they serve. Coming from Rome, originally one would have approached the church not over the nineteenth-century viaduct used today, but along a much narrower street that only gradually revealed the church and its dependencies from a lower diagonal viewpoint to the right.[21]

The plan of the interior (59) also depends on the Pantheon, but the elevation (60) has been totally transformed. Even more than in his two previous churches, Bernini strove for simplicity and consistency. His circular plan, like that of the Pantheon, is extended by eight

98

shallow recesses. But unlike the Pantheon's architect, Bernini insisted upon complete uniformity in their design. The frontal elevation of the high altar and the side chapels is identical, as is the sequence of fluted Corinthian pilasters that support the unbroken entablature. The scheme repeats that of the exterior portico but is richer and more luxurious in its use of the fluted Corinthian order.

One drawback of so fluid and symmetrical an interior is that it does not give adequate emphasis to the high altar. Unlike S. Andrea al Quirinale, Bernini's other circumfluent church, the chapel housing the high altar is at first glance virtually indistinguishable from its six neighbors. Closer inspection reveals some subtle differences, however. Not only is this chapel deeper than the others, it is the only one decorated in fresco, without windows, and artificially illuminated. By exploiting the ephemeral effects of light and color, Bernini led the worshipper discreetly through his idealized structure to those areas of greatest liturgical significance.

The subtlety of the interior orientation contrasts strikingly with the forceful frontality of the exterior. While it may seem that Bernini was more concerned with formal perfection than with religious expression inside the church, it is likely that his intention was to shift the spiritual focus from its traditional position in the presbytery out into the congregational space. Devotional concentration on the celebration of the mass at the altar was in part sacrificed for a more enveloping spiritual exhilaration. At Ariccia, one is not so much drawn forward to the altar as spirited up to the dome, the most exultant and lively part of the church. Like that of the Pantheon, the dome is drumless, with an oculus at its summit as the main source of illumination. The analogy with the allusive "dome of heaven" is reinforced by Cortese's fresco above the high altar in which putti scatter flowers in celebration of the Virgin's Assumption. These angelic figures are instrumental in directing one's eye heavenward to the "divine" light. Although the vocabulary is very different, the sense of spiritual ascension at Ariccia is not unlike that realized in Borromini's two centrally planned churches. With Counter-Reformation orthodoxy finally laid to rest, even such disparate souls as Borromini and Bernini were irresistibly drawn to the idea that supplication did not always have to precede salvation. More than ever, Italian churches gave a taste of heaven to the faithful on earth.

The church of the Assunzione was virtually complete by 1664, the same year Alexander VII asked Bernini to redesign a palace recently purchased by his family, the Chigi, in Rome. But for one wing of the

60. Bernini, S. Maria dell'Assunzione, Ariccia, interior.

Propaganda Fide and the prosaic Palazzo Ludovisi in Piazza Monte-citorio, Bernini had not been involved in the design of a major Roman palace since his early years at the Palazzo Barberini. The new commission called for a facade to mask a sixteenth-century building that already housed a handsome courtyard by Carlo Maderno. Bernini's achievement is best seen in an engraving (61) made before the building was doubled in length at the time of its sale to the Odescalchi family in 1745.

The engraving shows that the facade on the Piazza dei Ss. Apostoli was originally thirteen bays long, the same length as the formidable Palazzo Farnese (9). Like the Farnese, the Palazzo Chigi was also three stories high, accented with quoins at the corners, and fenestrated with linteled windows below and pedimented ones above on the *piano nobile*. To this popular prototype Bernini grafted ideas borrowed from a less frequently imitated monument of the Roman Renaissance, the Palazzo Senatorio on the Capitoline Hill, begun by Michelangelo in 1546. The novel features of the Senate building are the slight projection of its end bays and the superimposition of a giant order of pilasters over a rusticated base. Inspired by both palaces, Bernini ingeniously rearranged their component parts to form a totally new composition. Emphasizing but reversing the planar shifts of the Senatorio facade, he divided the Chigi front into three distinct horizontal sections, a scheme he used often in his sacred architecture. Instead of extending

61. Bernini, Palazzo Chigi, Rome, engraving of exterior.

PALAZZO DELL' EMIN. ET REV. SIG. CARDINALE FLAVIO CHIGI NEL RIONE DI TREVI LA PIANTA E L DIDENTRO E ARCHITETTVRA DI CARLO MADERNI LA FACCIATA DI FVORI DEL SIG. CAV. GIO. LORENZO BERNINI

the composition, however, as at Ariccia, here it served to scale down the existing building, which faced a shallow piazza. Bernini used the word *contrapposto* to describe the relationship between the actual size of a monument and the subjective impression one gains of it through an architect's ministrations.[22] However, scale was not his only concern at the Chigi. By contrasting the taller, classically ordered central block with the lower, rusticated sides, he was also able to direct the eye away from the local surroundings toward the grand entrance portal. The crowning balustrade with its Baroque statuary further emphasizes this section and lends elegance and refinement to the palace as a whole. So influential was the Palazzo Chigi's stately classicism that had he built nothing else, Bernini's reputation as a major architect would have been assured.

In the spring of 1665, while construction of the Chigi palace was still underway, Louis XIV asked Bernini to visit Paris to present designs for the east facade of the Louvre, then his principal residence. Other Italian architects, notably Pietro da Cortona and Carlo Rainaldi, had also been asked to submit drawings, but Bernini was the only artist invited to the French capital.[23] He was sixty-six years old and had never before been out of Italy, but the artistic rewards—and the political consequences for the papacy were he to refuse—made the offer irresistible As it turned out, the tangible results of his six-month visit hardly justified the expenditure of creative and diplomatic energies that the commission demanded.

Bernini made three proposals for the facade (62), two while still in Rome and one after he had arrived in Paris. The first dates from June 1664 but has surprisingly little in common with the contemporary Palazzo Chigi. Its flamboyantly curved and segmented plan could only have resulted from Bernini's attempt to satisfy French taste as he understood it. The elevation is an odd compromise between progressive Roman ideas and those suggested by a contemporary French craze for domed buildings with curved wings ending in square pavilions. Bernini might have seen the latter in engravings of Louis Le Vau's Collège des Quatre Nations in Paris begun in 1662, or in Antoine Le Pautre's designs for a chateau published in 1652, or—most likely—in Le Vau's own competing Louvre project which had been sent to Rome in 1664 for criticism by the Italian contestants.[24]

In his effort to adjust his design to French standards, Bernini underestimated both the changing Parisian taste and the practical concerns of his royal patron. By 1664 the king and his architectural advisor Col-

62. Bernini, three projects for the east facade of the Louvre.

bert were tiring of the Baroque style of Le Vau and Le Pautre and
sought more classical means of publicizing the grandeur of Louis' reign.
Thus, Bernini's first proposal stood little chance of being accepted.

In a second design sent to Paris in February 1665, Bernini eliminated the crowning drum, reversed the curvature of the central block,
and added a third story. Although more restrained and classical than
the first design, it too fell short of royal expectation, and the king asked

Bernini to come to Paris and discuss the matter in person. The final plan, made during his stay in France, presented a more disciplined facade, one that now resembled his work at the Palazzo Chigi. The multiphased curvature of the two earlier plans was abandoned in favor of a more rectilinear scheme rising in parallel planes. The elevation remained roughly the same, but the relationship between the five separate blocks was further clarified through the use of the classical order. As on the Chigi facade, the classical membering of the central block is discontinued on the recessed sections that flank it, but on this much larger facade, the order reappears on the corner pavilions. Bernini emphasized the authority of the center, where the royal apartment was to be located, by raising engaged columns there and placing pilasters at the sides. The columns and pilasters are dispersed with the dual aim of concentrating one's attention upon the entrance bays while avoiding monotony in the full elevation.

The foundations for the third project were laid in the fall of 1665, just three days before Bernini's return to Rome, but several factors weighed heavily against its completion. Among the decisions that remained unresolved were the height of the *piano nobile,* the arrangement of the royal apartments, and the design of the court elevation. The wings of the existing court had been built by three of France's greatest architects—Lescot, Lemercier, and Le Vau—and Bernini's desire to mask these elevations met with little enthusiasm. The Crown was also resistant to Bernini's assertion that the king's suite be placed in the center of the new East Wing, on the building's main axis. By Italian standards of decorum, this was the only appropriate location, but His Majesty thought that a suite over the entrance portal would be too noisy and he insisted it be moved to a quieter spot in the South Wing facing the river. Bernini's arrogant and imperious attitude toward local taste in the arts, which he considered to be utterly inferior to the Italian, only made matters worse. Despite his conciliatory modification of the third project in early 1666, the plans were abandoned and replaced by those of a Frenchman in the spring of the following year. Nationalism was on the rise in Louis' domain, and as one recent author has put it, "this decision saved Paris from the doubtful honor of having within its walls the most monumental Roman palazzo ever designed."[25]

Bernini's career had its ups and downs, but even in failure his work commanded worldwide attention. The French were influenced by his presence and traces of the Louvre designs eventually could be seen in government buildings throughout Europe and the New World. While his architectural practice declined after the death of Alexander VII in 1667 and the subsequent weakening of Roman patronage, it was just at that time, ironically, that the so-called Classical–Baroque conflict began to resolve itself in his favor. As taste changed and his rivals Borromini and Cortona died off, Bernini *architetto* finally received the acclaim that had come so much more easily to him as a sculptor.[26]

63. Cortona, Villa Pigneto, Rome, engraving of exterior.

5

Pietro da Cortona

Among Borromini's and Bernini's contemporaries, just two or three architects stand out. The most visible and talented was Pietro Berrettini, known as Pietro da Cortona for the town in southern Tuscany where he was born in 1597. Although he was trained as a painter, and excelled in that profession, he was at the same time an avid and successful architect, a vocation in which he seems to have been self-taught. Cortona arrived in Rome in 1612, at age 15, and for the next ten years occupied himself with the study of Roman antiquity and the classical tradition of the High Renaissance. By the mid-1620s he had won the recognition and support of some of Rome's most enlightened patrons, including the Sacchetti and Barberini families.

Cortona's first important building, the Villa del Pigneto (63), was commissioned by the Sacchetti sometime before 1629 for a wooded site just outside of Rome. It was destroyed in the nineteenth century, but several views and plans of it survive. As one might expect, the building is dependent upon a number of historical sources. Cortona undoubtedly began by studying Pliny's description of a classical Roman *villa suburbana* and went on to benefit, in various ways, from some of the most celebrated villas of the Renaissance. At the time of his death in 1669, Cortona owned architectural books by Vitruvius, Palladio, and Vignola, and of these, he was most influenced by Palladio's *Quattro libri*. The simple, symmetrical plan and concave wings of the Villa del Pigneto reveal Cortona's understanding of the phrasing of the Palladian winged villa, a Venetian structural type which he ornamented in the vocabulary of local Roman tradition. The picturesque stairways and terraces leading to the entrance hemi-cycle, on the other hand, seem to derive from Bramante's Belvedere court in the Vatican, the most fabulous axial landscape complex since antiquity. Given Cortona's passionate interest in antiquity, however, it is not surprising to learn that both sites share the ancient Roman sanctuary of Fortuna at Palestrina as a common source. In 1629, the Barberini bought the town of Palestrina and hired Cortona to reconstruct the sacred precinct, a commission that coincided with his work on the Sacchetti villa. His antiquarianism, then, was based on firsthand experience, unlike that of most of his contemporaries, whose knowledge of the past was more indirectly acquired.

Cortona's next major commission, the church of Ss. Martina e Luca, turned out to be the most important of his career.[1] A chapel dedicated to S. Martina had stood on the site since the seventh century, and in 1588 the Accademia di San Luca, the newly founded artists' society, acquired the property. Plans for a new building were soon formulated, but a shortage of funds delayed construction for nearly 50 years. In 1634, Cortona was elected director of the Academy and in the same year decided to build himself a funerary chapel in the crypt of the old church. It is one of the fortuitous accidents of Baroque architecture that during construction, workmen unearthed the bones of S. Martina and three other Christian martyrs. In celebration, Urban VIII offered indulgences and personally composed Latin hymns, while his nephew Francesco Barberini, the cardinal protector of the Accademia, made the more material offering of funds to rebuild the complete church. Cortona, who remained patron of the crypt, was naturally the architect chosen.

Construction began in the spring of 1635, and by 1664 the structure was completed, although the decoration of the interior lagged on for years. The plan (64) is a domed Greek Cross with arms that are longer and narrower than was customary. An open crossing is the core of the scheme, but the overall proportions and the relatively greater length of the longitudinal axis orients the visitor toward the high altar. Yet in designing the elevation, Cortona was less concerned with directional accents than with uniformly activating the wall surfaces throughout the interior (65). Like Borromini's contemporary church of S. Carlo alle Quattro Fontane, a boldly projecting order replaces the flat wall as the primary spatial boundary. Twenty-four free-standing columns and sixteen piers faced with pilasters interact to keep the eye constantly in motion. Slight differences in projection and occa-

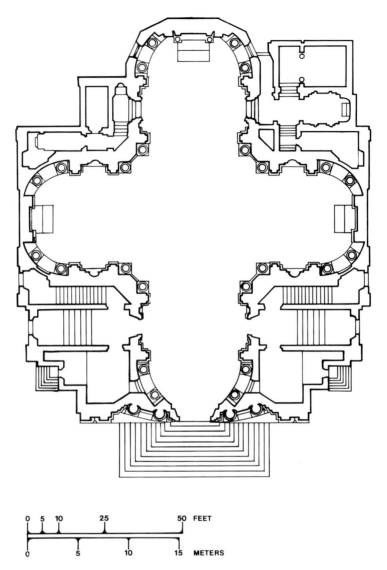

| 0 | 5 | 10 | 25 | 50 | FEET |
| 0 | | | 5 | 10 | 15 | METERS |

sional gaps for windows, doors, and niches create a varied and free-moving surface that comes to rest only at the three principal altars.

Like most Baroque churches in Rome, the interior of Ss. Martina e Luca is richly textured, even painterly, but makes little use of color. Except for three altar paintings, framed in marble, the limestone masonry unifies the space in a silvery monochrome that becomes more luminous as the height increases. The upper zone is also more freely conceived than that below. As the broken entablature leads the eye upwards, the simple classical shapes of the supporting order give way to

109

65. Cortona,
Ss. Martina e Luca,
Rome, interior.

denser, more complex surfaces (66). The dome and the main vaults
are covered with a heavy stucco relief of coffers and ribs trimmed with
Urban VIII's bees and laurel and Santa Martina's lily of chastity and
palm of martyrdom. Vaults with related structural and ornamental devices appear in the churches of Bernini and Borromini, but it is here
at Ss. Martina e Luca that such elements were combined for the first
time.[2]

In the vault above each altar, the window surrounds are composed
of a complex interweaving of scrolls, shells, garlands, and female heads,
all solidly formed and forcefully projecting into space. Their inspiration clearly came from Tuscany, where Buontalenti and other sixteenth-century Mannerist architects had used similar forms.[3] Cortona,
who traced his roots to this region, was unusual among his Roman
contemporaries in relying upon Tuscan sources, but he was hardly
unique in adopting Mannerist methods of composition. In the work

66. Cortona, Ss. Martina e Luca, Rome, interior vaulting.

of Borromini and others, neither the vocabulary nor grammar of that period-style ever disappears entirely, and, in fact, Mannerist principles guided the design of some of Rome's most renowned Baroque buildings.

The facade of Ss. Martina e Luca (67) is handsomely situated, overlooking the northeast corner of the Roman Forum. Among Roman churches, its plan and elevation are unique. The plan is divided into five sections with alternating straight and curved planes. The straight planes of the central and outermost sections form a stable, solid framework that seems to squeeze the two inner bays, bending them slightly. The tense equilibrium that this produces is rather like what Michelangelo achieved in the exterior flanks of St. Peter's. However, Cortona's facade—already under construction in 1635—marks the first appearance of curved planes on the front of a Roman church. The plan of the facade gives an adequate introduction to the interior, but the elevation is little more than a screen that gives few clues to the shape of the building behind it. Because the facade is nearly twice as wide as the entrance arm into which it leads, visitors may feel slightly constricted upon first entering the church. In concept, this sort of screen facade is related to Michelangelo's unexecuted model for the front of S. Lorenzo in Florence. Like his countryman, Cortona upheld the view that the facade is an independent urbanistic composition that need not correspond in all aspects to the interior.

The originality of the curved plan and full two-story elevation is tempered by the more traditional use of the classical orders. Like Maderno's facade of S. Susanna (14), Cortona's arrangement of pilasters and half-columns focuses our attention toward the center. The progression of planes, however, is less rigid, and the relationship between tectonic and decorative elements is handled more loosely. The columns of the lower story do not merely stand against the wall, they are pushed into it, displacing the cornices and moldings behind them. Their remarkable elasticity and pliability make the stone seem to yield like rubber. In the upper story, the membering is varied by substituting pilasters for columns, and columns for *piedroits* in the central bay. The density of these features and the freedom with which they are organized remind one of paintings that the artist did around the same time, such as *The Glorification of Pope Urban VIII* in the Palazzo Barberini.

We know from a drawing that Cortona had considered crowning the entire facade with a triangular pediment, but since the upper portion of the construction was not finished until after his death, we do

67. Cortona, Ss. Martina e Luca, Rome, facade.

not know whether it was his or a successor's decision to omit it. Without the pediment, more of the dome is visible behind the facade, and this may have been the deciding factor since the dome is one of the most striking and distinctive parts of the building. Its tall drum, pointed vault, and bulbous lantern rise to twice the height of the facade and are ornamented in the architect's characteristically lavish style. As in the interior, the decorative relief mixes tectonic and sculptural elements that become increasingly more voluptuous with height. Again, the vocabulary recalls Florentine Mannerist sources, but the overall prominence of the dome is unmistakably Baroque.

Between 1640 and 1647 Cortona spent most of his time in Florence, painting frescoes in the Palazzo Pitti. While there, he was also asked to draw up plans for a new Oratorian church to be dedicated to S. Firenze. The patrons were pleased with his proposals at first, but the project was abandoned soon after the foundation was laid because of criticism from local architects. Between 1645 and 1666, when he was finally dismissed, Cortona made three dozen drawings (now in the Uffizi) that provided for a longitudinal church of the type popular during the Counter-Reformation.[4] In this series of drawings Cortona attempted to transform the traditional Gesù type into a more lively Baroque composition. One idea he returned to again and again is the adoption of a columnar nave similar to that introduced by Mascarino at S. Salvatore in Lauro half a century before. Other studies explored ways of changing the rhythm and movement of the Gesù nave in even more imaginative ways. Six of the eight preserved plans even called for a curved facade, an uncommon frontispiece for an Italian longitudinal church before the eighteenth century.

After he returned to Rome in 1647, Cortona occupied himself for almost a decade with the painted decorations of S. Maria in Vallicella and the Palazzo Pamphili, and with the continuing construction of Ss. Martina e Luca. His most productive years, like Bernini's, began with the election of Pope Alexander VII in 1655. Alexander had a passionate love of architecture and urbanism, and during his twelve-year reign he succeeded in turning the papal city into one of Europe's most striking and impressive capitals.[5] Although Bernini remained the Pope's favorite architect, Cortona received three choice commissions for buildings in the heart of downtown Rome.

In 1656 he was asked to construct a new facade and to systematize the piazza in front of the existing church of S. Maria della Pace. In choosing this site in the densest quarter of the city, Alexander wanted both to unsnarl traffic congestion and to make a votive offering to the Virgin of Peace, who he hoped would protect Rome from the plague, which had claimed ten percent of the population that year, and from France, whose military aggression was viewed as an equal menace. Constructed in haste, the facade and a few necessary modifications to the interior were virtually complete by 1658, but work on the piazza continued into the next decade.[6]

The total enterprise (68–70) constituted some of the most clever town-planning of the seventeenth century. The church's relationship to the buildings in the surrounding trapezoidal piazza is like that of a stage to its hall.[7] By joining the solid and spatial elements in a fluid arrangement, Cortona went a step beyond the usual Renaissance practice of maintaining the distinctiveness of the individual parts—as in Michelangelo's Capitoline Hill complex. The available space was quite limited, measuring only about 45 × 100 feet after some of the surrounding buildings were partially demolished. He disguised its restricted scale by allowing the spatial boundaries of the church to fluctuate. The round portico projects into the space, whereas the upper concave wings recede from and expand it. This fluctuation in relief anticipates Bernini's slightly later design for the front of S. Andrea al Quirinale (53), but Cortona's complex columnar interrelationships and highly sculptural feeling for surface are much more energetic and Baroque than the measured cadences of Bernini.

Cortona's interest in Roman antiquity undoubtedly inspired the rounded portico, a motif that also appears in several of his historical paintings, where it often is associated with temples of Peace.[8] Using the low portico here, however, forced him to devise a separate elevation for the facade's upper story. This elevation is less original, for he did little more than revise his design for the upper story of Ss. Martina e Luca. The composition is now tighter and more compact, and, in keeping with the stark Tuscan simplicity of the porch, there is no decorative relief sculpture.

Seen from the front, the membering of the two stories is roughly in alignment, partially compensating for the inconsistency of their plans. The great crowning pediment also resolves the facade's vertical thrust more gracefully than does the straight cornice capping Ss. Martina e Luca. This pediment was of the currently fashionable compound or encased type. Tentatively introduced in several works by Michelan-

68. Cortona, S. Maria della Pace, Rome, engraving of piazza.

gelo, it made its first appearance in complete form in Rome on Della Porta's Gesù facade. Its full potential, however, was not realized for another seventy-five years, when in 1646, Martino Longhi the Younger made it the leitmotif of his ingenious facade for Ss. Vincenzo ed Anastasio (77). The architectural cross-fertilization at this time was such that Cortona unhesitatingly adopted from Longhi's design both the compound pediment and the innovative placement of free-standing columns at the corners of the facade, which guide the visitor toward the church entrance from either of two side streets leading into the piazza (71). From such diagonal perspectives, one's eye is first arrested by these bold columns, and then the adjacent columns of the portico lead one around to a frontal position on axis with the entrance. By 1656, this interest in the changing perceptual experience of architecture had become one of the main preoccupations of architects working in Rome.

Cortona lavished the same attention on the design of the house fronts which faced onto the piazza. While he desired a unified visual

116

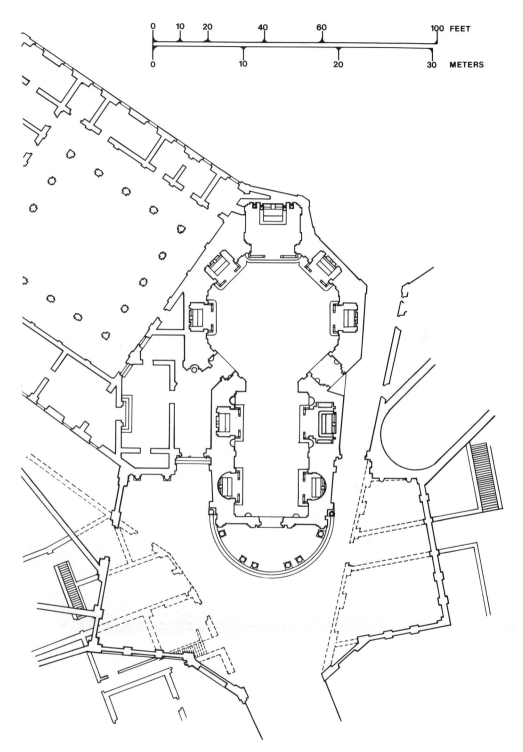

69. Cortona, S. Maria della Pace, Rome, plan.

70. Cortona, S. Maria della Pace, Rome, exterior.

71. Cortona,
S. Maria della Pace,
Rome, corner and
palace fronts.

ensemble, he was also careful to maintain the proper relationship between the sacred and secular forms. Using the wings of the church facade as transitional elements, he duplicated the sequence of orders that appear on the church on the slightly lower floor levels of the houses so that the sacred and secular zones would be distinguished by contrasts in plan and relief. The flat pilaster-ordered houses enhance rather than compete with the exuberant curvilinear rhythms and robust orders of the church. Indeed, the entire complex rather accurately reflects the relationship between worldly and spiritual concerns in Rome at the time.

The architect's sensitivity to the relation between a monument and its surrounding site is just as apparent in his next commission, also for a church facade. In 1658 the pope asked Cortona to construct a new front for the aged and venerable church of S. Maria in Via Lata. The

72. Cortona,
S. Maria in Via Lata,
Rome, facade.

Via Lata or, as it is now known, the Via del Corso, runs from the Piazza del Popolo to the present Piazza Venezia and has since antiquity been one of Rome's major thoroughfares. Because of the church's location on this narrow and busy street, Cortona was somewhat restricted in the kind of facade that he could build. An isolated curved front would have seemed inappropriate among the straight facades of neighboring buildings, and a fully open portico would have absorbed too much of the sight and noise of passing traffic. In adapting his design (72) to the circumstances, Cortona lessened the dramatic intensity of S. Maria della Pace while preserving much of its forthright character. His solution was to combine a proper straight front with an open narthex behind. On each story, a four-column loggia is buttressed by solid corner bays. The structural independence of these elements is emphasied at the points of their juncture by the multiplication and projection of the orders and by the triangular pediment which crowns only the central bays. Reversing the pedimental break of S. Maria della Pace, the middle section of the straight cornice now bends upwards instead of down, giving greater centrality and verticality to the facade, while mildly differentiating between its twin loggias. This so-called Syrian pediment—an arch set into a pediment—originated in Imperial Rome and, as its name indicates, was especially popular in the Eastern Provinces, where its use connoted special authority. Revised in the late Renaissance as a symbol of papal majesty, the motif appeared in Gregory XIII's loggia in the Sala Regia of the Vatican Palace and on the facade of Innocent X's family palace in the Piazza Navona.

Were it not for the decorum demanded by the site, S. Maria in Via Lata would surely suggest that Cortona had become a more restrained and classical architect. There is none of the Baroque exuberance of S. Maria della Pace or the Mannerist detail of Ss. Martina e Luca, but what brought about this stylistic change is a matter of debate. An examination of his subsequent works may help to reveal the true nature of his convictions.

Cortona's combined interest in architecture and urbanism coincided with similar inclinations on the part of Alexander VII. Because of the great expense of financing the piazza and colonnade of St. Peter's, several of the pope's lesser projects were destined to remain on paper. Among these was Cortona's proposal, recorded in a set of studies in the Vatican Library, to redevelop part of the Piazza Colonna.[9] Soon after the Chigi bought a palace in the piazza in 1658, Alexander commis-

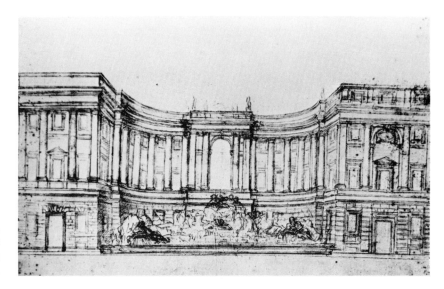

73. Cortona, project for the Palazzo Chigi in Piazza Colonna, Rome.

sioned Cortona to renovate the area, emulating what his predecessor, Innocent X, had done in the Piazza Navona.[10] The architect's most interesting suggestion (73) was to recloak the existing palace with a curved facade carrying a giant order over a rusticated base. More unrealistically, the project would have required moving the fountainhead of the Acqua Vergine—the Trevi Fountain—to the new site, where its waters would spring from stone outcroppings set into the facade's concave center. Although it was never executed, the design was pivotal in mid-seventeenth-century Roman architecture. An obvious and clever derivation from S. Agnese in Piazza Navona and the neighboring Fountain of the Four Rivers, it may also have been a catalyst for Bernini's slightly later designs for the Palazzo Chigi in Piazza Ss. Apostoli (61) and the East Facade of the Louvre (62).[11] The fountain design was not forgotten either, for when Nicola Salvi built the present Trevi Fountain in the eighteenth century, he too combined a classical palace front with an outcropping of rugged stone (108).

A few of Cortona's ideas for the Palazzo Chigi also appear in the architect's unsuccessful proposal for the East Facade of the Louvre, submitted to Louis XIV in 1664.[12] A giant order above a rusticated base is used once again to unify a series of straight and curved planes. Trying to lessen the monotony of that enormous front, and perhaps to make his design seem more French, Cortona devised an extraordinarily complex phrasing of individual bays. The rambling dissonance of the wings and the exaggerated grandiloquence of the dome, however, only guaranteed the project's rapid rejection. Unlike Bernini, he was not invited to submit another. Years earlier, Cortona had

74. Cortona, dome of S. Carlo al Corso, Rome.

written to his friend Cassiano dal Pozzo that he felt he was always unlucky in matters of architecture. It was an assessment that proved to be especially true of his secular commissions.

Cortona was more fortunate at S. Carlo al Corso, his last work, where he added the tribune and dome to a church that had already been under construction for more than half a century. Work began in July 1668, just ten months before his death. Not surprisingly, the design of the dome (74), which had yet to be finalized, presented him with more creative opportunities than the largely predetermined elevation of the tribune.

A comparison with his dome at Ss. Martina e Luca comes immediately to mind. Standing at opposite ends of his career, the two works reaffirm what was first apparent at S. Maria in Via Lata: that the architect eventually came to reject the ornamental complexity of his youthful style. S. Carlo al Corso is, without question, sparer and more classical than its predecessor. Foregoing the Florentine delicacy of the earlier drum, Cortona endowed this cupola with a tectonic strength that is typically Roman, recalling as it does Vignola's small domes at St. Peter's, executed a century earlier.[13] Only in the narrow and well-defined attic above the drum does classical restraint give way to the ornamental exuberance for which Cortona was famous. The lapse from his new classicism is only momentary, however, for the vault quickly restores the composition's essential purity. The only feature the two domes have in common is the lantern, a more or less standard fixture in Italian architecture throughout the seventeenth century. In many ways, the dome of S. Carlo al Corso perfectly expresses the changing architectural mood of the late 1660s. Blending classical poise with Baroque animation, it emulated the refinement of Bernini without sacrificing the vigor of Cortona's own imagination. As we shall see in the following chapter, this was a challenge that he did not face alone.

6

Other Aspects of the Roman Baroque

Borromini, Bernini, and Cortona were not the only architects active in mid-seventeenth-century Rome as any interested visitor to the city will quickly realize. The building boom in Rome was so extensive that a number of other architects were able to establish respectable careers for themselves independent of the influence of the three major masters. G. B. Soria, Martino Longhi the Younger, Carlo Rainaldi, and G. A. De Rossi, for example, designed buildings in styles that ranged from the most conservative and conventional to the most progressive and personal.[1] Together, their works reinforce one's impression of the remarkable variety and ingenuity of Roman Baroque architecture.

The oldest and most conservative member of the group was Giovanni Battista Soria (1581–1651), who has four Roman church facades to his credit. Soria was a versatile and ubiquitous figure, working as a wood-carver and lensmaker, publishing Montano's fanciful reconstruction of ancient temples, and at times, assisting Bernini. His most ambitious design was for the exterior of S. Caterina a Magnapoli (75), located just south of the Quirinal Hill. This was begun around 1638 and completed in 1640. As do several of his other facades, it consists of two stories of equal width, following a minor Roman tradition alternative to that of the Gesù.[2] Ignoring the double-ramped stairway, which was added in the nineteenth century, one is struck by the similarity of the arched portico to Bernini's S. Bibiana (42), a reflection of Soria's esteem for his younger and more famous contemporary. The upper story is identical to the one below, except for differences in the size and function of the arches. The arched niches above are also some-

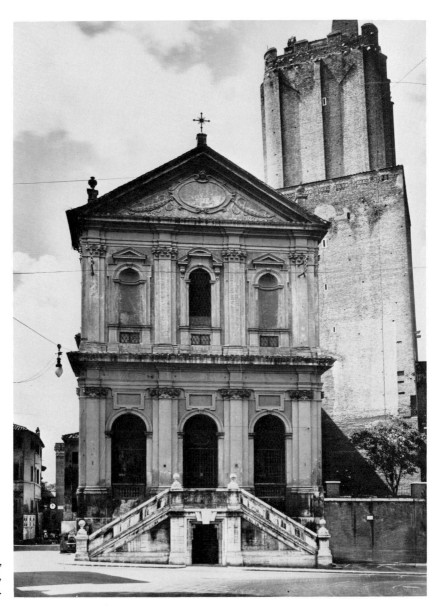

75. G. B. Soria,
S. Caterina a Magnapoli,
Rome, facade.

what awkwardly framed by pedimented surrounds. The arrangement
over the central window, which seems particularly clumsy, is in fact
derived from a motif that first appeared in Vignola's Gesù project (5)
and then was popularized by Maderno's circle. The most surprising
aspect of the facade is the weakness of its main structure. Soria seems
to have been untouched by the dramatic advances which Maderno had
realized years earlier at S. Susanna: both the massing of the wall and
the expression of the orders lack the concentration and animation that

one would expect in a facade of the 1630s. Equally surprising is the absence of motifs from the antiquarian volumes of G. B. Montano, which Soria himself had published in the 1620s. Although his crisp membering and fine sense of proportion have established him as the most interesting of the many traditional architects then practicing in Rome,[3] there is very little that could be called Baroque in Soria's architecture.

Martino Longhi the Younger (1602–1660) was a less conventional architect of the next generation. His father Onorio and his grandfather Martino the Elder were also architects, but neither had the "wild and licentious spirit," either temperamentally or artistically, that biographers of the younger Martino describe. His penchant for anti-social behavior and his frequent scrapes with the law make colorful reading, but they can hardly have helped to further his career as an architect.[4] While still in his twenties, Longhi designed the church of S. Antonio dei Portoghesi for the Portuguese community in Rome. The facade (76), begun in 1629 and not completed until 1695, is more interesting than the traditional cruciform interior. The basic structure of the facade is, of course, also traditional—a relatively flat, two-story composition articulated with pilasters—yet this familiar scheme has been modified to suit a more Baroque taste. Unlike its sixteenth-century predecessors, Longhi's facade achieves a true sense of richness through its ornamental use of the orders and its extensive use of sculpture. A putto hovers within each door pediment, the scrolls connecting the two stories are turned into telamons, the Braganza coat of arms embellishes the area over the central window, and trumpeting angels surmount the main pediment. The architectural membering is itself more vigorous, with deeply projecting compound pediments and a multiplication of pilasters around the central bay. The combination of these tectonic and sculptural features produces a facade which, while still modest in its methods, is as dramatic and pictorial as any designed in Rome before 1630.

Longhi's genius as a designer of church facades is even more apparent at Ss. Vincenzo ed Anastasio (77), constructed from 1646 to 1650. Sponsored by Cardinal Giulio Mazarin, First Minister to Louis XIV, this splendid and forceful facade, built in the Piazza della Fontana di Trevi in the heart of Rome, proclaimed the arrogance of the Cardinal's authority. As at S. Antonio, the facade bears some resemblance to Il Gesù, but at Ss. Vincenzo ed Anastasio we see a most re-

76. Martino Longhi the Younger, S. Antonio dei Portoghesi, Rome, facade.

77. Martino Longhi the Younger, Ss. Vincenzo ed Anastasio, Rome, facade.

bellious offspring. Longhi now used clusters of free-standing columns where, in the earlier facade, he had applied timid pilasters, creating a tectonic structure that is virtually independent of the wall behind it. On sunny afternoons a rich chiaroscuro plays over the columns and the sculpture, animating the robust ensemble of three-dimensional forms.[5] Closer study reveals the intricacy and sophistication of his bold design. One's first impression is that the upper story is identical to the one below, with the columnar triads running continuously through both levels. The actual functions of the columns on the lower story, however, are not the same as those above. On the upper story, each column in each triad supports (as is logical) one of the encased pediments that crown the facade. On the lower story, there is one less pediment, and two additional columns at the corners. The columns only support the larger of the two pediments; the smaller one floats uneasily above an impost block. Two of the three columns in each lower triad, then, support not pediments, but sections of straight entablature. It is visually tempting to link the outermost column in each triad with the corner column and see them as jointly supporting the entablature and enframing the end bay. Seen in this way, the lower triad dissolves before our eyes and the two stories become structurally disconnected.

Even closer scrutiny reveals the unusually subtle means Longhi used to reinforce the initial impression of the facade's consistency and logic. His attempts at optical persuasion included stretching the outer pediment of the lower story to make it seem to complement the largest pediment above, while increasing the intercolumniation of the upper triads to make their closely spaced counterparts below seem more unified than they actually are. As a consequence, one's third and final impression of the facade is of a more complex and exacting aesthetic than might first have been anticipated.

Martino Longhi, like most Baroque architects, was interested in the viewer's dynamic as well as static perceptions of buildings. Because Ss. Vincenzo ed Anastasio stands on a sharply angled corner, many visitors approach the building along its flanks instead of from the front. Taking this into account, Longhi positioned pairs of columns at the corners to help lead one's eye from the approaching streets to a full view of the facade. These columns, and the caryatids placed above them, are wholly typical, if not prototypical, of the scenographic and sculptural qualities found on the most progressive buildings of the mid-seventeenth century. Ss. Vincenzo ed Anastasio was, in fact, prophetic of later designs by Pietro da Cortona (70) and Carlo Rainaldi

(84). It was the first Roman facade to use free-standing columns, the first to be crowned with compound encased pediments, and the first to expand the traditional fixed point of view to include multiple and moving perspectives. Even in Rome, few buildings rival its ingenuity and irrepressible Baroque spirit.

Carlo Rainaldi (1611–1691) was another Roman architect whose works merit careful attention. Like Martino Longhi, he learned the practice of architecture from his father, working with him until the elder Rainaldi died at the age of 82. It was only then, at the age of 45, that Carlo became fully independent. Despite his late start, he went on to build several uncommonly interesting buildings during the third quarter of the century.

His earliest important work, S. Agnese in Agone (78), was the family church of the Pamphili pope, Innocent X. Set in the Piazza Navona, one of the choicest sites in Rome, S. Agnese is splendidly positioned between Girolamo Rainaldi's Palazzo Pamphili (1645–1647) and Bernini's Fountain of the Four Rivers (1648–1651). The history of its construction is rather complicated: it was begun by the two Rainaldi in 1652, was modified first by Borromini and then by Bernini, and was finally completed by Carlo Rainaldi.[6] Credit for the design must therefore be shared by four architects, none of whom contributed elements that are entirely characteristic of their individual styles. A study of the surviving preparatory drawings emphasizes the seminal role of the Rainaldi's earliest efforts, but the church's real significance transcends questions of attribution and personal style. In fact, the building is oddly impersonal in style, although it is uniquely typical of the architectural magnificence, and the papal grandeur, of its age. No Roman church since St. Peter's dared be so prepossessing.

And St. Peter's stands clearly in the background, consciously evoked in a variety of ways. Neither a case of plagiarism nor persiflage, S. Agnese fulfills some of the original intentions, and "corrects" some of the obvious flaws of the earlier, more famous basilica. Maderno's nave in St. Peter's not only ruined the symmetry of Bramante's centralized space, but also obscured the close view of Michelangelo's dome. Equally unfortunate was the failure to construct bell towers (18) on the foundations that Maderno had built for them at each end of the facade. Bernini's efforts (44) to raise the towers also failed, and despite a rash of subsequent proposals—including ones by each of the Rainaldi and by Borromini—the towers were never built. S. Agnese is

78. Carlo Rainaldi and others, S. Agnese in Piazza Navona, Rome, facade.

therefore the realization of what St. Peter's might have been: a centrally planned interior with a two-towered facade crowned by a visible dome. Like Bernini's adaptation of the Pantheon at Ariccia, S. Agnese is a respectful and imaginative revision of a venerable predecessor.[7]

But simple revival was not all the patron and the architects of S. Agnese had in mind. They intended to update the design and bring it more in line with contemporary practice. On the exterior, this was accomplished by introducing a complex arrangement of curved and straight planes, by coupling the orders, and by using a taller drum to raise the height of the dome. The resulting design encompasses considerable variety within a completely unified ensemble. The facade's firm center and corners stabilize the concave bays between them, while the curvature of the lower tier is reversed by the convexity of the dome above. Even the towers provide variations of motifs found elsewhere in the design. As is typical of the fully developed Roman Baroque, the exterior of this church is hierarchical in symbol and in function, and its greatness lies in its attainment of a perfect balance between tradition and innovation, creative freedom and formal discipline. In spite of its mixed background and complicated authorship, there is something almost inevitable about its final design.

Located in one of Rome's most prominent squares, S. Agnese plainly reflects the worldliness, the self-promotion, and of course, the good taste of its papal patron. As such, the church is as much a public and civic monument as it is a place of worship. It should not be surprising, therefore, to discover that the facade is more interesting and vital than the interior that lies behind it.

The plan of the church (79) is a Greek Cross whose design can be traced back to the Rainaldi's earliest studies. Here, as in St. Peter's, which once again provided the inspiration, four sharply bevelled main piers transform the crossing into a broad octagon (80). One thus perceives the Greek Cross as a more fully centralized space, for not only is the ritual axis quite short, the niches in the piers are richly embellished with large sculptural reliefs that illustrate the trials of four early Christian martyrs. Only the broad transverse axis—which, because of the shallowness of the site, is ten percent longer than the longitudinal axis—denies the symmetry and centrality of the total space. In actuality, the greatest dimension within the building is its height, which is twenty-five percent greater than the length of the longitudinal axis. The resulting impression of verticality is further emphasized by the linkage, *en ressaut,* of the colored marble columns to the tall arches

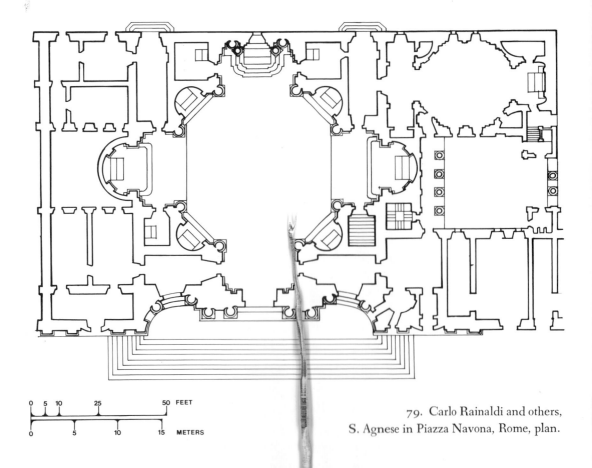

0 5 10 25 50 FEET

0 5 10 15 METERS

79. Carlo Rainaldi and others,
S. Agnese in Piazza Navona, Rome, plan.

above, as well as by the richly painted pendentives and cupola which
lead one's eye upward. Here, as in Borromini's church for the
Sapienza (31–32), the directional flow is as much vertical as it is horizontal. This perceptual experience is roughly analogous to changes
that had taken place since the end of the sixteenth century in religious
practice itself. Earthly penance gave way to more mystical attitudes
on the part of clergy and congregation alike.[8] Worship became more
exhilarating as one was encouraged to imagine salvation coming liter-
ally from above. S. Agnese is therefore significant not just for its stylistic relationship to St. Peter's, but as an expression of the new religious
attitudes of post-Counter-Reformation Catholicism, a message reiter-
ated in Ciro Ferri's fresco of St. Agnes in Glory in the dome, and in
Bernini's Fountain of the Four Rivers in the piazza in front of the
church. Through an elaborate conceit, Bernini causes one to witness
the worldwide subordination to the power of the Roman church under
the providential rule of Innocent X. S. Agnese is more abstract in its

language, but it is clearly a building conceived with the same unrestrained self-confidence.

Carlo Rainaldi's independent genius can be seen in his slightly later commission for the church of S. Maria in Campitelli (81–84),[9] where for the first time in his career he neither had to collaborate with his father nor suffer the intervention of other architects. He was also fortunate that the vast church was completed with unusual speed: the foundation stone was laid in 1662 and the consecration took place in 1675. An earlier church had stood on the site for only a few decades when in 1656 the Roman Senate decided to construct a new home there for an icon that it was hoped would protect the city from a plague then ravaging southern Italy. Like S. Maria della Pace, S. Maria in Campitelli was a votive offering to the Virgin for the deliverance of Rome in its time of need.

Rainaldi's original proposal (81) would have made the church a longitudinal oval with side chapels and an extended sanctuary. The

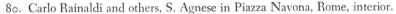

80. Carlo Rainaldi and others, S. Agnese in Piazza Navona, Rome, interior.

81. Carlo Rainaldi,
S. Maria in Campitelli,
Rome, project.

resemblance between the design he proposed for the interior and that of Bernini's contemporary church of S. Andrea al Quirinale is striking. The exterior, however, was just as strongly based on the work of Pietro da Cortona: in the version illustrated here, Rainaldi in effect joined the facade plan of Ss. Martina e Luca (64) with the elevation of S. Maria in Via Lata (72). What results is more vigorous and robust than either of Cortona's designs and clearly reveals its author's inclination towards progressive Baroque compositions.

No doubt practical and economic factors dictated the eventual substitution of a longitudinal plan (82) for the elliptical design, since it would have required the construction of one of the largest oval domes in the city. The executed plan, in some ways, is no less idiosyncratic, however. As we have seen, the Counter-Reformatory zeal for the traditional basilica plan had by the mid-seventeenth century given way to a renewed appreciation of centrally planned churches. Yet the longitudinal plan of S. Maria in Campitelli does not conform to the standard cruciform schemes of earlier Roman architecture either. The usual relationship between nave, transept, and crossing has been ig-

136

nored: the transept is quite shallow and the nave is traversed by a broad cross-axis, which reverses the spatial flow of the normal longitudinal plan and creates a sequence of independent centralized spaces instead. Although not totally unprecedented in Rome, such an arrangement was more familiar in northern Italy where sequential plans and bisected naves were more common in this period.[10] Similar plans are also known in Roman antiquity, but there is no evidence that Rainaldi was consciously aware of them.

One danger of the unusual plan was that it might distract worshippers from the ritual path leading from the entrance to the high altar. Bernini had faced a similar problem a few years before when he used a transverse oval for the plan of S. Andrea al Quirinale. In both churches, the architects' challenge was to neutralize the conflict between the ritual axis and the actual flow of the physical space. Even in a black and white photograph of S. Maria in Campitelli (83), it is ap-

82. Carlo Rainaldi,
S. Maria in Campitelli,
Rome, plan.

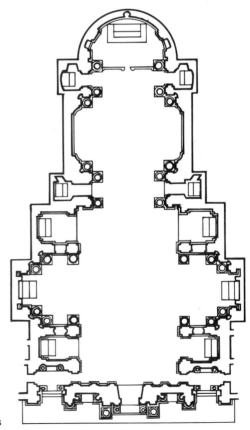

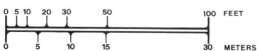

83. Carlo Rainaldi, S. Maria in Campitelli, Rome, interior.

parent that Rainaldi used both color and controlled illumination to accentuate the main altar. A lavish gilt bronze tabernacle containing the miraculous icon of the Virgin provides a visual focal point for the interior, which would have been even more spellbinding by candle-light.[11] The area around the high altar is also bathed in daylight more than any other part of the church, light which issues from a ring of large windows set into the base of the dome. From the moment one enters the building, this luminous, enclosed zone draws one forward through the dimly lit and monochromatic nave.

Rainaldi's second method of emphasizing the longitudinal axis was more architectonic. Two dozen free-standing columns are arranged to create a natural perspective that leads directly to the high altar. The dynamic function of the columnar groupings is similar to the sceno-graphic placement of columns on the slightly earlier facades of Ss. Vincenzo ed Anastasio (77) and S. Maria della Pace (70), or even in the interior of S. Carlo alle Quattro Fontane (25).

Rainaldi's interior is a perfect expression of the sensibility of the High Baroque. If one compares it with S. Salvatore in Lauro (12), one of the most inspired churches of the late sixteenth century, the evolution of Roman taste is made abundantly clear. Mascarino's pre-dilection for the columnar naves of northern Italy is now combined with the desire to emulate the monumentality of ancient Rome. Per-haps inspired by Michelangelo's transformation of the Baths of Diocle-tian into the church of S. Maria degli Angeli, Rainaldi surpassed Mas-carino in gravity and stateliness, while displaying the more flexible ap-proach characteristic of his own later generation. Spatial boundaries no longer are rigidly fixed, masses are broken and constantly shifting, and light is more carefully controlled. To enter the building is to have one of the most splendid and solemn architectural experiences possible in Rome.

Once the longitudinal ground plan had been substituted for the oval, it made sense to replace the proposed curved facade with the straight front that was customary for such basilican churches. The profile of the tall vaulted nave and broad side chapels naturally suggested the familiar model of Il Gesù: a two-story composition crowned by a pedi-ment and framed with scrolls that provide a transition between the broad lower and narrow upper stories. Instead, Rainaldi consolidated the two alternatives that Vignola and Della Porta had devised in their designs for the Jesuit church (5 and 6).[12] Like Vignola's unexecuted project, the facade of S. Maria in Campitelli consists of a series of stepped planes arranged to accentuate the central bay; like Della Porta's executed design, the composition is vertically unified by en-tablature breaks that connect the corresponding columns of the two stories. However, in the boldness of its expression, S. Maria in Campi-telli surpasses all of its prototypes. Even Maderno's facade for S. Su-sanna (14) seems weak and timid in comparison with the forceful, almost aggressive deployment of free-standing columns here. The broken compound pediments that crown the composition continue the vertical theme up to the roofline. In his preference for stark, jagged forms over pliable and elastic ones, Rainaldi clearly deviated from con-temporaries like Borromini and Pietro da Cortona.

84. Carlo Rainaldi, S. Maria in Campitelli, Rome, facade.

Altogether, the classical order is used 32 times on the facade of S. Maria in Campitelli (84), more than on any other church facade in Rome. Part of the building's fascination lies in the clever arrangement of these members in series of interlocking sequences. More fully developed on the lower story, the sequences form patterns that rise and fall as well as advance and recede. The main sequence consists of the stepped progression of pilaster, half-column, and full column that concludes in the central bay. Like musical counterpoint, this brisk series is retarded by the pair of recessed columns set in bays two and four, and is relieved by the secondary sequence of lower columns in bays one, three, and five. The profusion of columns and pediments standing independent of the wall is reminiscent of the spirit, if not the actual forms, of later antiquity—in this instance, the stage architecture of Roman theatres like that in Aspendus in Asia Minor (85). In a drawing done in 1665, Rainaldi softened the lines of this rigid tectonic structure by placing free-standing and relief sculpture in some of the available free space.[13] Unfortunately the idea was never carried out, which accounts in part for the severity of the facade as it appears today.

Soon after his election in 1655, Alexander VII began to commission the series of projects which have made his name synonymous with

85. Reconstruction of Roman Theatre, Aspendus.

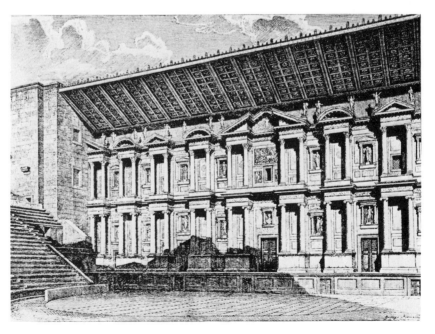

some of the most ambitious urbanistic undertakings of seventeenth-century Rome. Projects such as Bernini's colonnade at St. Peter's or Cortona's S. Maria della Pace combined innovative architecture with a special sensitivity to spatial setting and the larger urban surroundings. In the late 1650s, Carlo Rainaldi began to make studies for one of Alexander's most unusual projects, the construction of twin churches in the Piazza del Popolo (86). Since antiquity, the portal leading into the piazza had been the city's ceremonial entry for dignitaries visiting from the north. For the arrival of Queen Christina of Sweden in 1655—whose recent conversion to Catholicism had been a sensational event—Alexander commissioned Bernini to redesign the portal and hired Rainaldi to erect two symmetrical churches across the piazza at the juncture of the three main thoroughfares leading into the heart of the city. The building of these churches—S. Maria in Montesanto on the left and S. Maria dei Miracoli on the right—was ordered in a papal chirograph of 1661. After Alexander's death in 1667, work proceeded intermittently, and they were not completed until 1675 and 1679, respectively. During the course of construction, Rainaldi's own evolving ideas were modified by the participation of both Bernini and the young Carlo Fontana.[14]

Carlo Rainaldi originally designed the churches as Greek crosses, but his desire to increase the exterior dimensions of the dome eventually led him to formulate a more open plan, with a larger and more prominent cupola. Given the churches' prominence as frontispieces to the city, their external appearance was of greater importance than the design of the interiors. However, since the two wedge-shaped sites were not identical—the one on the left being somewhat narrower than that on the right—the perfect symmetry that Alexander had envisioned could only be achieved as an illusion.

By using an oval plan for S. Maria in Montesanto and a circular plan for S. Maria dei Miracoli (87), Rainaldi made the domes appear to be identical from the frontal view. Possibly Bernini, who was associated with the Montesanto in the later years of its construction, had a role in the decision to employ non-uniform plans to attain uniform elevations. Certainly the concept fits with his own practice at S. Andrea al Quirinale and the Scala Regia, and it exemplifies his idea that "the highest merit lay in . . . being able to make do with little, to make beautiful things out of the inadequate . . . to make use of a defect in such a way that if it had not existed, one would have to invent it." Nevertheless, there is no evidence to discount Rainaldi's own claim to this ingenious solution. The plan of S. Maria in Montesanto is, after all, not so different from his own earlier oval project for S. Maria in Campitelli.

On the exterior, Bernini's intervention is more precisely identifiable. There we know that he eliminated the attic that Rainaldi had planned for the top of each facade. This simple change gave greater emphasis to the dome and a crisper, more classical character to the free-standing portico—exactly what he had hoped to do earlier with the facade of St. Peter's. Such an alteration seems relatively insignificant, however, when compared with the changes in Rainaldi's own style during these years. Nowhere in these buildings does one find the broken masses or the complex rhythms of S. Maria in Campitelli. Instead, the facades—the first free-standing temple porticoes in Rome since antiquity—are reductive and pure in their classical equipoise.

Rainaldi's new classicism has been traced to his association with Bernini and Carlo Fontana. Several other factors may also have influenced him however. Clearly, an abstract and simplified design was essential for a facade that would be seen first from a great distance. Such prominent twin facades could hardly be whimsical or indecorous either. More elaborate schemes may have been impractical economically as well. We know, for instance, that the half-columns Rainaldi planned for the interior of S. Maria dei Miracoli were replaced with pilasters because they were cheaper.

The boom in construction during this period unfortunately was not matched by an expansion of papal revenues. After the death of Urban VIII in 1644, the papal state faced bewildering economic problems, which originated with the profligacy of Urban himself and were compounded by natural disasters, economic competition from abroad, and the necessity of increasing military expenditures. As early as 1648, the populace began to grumble about how their taxes were spent, and graffiti appeared that read:

> *Noi volemo altro che Guglie, et Fontane*
> *Pane volemo, pane, pane, pane*

> We want more than obelisks and fountains
> bread we want, bread, bread, bread

Combined with the program in the Piazza del Popolo, Alexander's

86. Carlo Rainaldi and others, S. Maria in Montesanto and S. Maria dei
Miracoli, Rome, exterior.

even more extravagant patronage of the colonnade at St. Peter's virtually depleted the papal treasury and halted large-scale construction
in Rome for the next fifty years.

The new buildings that were constructed in Rome during the last
quarter of the seventeenth century are markedly different in temperament from those of earlier decades. One should be cautious in attrib-
uting the change to economic conditions, however, for a shift in architectural taste also seems to have taken place during these years. It can

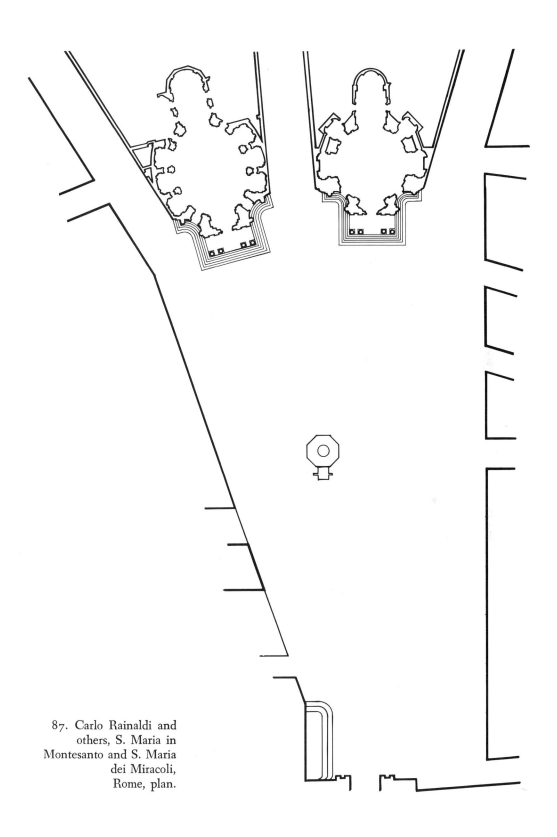

87. Carlo Rainaldi and
others, S. Maria in
Montesanto and S. Maria
dei Miracoli,
Rome, plan.

be seen in works Rainaldi designed on his own after the death of Alexander in 1667. The church of the Gesù e Maria (88) is perhaps the best known of his late commissions because of its location on the Via del Corso, only three blocks from the Piazza del Popolo.

Between 1671 and 1674, Rainaldi added a facade to the pre-existing church as part of a larger decorative program that lasted until 1685.[15] Several factors might explain the unexpectedly simple nature of his design. On one hand, economic restrictions are known to have been a problem before private support was made available in the later 1670s for the lavish decoration of the interior. On the other hand, the location of the church on Rome's busiest and most important street would undoubtedly have restrained Rainaldi from proposing anything really flamboyant, perhaps just as it had in the case of Cortona's S. Maria in Via Lata. Finally, there is the question of stylistic choice alone, free from all practical considerations. The ascetic appearance of this flat facade reflects a sensibility that plainly was at odds with the exuberance of S. Maria in Campitelli, designed just a decade earlier. One assumes that Bernini's S. Andrea al Quirinale (53) was decisive in Rainaldi's thinking. The single aedicule formed by giant pilasters and a pristine triangular pediment is so similar on both facades it could hardly be coincidental. In adapting the composition to the longitudinal plan of the Gesù e Maria, Rainaldi simply added an extra bay at either side to mask the projecting side chapels. He also doubled the pilasters and eliminated the projecting porch to make the facade even flatter and less vigorous than that of its prototype. The result is neat, but it completely repudiates the progressive tendencies for which the architect was renowned.

Rainaldi's other late church facades were less influenced by Bernini, but they are just as sedate as the Gesù e Maria. Indeed, they epitomize the spirit of a generation that praised discipline over vitality, preferred the pilaster to the column, and sought to reestablish the primacy the flat wall had had in the late sixteenth century. By the 1670s, the conservative forces led by Bernini had finally surpassed the progressive styles of Borromini and Cortona, who both had died at the end of the 1660s, leaving no artistic successors. And like Rainaldi, who lived on until 1691, even Cortona, in his late works like S. Maria in Via Lata (72) and S. Carlo al Corso (74), had become a convert to the new discipline.

At its best, the style of the later seventeenth century was one of con-

88. Carlo Rainaldi, Gesù e Maria, Rome, facade.

89. G. A. De Rossi, Palazzo D'Aste, Rome, facade.

siderable refinement. Examples of this refinement can be found in the work of Giovanni Antonio de Rossi (1616–1695), an architect who at times also reflects the more pedestrian side of the period as well. De Rossi was born in Rome, and after an early apprenticeship to a minor architect, went on to develop an independent style, which in its flatness and its detail recalls that of the older Giovanni Battista Soria.[16]

Unlike his more famous contemporaries who devoted most of their energies to the construction of sacred buildings, De Rossi's oeuvre includes an equal number of secular commissions. The finest of these is probably the Palazzo D'Aste of 1658–1665, located at the head of the Via del Corso facing the present Piazza Venezia (89). This handsome palace is pivotal in the history of Roman Baroque architecture, for while its lilting pediments and bevelled corners look back to Borromini, it also quickly became the prototype for a series of palaces that continues into the eighteenth century. Part of its charm stems from the compact proportions of its main facade, which is four bays narrower than the side elevation on the Corso. The three stories are crisply articulated with moldings, pilasters, and pediments that discreetly relieve the monotony of the flat wall. Despite its relatively early date, the delicacy of this design is more akin to the aesthetic of the Rococo than to the Baroque of its own time. This makes it all the more unfortunate, and puzzling, that in his later palaces, De Rossi seldom achieved the same degree of elegance and refinement that he did here.

De Rossi enjoyed equally sporadic success in his ecclesiastical commissions. Active at a time of reduced demand on the part of the religious orders, this work mostly involved small scale enterprises like designing chapels or modernizing lesser churches. Among the most interesting of these commissions was the completion of the interior of S. Maria Maddalena (90). In 1695, the year of his death, De Rossi redesigned the nave of this earlier church whose ritual end had already been rebuilt by Carlo Fontana in the 1670s. De Rossi's ingenious solution can be taken as the century's final statement on the conflicting virtues of longitudinal and centralized planning. A perfect compromise, the interior of the Maddalena combines the advantages of each. The substitution of an elongated octagon for the traditional rectangle opens up the nave, and in effect creates a mild cross-axis that balances the directional impulse. Yet De Rossi avoided the tension of Rainaldi's interior of S. Maria in Campitelli by reducing the number of side chapels and arranging them so that they do not reinforce the transverse axis. One's interest is thus contained within the boundaries of

90. G. A. De Rossi,
S. Maria Maddalena,
Rome, plan.

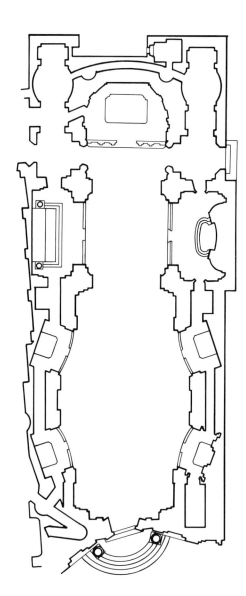

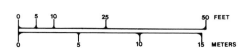

the main space, and the flanking chapels remain independent and subordinant.

Although it was only a modest innovation, De Rossi's expansion of the nave at S. Maria Maddalena breathed new life into the moribund Latin-cross plan. In the eighteenth century his idea was revived, particularly in central Europe, where the distended nave became a favorite device of architects like Balthasar Neumann.

The temper of the late seventeenth century is best reflected in the work of Carlo Fontana (1638–1714). For this architect, virtue lay in orthodoxy, and his life, like his work, was grounded in academic tradition. He served an unprecedented nine terms as director of the Accademia di San Luca, the institutional arbiter of classical taste; he made and preserved dozens of volumes of carefully executed drawings; he published scholarly discourses; and he taught large numbers of students, some of whom, like Filippo Juvarra, went on to establish greater reputations than his own.[17] After his arrival from northern Italy in the early 1650s, he served as an assistant to Bernini, Cortona, and Carlo Rainaldi, and he continued to collaborate with these masters occasionally, even after he began his independent practice in the 1660s.[18]

The facade of S. Rita (or S. Biagio in Campitelli as it is sometimes called) offers a good example of Fontana's early talent. The octagonal church was built by an anonymous architect ca. 1650 and received Fontana's facade ca. 1660–1665 (91). It was moved to its present location in the Piazza Campitelli earlier this century from the foot of the Capitoline Hill. For the basic composition, Fontana was probably inspired by Bernini's earlier front for S. Bibiana (42), where a similar arrangement of arched and pedimented elements also appears. The motif of the illusionistic arches—slanted to look deeper than they are—certainly derives from Bernini, who had used it several times before.[19] The most unconventional feature of the facade, however, is its unusual treatment of the upper story where the concave end bays are sharply folded across the corners. This probably was done in deference to the spectator viewing the church laterally from the narrow street in which it originally stood. Not surprisingly, perhaps, Bernini had planned to use a similar scheme years earlier in an unexecuted design for a tomb.[20] Beyond any such direct and specific borrowings, S. Rita is most Berninesque in its general concept. In his preference for the pilaster, and his use of secondary, oblique points of view, Fontana reaffirmed two of Bernini's favorite practices. The rise in Fontana's reputation did little, therefore, to diminish the legacy of Bernini, but it soon signalled the end of the adventuresome spirit of the Roman High Baroque.

The indisputable masterpiece of Fontana's career was the facade of S. Marcello al Corso (92), constructed, like so many others of the period, for a previously existing church. This facade, built in 1682–1683, is unusual for two reasons. First, it is composed entirely of curved planes, and secondly, it reaffirmed the free-standing order at a time

91. Carlo Fontana,
S. Rita, Rome, exterior.

when such robust membering had fallen mostly into disuse. It might
seem that Fontana was reverting to the more dramatic style of the previous generation, but closer analysis of the facade reveals that much
of the drama is shallow, or perhaps even unintentional. To begin with,
the concave curvature may have been the result of another architect's
abortive effort to construct the facade a decade earlier,[21] rather than a
free invention of Fontana's.

A study of the orders provides more useful insights into the true
nature of the facade. Because the church is set back from the street in
a broad but shallow piazza, a cluster of free-standing columns may

152

92. Carlo Fontana, S. Marcello al Corso, Rome, facade.

PALAZZO DELL ILL.^{mo} SIG CON^e GIO ANTONIO BIGHAZZINI NELLA PIAZZA DI S. MARCO RIONE DI PIGNA LA FACCIATA ARCHITETTVRA DEL CAV^e CARLO
FONTANA CON PARTE DEL DI DENTRO

93. Carlo Fontana, Palazzo Bigazzini, Rome, engraving of facade.

have seemed the best way to emphasize the entrance. Yet the boldness of this frontispiece is diminished by the steady, almost mechanical progression of its orders. Only pilasters and full columns are used; there are no intermediate members, and no secondary orders relieve the monotony of the regular sequence. On the upper story, the sequence is reversed, but the consistency of the overall composition remains as clear as that of Maderno's S. Susanna (14), designed nearly a century earlier. By avoiding the complexity and texture of interlocking orders and encased pediments, Fontana created a facade that is more static and abstract than it is dynamic and sensuous. The easy legibility and lack of ambiguity attest to its author's continuing allegiance to the most important principles of Bernini's classical ideology.

Just before its completion, Fontana made some last-minute changes at S. Marcello. These changes, confined mainly to the central bay of the upper story, introduced the facade's few unorthodox features. To accommodate a small window that already existed in the front of the church, he sacrificed a normative pedimented window—known from preparatory drawings—and used instead an illusionistic arch similar

154

to those he employed earlier at S. Rita. He also set a small aedicule into the space between the two segments of the lower pediment. This aedicule very likely was intended to house a sculptural relief, but as far as we know, it remained unexecuted.

Given the circumstances of the period, the facade of S. Marcello was a remarkable achievement. Its surface may be slightly chilled, but its structure is far from being completely frozen. Certainly it shows more imagination than Fontana's most ambitious secular building, the since destroyed Palazzo Bigazzini (93), which once stood in the Piazza di S. Marco. This dry and repetitive elevation was built from 1676–1680, not long after Fontana had been Bernini's assistant at the Palazzo Chigi in Piazza dei Ss. Apostoli (61). But Fontana was unresponsive to the refinement of both the Chigi and the nearby D'Aste palaces, following more traditional sixteenth-century models like the Farnese and Lateran palaces (8 and 9). Carlo Fontana was not alone, however, in preserving the ideal of the three-story palace with pedimented windows, rusticated corners, and no classical order: Giovanni Antonio de Rossi had created similar facades for several of his own later palaces.

One should consider, of course, the likelihood that such thoroughly conventional designs are less revealing of the creativity of an architect than of the expressed desire of a patron to remain inconspicuous. Count Giovanni Bigazzini, who was not from one of Rome's most noble families, may have deliberately intended to downplay his status as a parvenu in a residence that stood across the square from Paul II's Palazzo di S. Marco (now Palazzo Venezia), one of the city's most imposing Renaissance structures.[22]

Fontana's reputation doubtless would be much greater today if he could have built any of three large urban projects that he designed after 1690. The proposals were as ambitious as any conceived under Alexander VII, but by this time the papacy had neither the means nor the determination to execute any of them. In fact, Innocent XII (1691–1700) is said to have told Fontana, "You astonish us, Cavaliere, proposing building projects prohibitive of our exhausted treasury. You will have to change the tune of these ideas of yours."

Not only did the papacy become more financially responsible in these years, but it started to pay more attention to the social needs of the Roman population as well. Fontana's commission to transform the Palazzo Ludovisi in Piazza Montecitorio, a residence Bernini had built

94. Carlo Fontana, project for a church in the Colosseum, Rome.

for a papal nephew many years earlier, into the *Curia Innocenziana* or Court of Justice, was as symptomatic of this change as was Innocent's rejection of the architect's related plan to greatly enlarge the piazza which stood in front of it.[23]

Rivalling his project for the expansion of the Piazza di Montecitorio was Fontana's equally grand proposal to enlarge the Piazza of St. Peter's by creating a trapezoidal space in front of the oval colonnade and constructing a tall frontispiece there to isolate the square from the crowded neighborhood that surrounded it. The opportunity to realize this clever scheme was also passed up by the pope. Fontana's last major Roman project, conceived under Clement XI (1700–1721), called for transforming the Colosseum into a religious shrine by building a centralized church at one end of the open amphitheatre (94).[24] Although it was no more successful than Domenico Fontana's efforts in the late sixteenth century to turn the Colosseum into a yarn factory, it does prove that Carlo and his generation were not completely unimaginative. The enormous statue of the pope that was intended to surmount the dome is also a clear indication that the papacy saw no diminution of its role as the unassailable leader of a still triumphant world church.

Architecturally, Fontana's Colosseum project was less remarkable. Despite the vigorous massing of the dome, towers, portico, and enclosing cloister (invisible here), the overall effect of the composition is rather bland and expressionless. Fontana's exclusive use of pilasters

156

yields an undifferentiated and indifferent surface, while his eclectic vocabulary seems oddly familiar. Borrowing freely from both Bramante's Tempietto (1502)—as originally intended within a colonnaded courtyard—and S. Agnese in Piazza Navona (78), Fontana created a design of characteristic reticence and good manners. One senses in this style the exacting mentality of the Accademia di San Luca, the conservative institution which Fontana headed from 1692 to 1700, where student assignments similar to this soon became standard practice. Indeed, Fontana's work occupies a pivotal position between the seventeenth and the eighteenth centuries. As we shall see in the next chapter, with the renewal of architectural activity in Rome ca. 1725, his few buildings were a stimulus—both positive and negative—for the generation of builders that succeeded him.

95. G. O. Recalcati, S. Agata in Trastevere, Rome, facade.

7

Rococo and Academic Classicism in Eighteenth-Century Rome

Roman architecture in the early eighteenth century was of two temperaments: one stern, formal, and rather officious—the legacy of Bernini and Fontana—and the other sprightly, flexible, and, though ornate, more modest in its intentions—the outcome of a renewed interest in Borromini. This second style is usually known as the Rococo, but the split between it and contemporary classicizing trends was less identifiable with individual architects than the progressive/conservative schism had been in the seventeenth century.[1] Now there were few dominant figures, and the most challenging commissions were more evenly dispersed among a greater number of architects.

The Rococo's gradual emergence was the more interesting of the two developments. It was in 1710 with Giacomo Onorato Recalcati's church of S. Agata in Trastevere that it made one of its first appearances. Within the framework of a conventional Gesù-type facade (95), Recalcati introduced details that would certainly have offended a conservative critic like Carlo Fontana. Among the unconventional details are upper story pilasters with unfinished capitals, and an oval window framed with angel wings. Both features, of course, had appeared decades earlier in Borromini's facades of the Oratory of St. Phillip Neri and the church of S. Carlo, works which until now had produced no offspring. In combining these features with fanciful pediments and other discreetly unorthodox details, Recalcati clearly expressed his impatience with the conformity of his classicizing contemporaries.

159

The facade of S. Agata was especially prophetic of the Rococo in its affinity for the ornamental rather than the spatial or structural qualities of Borromini's architecture. Few architects of the period tried to match the complexity of Borromini's plans or the elasticity of his elevations, although occasionally there were some delightful exceptions to this rule. Giuseppe Sardi's little church of S. Maria del Rosario in Marino is one of the most intriguing and perhaps unfamiliar of these rare exceptions. Marino is a small town to the south of Rome, across the Lago di Albano from Castel Gandolfo. In the early 1720s, Sardi (ca. 1680–1753) built a circular chapel within the walls of the town's Dominican convent. The centralized interior space (96) is formed from a ring of eight Tuscan columns that support a low arcade. The arcade frames both the entrance and chapel arms on the orthogonal axes and the niched piers on the diagonal axes. The late Baroque ornamental vocabulary, as well as the interior's malleable and perforated spatial boundaries would be unthinkable without the example of Borromini. But Sardi's search for inspiration did not end there. In designing the unconventional ribbed and pierced dome, he must have turned to the work of Guarino Guarini (1624–1683), the Piedmontese creator of some of the seventeenth century's most bizarre and fanciful vaulting. A glance at Guarini's dome of S. Lorenzo in Turin (130), completed in 1687, reveals some basic similarities in the treatment of the interwoven ribs and the perforated shell-like vault. These forms, in their lightness and buoyancy, are the direct precursors of the even more sprightly Rococo interiors of southern Germany. By Roman standards, the church of the Rosary must have been a welcome relief from the academic constraints that had inhibited architects for nearly half a century.

During the second quarter of the eighteenth century, despite the lack of discernible improvement in the papacy's fortunes, pontiffs like Benedict XIII (1724–1730) and Clement XII (1730–1740) promoted the construction of a surprisingly rich assortment of new buildings and urban projects, ending a long period of uninspired patronage. The striking Via del Corso wing of the Palazzo Doria-Pamphili (97), commissioned by descendants of Pope Innocent X in 1730–1735, is an excellent example of the vitality and increased scale of these projects. This imposing structure was built to house a picture gallery on the *piano nobile* while giving Rome's most important street an appropriate frontispiece for the complex of buildings that then fronted onto a nearby piazza. The architect, Gabriele Valvassori (1683–1761), re-

96. Giuseppe Sardi, S. Maria del Rosario, Marino, interior.

97. Gabriele Valvassori, Palazzo Doria-Pamphili, Rome, Corso facade.

ceived his training at the Accademia di S. Luca during Carlo Fontana's presidency, but his lively design for this long facade makes few concessions to academic taste. The seventeen bays of the upper stories are divided into seven groups by rusticated wall strips. The seven vertical divisions both stress the entrance bays and retard the tempo of the rows of windows between them. By this means, and by visually linking the windows of the two lower stories, Valvassori managed to bring the considerable length of the facade—one of the longest on the Corso—into greater harmony with its standard height of three stories. In contrast to earlier Roman palaces, the size and projection of the windows is also greatly increased relative to the surrounding wall surface, significantly reducing the expressionless areas of the facade.

162

Naturally, it is the architecture of Borromini—especially the exterior of the Propaganda Fide (39–40)—that must have inspired the high relief and dramatic enframement of the windows and doorways of the *piano nobile*. The creative impoverishment of the late seventeenth and early eighteenth centuries was now giving way to livelier modes of expression.

Despite the Baroque flavor of its bold ornament and unabashed emulation of Borromini, the Palazzo Doria-Pamphili is a characteristically Rococo building. During the seventeenth century only De Rossi's Palazzo D'Aste (89) had dared redress the solemnity of the traditional Roman palace front. The D'Aste was not imitated in its own time, but standing so prominently in the Piazza Venezia, just a few yards up the Corso, with its beveled corners and freely conceived pediments, it may have been the impetus for the creation of the Doria-Pamphili and several other eighteenth-century domestic buildings stylistically related to it.

Filippo Raguzzini (ca. 1680–1771) was another imaginative architect of Sardi's and Valvassori's generation. He was born in Naples, began his career in nearby Benevento, and in 1724 followed his newly elected compatriot Pope Benedict XIII to Rome, where he enjoyed an active and varied practice for the six years that his patron reigned.[2] In Rome, Raguzzini's attachment to Neapolitan tradition gradually lessened, and he soon became one of the most engaging of Roman Rococo architects. Less rhapsodic than Sardi or Valvassori, and less self-conscious than Recalcati, Raguzzini's architecture is low-keyed, informal, and at times closely related to the Roman vernacular. Instead of marble, he preferred inexpensive stucco, an ideal medium for his simple, unpretentious style, and an economic benefit for his curiously austere and unworldly papal patron. Indeed, the importance of stucco cannot be overemphasized in the history of the Rococo. Its pale color and delicate texture were as much a part of its charm as its low cost was a stimulus to ornament great numbers of previously unornamented domestic and secular buildings. Now, for the first time, modest houses and income-producing apartments were sometimes as artfully designed as aristocratic palaces and religious buildings.

In 1727 Raguzzini began construction of a group of multi-family dwellings in the Piazza di S. Ignazio (98, 99), a small square facing a seventeenth-century church dedicated to the founder of the Jesuit order.[3] The church is a large, uninspired, late derivative of the Gesù,

98. Filippo Raguzzini,
Piazza di S. Ignazio,
Rome, isometric view.

with a broad facade looming ponderously over the shallow piazza.
Raguzzini first transformed this infelicitous space by redirecting the
narrow access streets so they entered the piazza obliquely rather than
on axis, as was traditional with such sites. By doing so, he slowed the
pace of approach and created as many as six possible entrances from
the north side of the square. Even after many visits, one experiences
a keen sense of discovery upon issuing from these narrow passages into
the open piazza.

In Cortona's comparable scheme for the piazza of S. Maria della
Pace (68), one, of course, entered on axis, and the church's facade
was the climax of the composition. Here, by contrast, Raguzzini diminished the impact of the pre-existing church by focusing one's attention
on the secular buildings. In authorizing the project, Benedict XIII re-
ferred to it as a *fabbrica teatrale,* and while no theatrical performances
are known to have taken place in the square, the shape and placement
of the new buildings do suggest the insubstantial forms of stage designs. Each of the three polygonal buildings that face the church has

164

a curved facade formed from segments of an equal number of tangential ovals. These gracefully curved facades utter an appropriately Rococo response to the cumbersome Baroque front of S. Ignazio. The low four-story elevations are delicately worked with thin string courses and pilaster strips. Only the third level of windows is lightly pedimented, and the rest of the ornamentation consists of thin ironwork balconies and fine encrustations of stucco.

The very concept of this secular enterprise is alien to propagandistic and rhetorical seventeenth-century ensembles like S. Maria della Pace. Through refined understatement and a bit of ingenuousness, Raguzzini succeeded in shifting the focal point of the piazza from the church to the apartment houses that stand opposite it. Like a light dessert after a heavy meal, the Piazza di S. Ignazio served eighteenth-century Rome

99. Filippo Raguzzini, Piazza di S. Ignazio, Rome, view.

100. Filippo Raguzzini,
S. Maria della Quercia,
Rome, facade.

an easily digestible alternative to its traditional view of urban space.
Part of its charm, of course, is its very uniqueness, for nothing like it
was ever built again in Rome.

In 1727, the year that work began on the piazza, Raguzzini was also
commissioned by the Roman guild of butchers to rebuild the tiny centralized church of S. Maria della Quercia in an old quarter of Rome
near the Palazzo Farnese. Although he was superseded by another architect after his papal protector died in 1730, his refined and genteel
style is easily recognizable on the church's disarmingly small facade
(100). Originally fronting on a more constricted piazza than exists today, this facade is a perfect example of Raguzzini's ability to adjust the

weight of the ornament to the site and scale of the building. The gently undulating wall is reminiscent of Borromini, but the delicacy of Raguzzini's treatment of the classical order is quite unlike the brawny strength of buildings like S. Carlo alle Quattro Fontane. On this facade, the order is reduced to thin pilasters that are folded and paneled to diminish their bulk. The pilasters combine with crisp wall panels and moldings to create a finely vibrating pattern of light and shade that plays over the entire surface. Raguzzini's undoctrinaire approach to architecture is most obvious in the lack of classical pediments over either the door, window, or full frontispiece. Apart from Borromini, few architects in Rome would have dispensed with the traditional pediment as the crowning feature of a church facade. Here at S. Maria della Quercia, Raguzzini substituted a simple curved panel for the pediment, enhancing the restrained and unassuming nature of the stucco exterior. Crests of this type were a common sight in Naples at the time, and such a treatment on this facade may have been prompted by the architect's recollection of his pre-Roman experience.

Benedict XIII's death in 1730 brought Raguzzini's career in Rome to an abrupt halt. The victim of jealous rivals, he was temporarily imprisoned during the scandalous aftermath of his countryman's papacy, and ultimately paid the price for the success he owed to Benedict's regional chauvinism. Despite the professional demise of this gifted architect, the Rococo style continued to survive in the works of a few contemporaries who shared his ability to create interesting and fanciful buildings on a modest scale. The little Oratory of the SS. Annunziata (101), built by Pietro Passalacqua (d. 1748) in 1744–1746, is an example of such a building. Like S. Maria della Quercia, its delicately articulated interior is too small to be reproduced adequately in a photograph, but the crisp linear patterns created by its refined pilasters and moldings are a delight to experience first-hand. The exterior, which masks utilitarian dependencies above and alongside the oratory proper, is modelled with a vigorous, painterly touch. In the central portion, a tall aedicule encloses a doorway framed with a secondary order and surmounted by an oval window.[4] Closer inspection reveals that Passalacqua enlivened this simple design by gently bending the planes of the background wall. Even more unusual is the central wall plane running between the Giant columns of the aedicule. Creased at either side in an uncinated (hook-like) curve, it proclaims the architect's indifference to the standard geometry of classical architecture. Like many Rococo inventions, in painting and in architecture, this modest

101. Pietro Passalacqua, Oratory of SS. Annunziata, Rome, facade.

stylization was probably intended for the knowledgeable connoisseur rather than the everyday churchgoer.

The flanking wings and the area above the main pediment are more densely ornamented than the central portion of the facade. Passalacqua's ornament is not as refined as Raguzzini's, but is a good deal friskier and more playful. In places, reminiscences of Borromini can still be detected, now fully absorbed into the mature Rococo idiom. Passalacqua's training at the Accademia di S. Luca did not seem to have made a lasting impression on him.

The most ambitious Rococo undertaking was the Scalinata di Spagna, or Spanish Staircase, constructed on the designs of Francesco de Sanctis (d. 1731) between 1723 and 1726 (102, 103).[5] In contrast to the intimate scale and inconspicuous location of the Piazza di S. Ignazio, the Spanish Staircase—which ascends the Pincian Hill between the Piazza di Spagna and the church of the Trinità dei Monti— is lavish in scale. Many attempts had been made to tame the steep hillside in the seventeenth century, but for various reasons, all had failed. Since the property belonged to the French Minims of the Trinità dei Monti, the obstacles were diplomatic as well as practical. Just before his death in 1661, Cardinal Mazarin, then Prime Minister of France, had Bernini design a project with a lifesize equestrian statue of Louis XIV as the central feature, a monument hardly calculated to please Pope Alexander VII at a time of increasing tension between the two sovereigns. Bernini's proposal for the stairway, which consisted of a series of straight and curved ramps separated by broad landings, nevertheless did prefigure the final design in the diversity of its paths of approach. De Sanctis probably was inspired by a group of projects executed by Alessandro Specchi in 1717–1721, which had also explored the dynamic possibilities of expansion and contraction along a shifting series of axes.[6]

The staircase consists of an alternating sequence of single and divided ramps linked with spacious landings that offer the visitor a scenic and unhurried passage in either direction. Although the grandiloquence of the scheme remains in the Baroque tradition, the graceful fluidity and flexible contours of the design are unmistakably Rococo. De Sanctis, moreover, also expressed the typical eighteenth-century concern with function and convenience. In a memorandum accompanying a project he submitted to Clement XI, the architect repeatedly stated that he wanted to create "an inviting place that will offer the utmost

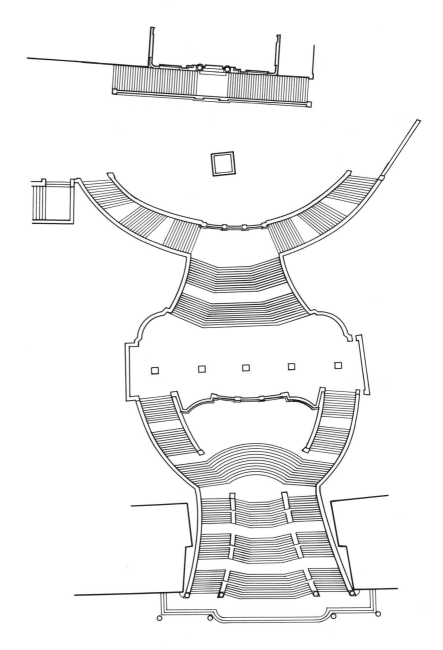

102. Francesco de Sanctis,
Spanish Staircase,
Rome, plan.

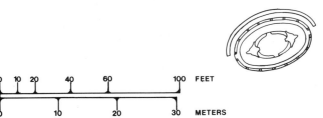

0 10 20   40   60   100 FEET

0   10   20   30 METERS

repose to the people." Trees were to provide relief from the sun, statuary was to soften the outline of the balustrades, and a fountain was to
be the focus of the principal landing. From the beginning, De Sanctis
intended the site to function as a piazza (the term he used for the
main landings) and as a thoroughfare. He would probably not be dis-
appointed if he could return today to find it filled with crowds of
breathless tourists and self-employed craftsmen displaying their goods.
Ironically, the Spanish Staircase is probably more attractive now than
it was in the eighteenth century for the simple reason that, unlike so
many other public spaces in Europe, it is never choked with vehicular
traffic.

For De Sanctis, the commission for the Scalinata ended unhappily.
In 1728, the site was badly damaged in a rainstorm, and he was named
the respondent of a long and messy lawsuit. He was to receive no fur-

103. Francesco de Sanctis, Spanish Staircase, Rome, view.

104. Alessandro Galilei, S. Giovanni in Laterano, Rome, facade.

ther commissions, and he died in 1731. The damage was not repaired until six years after his death.

Thus far it would appear that the Rococo faced little competition from the proponents of opposing styles. Indeed, after Carlo Fontana's death in 1714, nearly two decades passed before his punctilious late style found its true successors. The revival began in 1732 with a competition for the facade of S. Giovanni in Laterano, the cathedral church of Rome which had stood on the same site since the fourth century. Twenty-three architects from all over Italy submitted projects to a jury chosen by the Accademia di San Luca and chaired by its president. Raguzzini, Passalacqua, and others proposed that this large and officious facade be designed in a discreetly Rococo manner, but their more classical-minded rivals provided stiff competition. A few of the Rococo designs were praised by the judges, but, not surprisingly, considering the background of the jury, the prize was awarded to a classical project. Pope Clement XII made the final decision from choices he was given, and he selected the entry of his virtually unknown countryman, Alessandro Galilei. The cost of construction was creatively financed by a lottery that Clement introduced in 1731.

Galilei (1691–1737)—a distant relative of the seventeenth-century astronomer—was born in Florence, worked briefly in Rome, and spent an extended period in England before settling in the papal city in 1731. His facade (104) has been said to reflect his familiarity with English architecture, but its sources can also be traced to Roman traditions.[7] The idea of framing superimposed loggias with the giant order is found in Bernini's studies for the Louvre (62), particularly the court elevation of the engraved third project, while the narrow aedicule enclosing the secondary order of the entrance bay clearly recalls Maderno's facade of St. Peter's (17). Galilei skillfully blended these sources into a composition of impressive decorum and propriety, but one with hardly a trace of Rococo charm or whimsy. Since the church is normally first seen from a distance, plain legibility was evidently one of his primary concerns.

Like St. Peter's, the facade of the Lateran masks a deep narthex. A strength of Galilei's design is that he exposed this narthex to light by eliminating all unnecessary wall surface on the frontispiece. Not only does this make the pilasters and columns seem more structural, the entire composition is made bolder and more dramatic when seen from afar. The spirit of the facade therefore depends only in part on the usual interplay of solid forms, for the juxtaposition of solids and voids now plays an equally prominent role. Such a treatment reconstitutes a basic principle of Bramante's High Renaissance architecture, which also sought to reduce the expanse of inert wall while giving greater emphasis to a framework of classical members.

Because Galilei employed a limited vocabulary in a highly regular composition, the Lateran facade appears stable and rather static. Compared with Fontana's facade of S. Marcello al Corso (92), its classicism is purer and more abstract, but the difference is more one of degree than of basic motivation. Despite its austere grandeur, the facade remained firmly in the Baroque tradition, not yet as archaeologically derivative or rigidly disciplined as the Neo-Classical style that was to follow in the second half of the eighteenth century.

Nevertheless, the Lateran facade was a turning point in Roman architecture. Suddenly, and with little warning, the classical style became more fashionable than the Rococo. After the completion of the Lateran in 1736, the surviving Rococo architects—men like Sardi, Valvassori, and Raguzzini—produced little that truly could be called Rococo. Only Pietro Passalacqua and Domenico Gregorini (d. 1777) seem to have succeeded in constructing important Rococo designs after that date. An interesting forerunner of Passalacqua's lively Oratory of the SS. Annunziata of 1744–1746 (101) is the facade and narthex of the medieval church of S. Croce in Gerusalemme (105), which Gregorini designed and Passalacqua helped execute in 1741–1744 under the patronage of the new pope Benedict XIV (1740–1758).[8] Like the Lateran, S. Croce was one of the seven cardinal basilicas and chief pilgrimage churches of Rome. The award of this important commission to a Rococo architect must therefore have come as something of a surprise. Nevertheless, Gregorini, undoubtedly aware of the disfavor into which the Rococo had fallen, compromised his normally vivacious manner with strong reminiscences of the severe front of the Lateran. The plan of S. Croce's facade bears an unexpected resemblance to Cortona's Ss. Martina e Luca (67), but the elevation's austere giant pilasters, open portals with a central Palladian motif, and crested balustrade all derive from the Lateran. The few Rococo touches are limited to such minor embellishments as the fragmentary cornice over the central doorway and the "dripping" scroll over the oval window.

S. Croce and the church of the Lateran stand fairly close to one another on the eastern outskirts of the city, and during these same years Benedict XIV had a broad avenue laid out to connect them. Comparisons inevitably must have been made between the two facades. While S. Croce might have been viewed as a tame derivative of the Lateran, it could also have been seen as a politely critical Rococo revision of Galilei's classical manifesto. We have no way of knowing the real motivation behind Gregorini's imitation of the earlier building, but what sometimes passes for simple emulation of works of art may actually be satirical comment.

Behind the facade of S. Croce is an oval narthex that ranks among the most interesting spatial inventions of eighteenth-century Rome. Set perpendicular to the principal axis, this narthex consists of a ring of eight piers supporting an alternating series of arches and lintels that form a continuous Palladian motif identical to the facade's. An oval dome, supported by the low ring of piers, provides illumination and a

105. Domenico Gregorini assisted by Pietro Passalacqua, S. Croce in
Gerusalemme, Rome, facade.

106. Ferdinando Fuga, S. Maria Maggiore, Rome, facade.

sense of spaciousness. This kind of open, shell-like vestibule, though fairly uncommon in Rome, became a popular feature of Rococo architecture in other parts of Europe.

The renovation of the most venerable Early Christian churches was a dominant theme in Benedict XIV's patronage. At the same time he was sponsoring the work at S. Croce, he commissioned a new facade for a third major pilgrimage church, the basilica of S. Maria Maggiore (106). Its architect, the Florentine Ferdinando Fuga (1699–1782), had worked in Naples and Sicily before coming to Rome in 1730 to serve as papal architect to his countryman Clement XII. Fuga's early work displayed mild affinities with the Rococo, but as time went on, his designs became more classical in expression. His facade for S. Maria Maggiore (1741–1743) was both the high point and the stylistic midpoint of his career.

Fuga's challenge at S. Maria Maggiore was to create a frontispiece in harmony with the late sixteenth-century forms of Flaminio Ponzio's adjacent sacristy while preserving the view of some early mosaics on the upper level of the church's existing end wall. He accomplished this by following Galilei's example of eliminating most of the wall surface between the load-bearing structural members. The absence of curved planes and Rococo ornament may likewise reflect the influence of the Lateran on his thinking. Yet Fuga's commitment to classical ideals was by no means as strong as that of Galilei: he eschewed the Lateran's giant pilasters for two superimposed tiers of full columns, its single unbroken triangular pediment for four broken ones, and its spare lower elevation for one ornamented with free-standing sculpture. He also reinstated the traditional basilican profile of three bays over five. Thus despite its classical structure, the facade's rich texture and varied rhythms avoid any hint of academic rigidity.

Before he left Rome in 1751 to settle permanently in Naples, Fuga designed several palaces that reveal his increasingly conservative attitude towards design. Among his last Roman commissions was the facade of the Palazzo Cenci-Bolognetti in the Piazza del Gesù (107), built ca. 1745 to mask a pre-existing building. Fuga's design is a striking contrast to the lighter, more felicitous handling of Raguzzini's Rococo palaces in the Piazza di S. Ignazio just a few blocks away. Instead of modelling with lightweight panels and delicate moldings, Fuga relied entirely on the classical order to create his solemn and stately exterior. By Roman standards this was unusual. Previously, when the classical order was used on a secular building, it usually was

107. Ferdinando Fuga, Palazzo Cenci-Bolognetti, Rome, facade.

to create a discreet vertical accent, as, for example, on the corners of
the Palazzo D'Aste (89). Not since Bernini built the Palazzo Chigi
in the 1660s (61), had anyone but Fuga and his contemporary Nicola
Salvi dared use the orders so conspicuously. Bernini was now as much
the inspiration for this revival of classicism as Borromini had been for
the creation of the Rococo. Following the example of the Palazzo
Chigi, Fuga placed a giant order over a low base and emphasized the
central bays by bringing them slightly forward and spacing them differently than those to either side. However, Fuga stressed even greater
regularity in his design by continuing both the lower rustication and
the upper balustrade across the full width of the facade.

The original patron of the Palazzo Cenci—a little-known family
named Petroni—were of much lower social and financial status than
the Chigi had been when they commissioned Bernini to build their
palace, during the reign of their relative Alexander VII in the 1660s.

178

In the eighteenth century, fine architecture was no longer the exclusive domain of privileged church aristocrats. So prepossessing a design might also reflect the period's taste for regular urbanistic ensembles. Here in the Piazza del Gesù, Fuga's palace stands opposite the Palazzo Altieri—the elegant family residence of Clement X—and next to the imposing front of Il Gesù (6). The square itself, moreover, lay right on the papal processional route from the Vatican to the Capitoline Hill and was an area of some ceremonial importance.[9]

A better known and related work of the period is the Trevi Fountain (108), the terminal point of the aqueduct known as the Acqua Vergine. Its designer, Nicola Salvi (1697–1751), was selected from among sixteen architects in a competition held in 1732.[10] As in the Lateran competition, a number of Rococo proposals were passed over

108. Nicola Salvi, Trevi Fountain, Rome.

in favor of a strongly classical project. The winner, like Alessandro Galilei, was an unfamiliar figure in Roman circles.

The fountain consists of two distinct parts: an architectural backdrop and a cascade and basin containing an allegorical tableau of seahorses and tritons guiding the chariot of Oceanus. Like the Spanish Staircase, the design drew upon proposals that had already been made in the seventeenth century. One of these was a project by Bernini intended for the same site, while another, by Pietro da Cortona, would have moved the fountain to the Piazza Colonna to become the principal facade of a second Chigi palace which was located there (73).[11] The central feature of Bernini's and Cortona's proposals was a broad hemicycle, and this element was adopted by nearly all the entrants in the eighteenth-century competition. Salvi, however, straightened this unclassical curve and instead substituted an imposing triumphal arch as the centerpiece of the nine-bay palace facade. Formally, this elevation still relates to Bernini in the hierarchical tripartite arrangement of its center and side sections. Again the Palazzo Chigi in the Piazza di Ss. Apostoli comes to mind. If Salvi did not know it in 1732, he certainly did later, for he was the architect who in 1745 so ungraciously enlarged it from 13 to its present 27 bays. Berninesque, too, is the membering of the facade's central niche which recalls the majestic entrance to the Scala Regia in the Vatican (49).

Although the formal structure of the Trevi Fountain is not so rigid as that of the Lateran facade, its classical temperament is, in other ways, even stronger. The sources of the Lateran all stem from the Baroque tradition, but the Trevi combines that tradition with more direct borrowings from antiquity. Earlier Roman fountains had also been inspired by triumphal arches, but none was so consciously antiquarian as this in its derivation from the Arch of Constantine, a monument which Clement XII was having restored during these very years. Even the sculptural program is based on classical sources, and the imagery is devoid of religious reference.[12]

Despite its erudition, the Trevi Fountain is probably the most popular public monument in Rome. Not even the Spanish Staircase can rival the operatic spectacle of so much water pouring into so small and enclosed an urban space. Nathaniel Hawthorne called it "as magnificent a piece of work as ever human skill contrived," and tourists today still find it an irresistible attraction, although possibly less for its architecture than for its sculptural and aquatic enjoyments. For Salvi, the commission had a less happy ending. He died in 1751, supposedly

109. Carlo Marchionni, Villa Albani, Rome, garden facade.

from a chill caught in the culverts of the Acqua Vergine, and missed the fountain's completion eleven years later.

The last important architect of the Roman Baroque was Carlo Marchionni (1704–1780). Between 1748 and 1762 Marchionni constructed a large villa for Cardinal Alessandro Albani outside the Porta Salaria gate of the city wall.[13] The garden facade (109) introduces yet another aspect of eighteenth-century eclecticism: the revival of the classical architecture of the late Renaissance. Here, Marchionni combined the upper story of Michelangelo's Capitoline palaces in Rome (begun in 1563) with the rusticated Palladian loggia of the Villa Mondragone in nearby Frascati (1614–1621), limiting his own invention to the design of the discreetly Rococo upper window frames. Foreswearing the traditional hierarchical composition of the Baroque, he did little to differentiate the facade's long sequence of nine bays. In its lack of a central focus, Marchionni's design abandons one of the most cherished principles of Baroque design.

The villa housed Cardinal Albani's extensive collection of ancient art. The curator of this collection was Johann Joachim Winckelmann, whose publications in the 1750s and 60s were instrumental in the rediscovery of the culture of ancient Greece. Under Winckelmann's influence, Marchionni built three miniature temples on the site—one an artificial ruin patterned on Greek models—just as the main villa was nearing completion ca. 1760. Although such "garden follies," as they were known in England, remained rare in Italy and were ultimately distinct from the main developments of Italian Neo-Classicism, they and the villa itself are clear signs of the demise of the Baroque as a vital creative force. With Anton Raphael Meng's unsenuous and rigorously classicizing fresco of *Parnassus* painted in 1761 on the ceiling of one of the villa's rooms, the whole complex heralds the values of the coming Neo-Classical age.

8

Northern Italy in the Seventeenth Century

In the cities of northern and central Italy—Milan, Turin, Bologna, Venice, and Florence—distinctive architectural styles sprang up from indigenous traditions that usually were independent of Roman influence. Indeed Rome was as often the beneficiary as it was the source of innovative ideas that became popular throughout Italy. During the first third of the century, Milan and surrounding Lombardy rivalled the papal city as a prolific architectural center. It should not be forgotten, either, that Domenico Fontana, Carlo Maderno, Francesco Borromini, and Carlo Fontana were all Lombards who went to Rome with their minds already set on architecture.

The first significant Milanese building of the seventeenth century is the church of S. Alessandro, begun in 1602 and completed ca. 1710, mostly according to the original plan. It was designed by a Barnabite monk, Lorenzo Binago (1554–1629), for his own order, which had been founded in the mid-sixteenth century during the Catholic Counter-Reformation. The spirit of the Counter-Reformation was especially strong in Milan, since one of the movement's leading figures, Charles Borromeo, was archbishop of the city from 1560 until his death in 1584. Even before his canonization in 1610, Borromeo's *Instructiones Fabricae Ecclesiasticae* were instrumental in applying Tridentine decrees to the practice of architecture. As we shall see, the author's preference for "la forma di croce allungata" (the elongated cross) over "la forma rotonda" (the circular plan) was interpreted differently in Milan than in Rome. Earlier Roman architects almost invariably employed the Latin Cross for major churches, but in Milan,

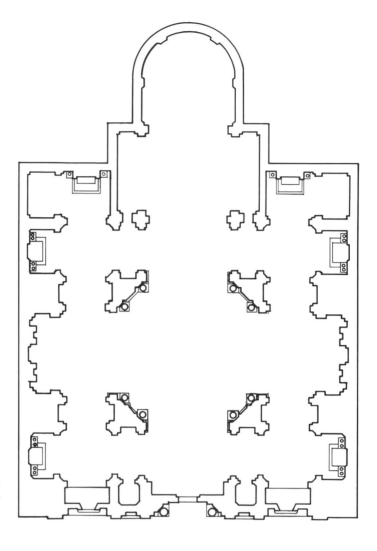

110. Lorenzo Binago,
S. Alessandro,
Milan, plan.

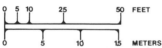

a sharper distinction was made between the less "appropriate" circular plan and the centralized Greek Cross plan.[1]

Binago's ground plan for S. Alessandro (110) is a Greek Cross rather like the one Bramante used a century earlier in his original plan for St. Peter's in Rome. The parallel between the two churches does not end there: as Binago was undertaking S. Alessandro, his contemporary, Carlo Maderno (1556–1629), was charged with completing the still unfinished St. Peter's. In typical fashion, Maderno extended the cruciform space by adding a nave (15); Binago, on the other hand, expanded the cross in the other direction by introducing a domed sanctuary between the crossing and the apse. Thus the interior of S. Alessandro seems compartmentalized as one moves from one independent domed space to another. In northern Italy, the sequential arrangement of distinct spatial units was as traditional as the fully unified space was in Rome. The contrast is exemplified by Palladio's S. Giorgio Maggiore in Venice and Vignola's Gesù in Rome, begun in 1566 and 1568, respectively. In Milan, an example of a typical northern plan is Pellegrino Tibaldi's Jesuit church of S. Fedele, begun in 1569, which consists of three independently vaulted units. Binago also followed S. Fedele by using free-standing columns to support the central cupola, a structural innovation that may have been the cause of its near collapse in 1626, and complete reconstruction in 1693.

The interior of S. Alessandro (111) is dim and murky, the result of too little fenestration and too much dark decoration. Despite the somewhat gloomy atmosphere (and insensitive modern attempts to rectify it with harsh artificial light), the interior still presents a varied and fluid sequence of spatial experiences. In most respects, it is considerably more interesting than its contemporary Roman counterparts.

The facade of S. Alessandro was the last part of the church to be built, and its upper story was completed in an extravagant Rococo style that has little to do with Binago's original intentions. Nonetheless, the basic conception of a stately silhouette composed of a prominent dome and two flanking towers was carried out. This, of course, was what Bramante had originally intended but never realized at St. Peter's.

Upon his death in 1629, Binago was succeeded at S. Alessandro by his former pupil Francesco Maria Ricchino (1584–1658). Following his apprenticeship with Binago, Ricchino had spent a year in Rome before embarking on an independent career in 1603. He subsequently received dozens of commissions in and around Milan, as well as at Milan Cathedral, which was still under construction. His best known work is probably the church of S. Giuseppe (112–114), begun in 1607 and completed in 1630.

The interior of S. Giuseppe resembles that of S. Alessandro in its sequential arrangement of two rather distinct spatial compartments, the first of which is larger than the second. Lacking the ambulatory and side chapels of Binago's church, the ritual axis in S. Giuseppe is stronger and the interior space is more compact and unified. In typical northern Italian fashion, Ricchino used columns where his Roman

111. Lorenzo Binago, S. Alessandro, Milan, interior.

counterparts would ordinarily have used pilasters. He also enhanced the sculptural quality of the architecture by cutting away the piers under the main dome to form choir stalls and niches for statuary. Ample illumination and the absence of painted wall decoration reinforce the impression of structural clarity and coherence.

The exterior of S. Giuseppe is somewhat less well-resolved. Ricchino joined the type of flat frontispiece traditionally used on longitudinal churches with the full-bodied octagonal mass of the structure behind. The resulting composition accommodates diagonal as well as frontal views, but the relationship between the front and sides of the upper story is rather awkward. Those accustomed to Roman practice will also

112. Francesco Maria Ricchino, S. Giuseppe, Milan, plan.

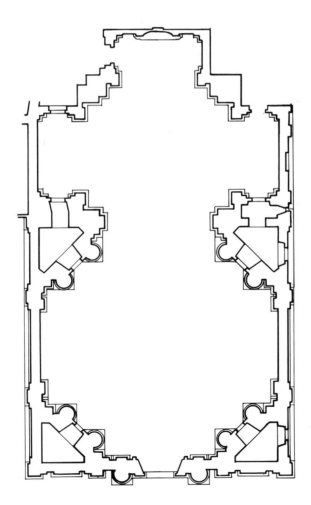

113. Francesco Maria Ricchino, S. Giuseppe, Milan, interior.

find the enclosure of the dome within an octagonal drum unfamiliar. Just as remarkable for this early period is the multiplication of pediments on the facade's upper story. In Rome, the encased pediment first appeared in a minor role on the facade of the Gesù, but it was not until much later, at Ss. Vincenzo ed Anastasio of 1646–1650, (77) that the motif was prominently featured as the crowning element of a two-story composition. However, at S. Giuseppe, the classical order and some of the lesser details were not handled with the same originality and sophistication. The half-columns on the upper story make the flatter portions of the lower order seem weak, while the sculptural detail on both stories is somewhat awkwardly proportioned and untidy.

114. Francesco Maria Ricchino, S. Giuseppe, Milan, facade.

Despite these flaws, Ricchino's church, like Maderno's S. Susanna (14), was a remarkable forerunner of the richly textured and dramatic facades of the coming Baroque. In Milan, it must be' said, succeeding generations of architects failed to develop these ideas with the enthusiasm of their Roman counterparts during the second third of the century.

One of Ricchino's finest but least known works is the portal he designed ca. 1640 for the Seminario Maggiore in Milan (115). Like his more famous facade of the Collegio Elvetico, this was a frontispiece for a clerical college founded years earlier by Charles Borromeo. In both buildings, a vast two-story courtyard consisting of superimposed open colonnades forms the heart of the complex. In the court of the Seminario (1602–1608), the columns are paired instead of spaced singly as in the Elvetico (begun in 1608), but both designs are marked by a severity that reflects Borromeo's own chaste piety. The two exterior elevations, on the other hand, show no trace of austerity. A broad elliptical curve enlivens the entrance of the Elvetico, and the much later portal of the Seminario Maggiore is ornamented with a rich assortment of tectonic and sculptural devices. Continuing a local tradition, Ricchino used caryatids personifying the Christian Virtues to support the main pediment. The lower section of these members is adorned with books fastened with ribbons, the upper part by festooned masks; together they provide the appropriate references to clerical instruction while offsetting the crude texture of the background rustication. Above the crisp pediment, a low attic supports the Borromeo insignia *Humilitas*. The self-indulgent nature of these forms, right in the Cardinal's own Archiepiscopal Seminary, suggests that by the middle of the century, the orthodoxy of the Counter-Reformation had finally been superseded in Milan, as in Rome, by more expansive views.

The most unusual manifestation of religious devotion in northern Italy was the creation of "Sacred Mountains" in the provinces of Lombardy and the Piedmont. The Sanctuary at Varese (1604–1680), just north of Milan, provides one of the best examples of the intense realism that often characterized religious narrative in this period.[2] Fourteen chapels representing the Stations of the Cross are spaced along the steep grade of a mountain whose elevation is nearly 900 meters. The sealed interiors of these tiny chapels are filled with lifelike *tableaux* in painting and sculpture depicting scenes from Christ's Passion. Although there are stylistic interrelationships among the chapels, each one has a unique plan and elevation. The architect, Giuseppe

115. Francesco Maria Ricchino, Seminario Maggiore, Milan, portal.

Bernasconi, who was from Varese, balanced progressive and conservative elements in formulating the overall architectural program.

The fourth chapel (116) is among the most engaging in the series. Four aedicular entrances extend the cylindrical interior into a Greek Cross, and the arms of this cross, in turn, are transformed back into a circle by low arcades that link them together. Thus the elevation is animated by an interplay between open and closed forms of varying shapes and sizes. The Sacro Monte at Varese offers the visitor an unusual rustic treat: fine art within a series of lively buildings in a magnificent pre-Alpine setting.

191

116. Giuseppe Bernasconi, Sanctuary at Varese, fourth chapel.

In the tradition of the itinerant medieval builders from this region who were known as the *magistri comacini*, Lombard architects were willing to travel long distances to practice their trade. Giovanni Ambrogio Mazenta, or Magenta (1565–1636), who was born in Milan, worked in Piedmont, Emilia, Tuscany, the Marches, and Rome, as well as his native Lombardy. Like Lorenzo Binago, he took Barnabite vows, and in 1612 he was elected General of his order. Mazenta's most important work is in Bologna, where in 1605–1606 he designed two new churches and a facade for a third.

One of the new churches, S. Salvatore (117–119), combines the architectural traditions of Milan and Rome. The ground plan is the compact Latin Cross of the Gesù, complete with connecting side chapels, domed crossing, and rounded apse. The nave bays, however, are of unequal size, are framed with free-standing columns, and are independently vaulted, which speaks persuasively for a Milanese derivation. Of course, these northern influences might have been reinforced by Roman anomalies like Michelangelo's S. Maria degli Angeli (begun in 1561) or Mascarino's S. Salvatore in Lauro (12; begun in 1591). In considering the interesting and complex cross-fertilization

117. Giovanni Ambrogio Mazenta, S. Salvatore, Bologna, plan.

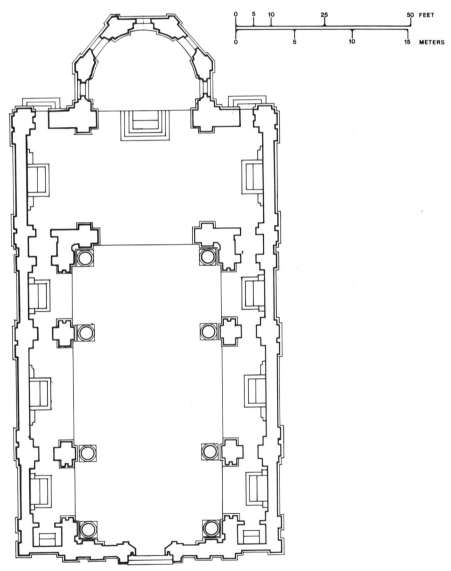

118. Giovanni Ambrogio Mazenta, S. Salvatore, Bologna, interior.

119. Giovanni Ambrogio
Mazenta, S. Salvatore,
Bologna, facade.

between northern and central Italy one should remember that Bologna, alone among northern cities, belonged to the papal states at this
time.

As Rainaldi was later to do at S. Maria in Campitelli, Mazenta positioned columns in the nave to draw visitors past the cross-axis formed
by the prominent side chapels and to lead them ahead to the high
altar. The fine fluting of these Corinthian columns adds a crisp texture
to an otherwise spare, monochromatic interior. The architectonic grandeur of the space is, in fact, unusual among early Baroque churches in
that it was spared the overlay of later decorative programs.

The exterior of S. Salvatore (119) is more or less typical of all three
of Mazenta's churches in Bologna. In 1605 when it was designed, and
1613–1623 when it was constructed, this type of flat, two-story facade
was perhaps the biggest cliché in Italian architecture. In some respects,
it is even more conservative than the prototypical Gesù in Rome. Un-

120. Bartolomeo Provaglia,
Palazzo Davia-Bargellini,
Bologna, facade.

like Vignola's unexecuted project (5), the planes do not consistently
project towards the center; unlike Della Porta's final design (6), the
pilasters of the two stories are not vertically linked. Mazenta was not
unaware of these nuances for he did use Vignolesque projections on
his contemporary facade of S. Paolo in Bologna.

Mazenta was Milanese, but Bolognese architecture itself was rather
tradition-bound during the seventeenth century. The city's best known
seventeenth-century palace, the Davia-Bargellini of 1638–1658 by Bartolomeo Provaglia (120), is little more than a recycling of the Palazzo
Bentivoglio in Bologna or any number of other sixteenth-century man-
sions that derived from the Palazzo Farnese in Rome. Provaglia's vari-

ation on the standard model was to embellish the doorway with atlantes, a motif that sprang from the same Lombard sources as Ricchino's caryatids on the portal of the Seminario Maggiore in Milan.

A similar situation existed in Genoa, where the strong sixteenth-
century tradition of Galeazzo Alessi (1512–1572) persisted into the
seventeenth century. Alessi was the creator of a refined palace type for
the Strada Nuova (now Via Garibaldi), a well-planned, patrician
street laid out in the center of the city in the 1550s. Three-quarters of
a century later, Genoa's most important Baroque architect, Bartolomeo
Bianco (1590–1657) designed a Jesuit College (now the City University) on the Via Balbi, a short distance away (121).[3] While the college is an extremely handsome building, there is little about its design
that suggests it was built as late as 1634–1636. The exterior is not sub-
stantially different from the varied facades on the Strada Nuova, and
its plan, splendid though it is, derives from the neighboring Palazzo

121. Bartolomeo Bianco, University of Genoa, courtyard.

Doria-Tursi, built more than sixty years before. Like his predecessor, Bianco took advantage of Genoa's steep terrain by constructing an oblong courtyard between the entrance staircase and the main staircase. The ascent along an axis to the *piano nobile* is interrupted by a pleasant stroll in the level courtyard—the whole a masterpiece of elegant design. The court is enclosed by superimposed arcaded loggias that rest on paired columns, a fairly familiar arrangement in Lombard and Ligurian architecture of the sixteenth century.[4] Without carved soffits or other ornament, the court is simple and pristine but not overly severe. The main staircase at the end of the court is more important historically, both for its central position within the palazzo and for the size and complexity of its plan.[5] Despite his imitation of the earlier stairway at the Doria-Tursi, Bianco must be credited with recognizing promising possibilities and realizing them with good taste. The Jesuit College is both his own and his city's greatest secular masterpiece.

Florence in the seventeenth century seemed content to remain an anachronism. The majority of architects strove to sustain the spirit of the Renaissance rather than to develop a Baroque style of their own. Several of Pietro da Cortona's imaginative architectural projects were rejected in Florence at a time when his reputation was steadily increasing in Rome.[6] As nowhere else in Italy, it was the Mannerist style of the late Renaissance that made the strongest impression on Florentine architects of the 1600s. Indeed, most of the important buildings from the first half of the seventeenth century were designed by men who had studied or collaborated with Bernardo Buontalenti (1531–1608), Florence's most idiosyncratic Mannerist architect.

Matteo Nigetti (1560–1648) and Gherardo Silvani (1579–1675) were among those who transformed Buontalenti's excesses into a style more palatable to the seventeenth century's classicizing taste. Although Nigetti spent forty years overseeing the construction of Buontalenti's Cappella dei Principi at S. Lorenzo (begun in 1603), his own contributions are not easy to discern amidst the gaudy incrustation of the interior and the massive hulk of the exterior. That this enormous funerary chapel was the central monument of Medici patronage is, in itself, a revelation about Florence in these times. Nigetti's facade of the church of the Ognissanti (122), on the other hand, tells us more about his own stylistic inclinations. It has often been pointed out how closely this facade (constructed from 1635 to 1637) follows that of S. Stefano in Pisa, built in 1593 by an earlier collaborator of Buontalenti.

122. Matteo Nigetti, Church of the Ognissanti, Florence, facade.

Nigetti copied both the outline and essential structure of the Pisan church, but he borrowed various ornamental details directly from Buontalenti himself. This is most apparent in the treatment of the pediments over the side windows of the upper story. Following the example of Buontalenti's Porta delle Suppliche at the Uffizi, Nigetti split a rounded pediment and reversed the two halves so that they each rise from the center to the sides. Nowhere on the facade, in fact, are there elements original enough to offset the impression that Nigetti was retrogressive, if not deliberately counter-Baroque, in style and outlook.

Similar attitudes are revealed in the work of Gherardo Silvani. His chief accomplishment, the facade of S. Gaetano (1645–1648) is little more than an embellished version of Buontalenti's facade of S. Trinità in Florence (1594). Silvani was Buontalenti's biographer as well as his student, and many of his buildings are reminiscent of his master's work. The Palazzo Fenzi on the Via Sangallo (123) of 1634 is the most interesting of the several secular commissions that he received. The temperament of its severe facade is in the tradition of the cold and precise late Mannerism of Ammannati and Dosio. A smoothly stuccoed two-and-a-half story elevation is horizontally divided with a single string course; the simple window surrounds are uniform on each story; and there are no vertical accents apart from the corner quoins. The building would be extremely dull had Silvani not relieved its starkness with some lively, well-placed sculptural ornament. A pair of emaciated harpies flank the portal and support a heavy, elaborately carved balcony. These grotesque figures are descendants of the creatures that Buontalenti devised for the nearby portal of the Casino Medicco and the grotto behind the Palazzo Pitti. More discreet and gratuitous are the tiny turtles that support the lower story window grilles. The "hardness" of the Ammannati-Dosio decorative idiom is further relieved by the Buontalentesque "softness" of the portal archivolt, the lower story cornice, and the family crest on the top floor.[7] At the Palazzo Fenzi, Silvani thus combined the two alternative traditions of late sixteenth-century Florentine architecture. This, alas, was to be the most significant accomplishment of the seventeenth century in Florence.

During the second third of the century, Venice came to surpass Milan as the leading architectural center outside of Rome. In earlier decades, Vincenzo Scamozzi (1552–1616) had produced tame classi-

123. Gherardo Silvani, Palazzo Fenzi, Florence, facade.

cizing variations on Palladio (d. 1580), which followed the pattern of development seen in regional styles in other areas where strong local traditions existed in the late Renaissance. The emergence of a full Baroque style in Venice coincided with the maturity of Baldassare Longhena (1598–1682), an architect who is chiefly remembered today for one extremely fine building, the church of S. Maria della Salute (124–126). Prominently situated near the head of the Grand Canal, it was erected as a votive offering to the Virgin after the pestilence of 1630. Construction began in 1631, and the church was consecrated in 1687.[8]

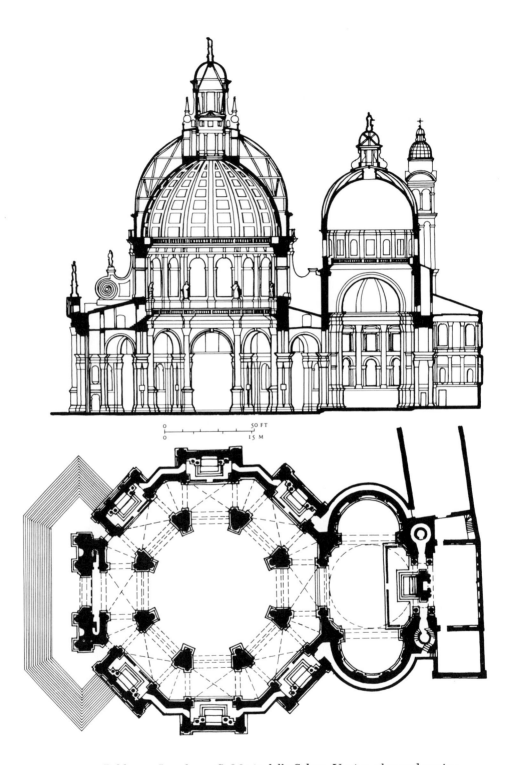

50 FT

15 M

124. Baldassare Longhena, S. Maria della Salute, Venice, plan and section.

Longhena's project was chosen from among eleven entries in a public competition which stipulated that all entries satisfy certain conditions of visibility, illumination, and ritual emphasis. The stipulations did not, interestingly enough, dictate the basic shape of the church. It is not surprising, therefore, that the two finalists proposed the fundamental alternatives of a longitudinal and a centrally planned church. Fifty years earlier an almost identical situation had occurred in Venice during the planning of another plague church, Il Redentore. There, Counter-Reformation orthodoxy prevailed and the architect, Andrea Palladio, was made to abandon his initial central plan for one that was essentially longitudinal. For the Salute, as for the Redentore, the final decision was made by the Venetian Senate, but this time it was the central plan that was approved.

The acceptance of Longhena's central plan could be construed as the product of yet another shift in the post-Renaissance conflict between liturgical pragmatism and the desire for aesthetic perfection in architecture. Here, in fact, the stipulations clearly stated that the new building "had to harmonize with the site and had to make a grand impression," while not mentioning the symbolism of its form. Longhena was not unmindful of iconography, however, for in a memorandum he declared "the dedication of this church to the Blessed Virgin made me think . . . of building the church in *forma rotonda,* that is in the shape of a crown."[9] The crown was emblematic of the Virgin as Queen of Heaven, the watchful figure believed to be responsible for ridding Venice of the plague. She was exalted in the church's narrative decoration and venerated in the early votive services.

The design of S. Maria della Salute is among the most ingenious of the seventeenth century. Its typological sources range from the Middle Ages through the Renaissance and combine a wide variety of architectural traditions. The notion of creating a longitudinal axis through a series of independent spatial units is, of course, distinctly northern Italian in character. The ambulatory in the main octagon is less common and was possibly inspired by churches of the early Christian and Byzantine periods, such as S. Vitale in Ravenna. Nonetheless, the most important influence on Longhena was the work of Andrea Palladio (1508–1580), Venice's most distinguished architect.

Palladio's two nearby churches, S. Giorgio Maggiore (begun in 1566) and Il Redentore (begun in 1576), provide the essential background for Longhena's design.[10] The lower story of the Salute's octagon suggests a centralized adaptation of the nave of S. Giorgio, while

125. Baldassare Longhena, S. Maria della Salute, Venice, interior.

the transverse sanctuary and appended choir recall similar features of
Il Redentore. More important, the visual linkage of these three spatial
elements through decoration and architectonic repetition demonstrates
Longhena's understanding of Palladian syntax and scenography. The
lesser structural embellishments used by Palladio—high pedestals,
broken entablatures, and bichromatic effects—were revived by Longhena as well.

In addition to the main axis that runs from the single entrance to
the high altar and choir, a number of minor axes run through the
church. Three cross-axes link the opposing side chapels, and there are
pronounced vertical axes in the rotonda and sanctuary. When standing
in the rotonda, one is particularly impressed and uplifted by the tall,
well-illuminated cylinder whose vertical members are so emphatically
linked through the three stories of the elevation. Had the cupola been
painted, as was originally intended, the upward thrust would be even
stronger than it is. It should be remembered, moreover, that Longhena

126. Baldassare Longhena, S. Maria della Salute, Venice, exterior.

127. Baldassare Longhena, Palazzo Pesaro, Venice, facade.

designed his church years before comparably Baroque solutions began
to appear in Rome or elsewhere in Italy.

Visible from a multitude of perspectives, the exterior of S. Maria
della Salute is undeniably the most splendid of its time. The main
frontispiece, which adopts the standard motif of the triumphal arch,
gracefully subordinates the modest fronts of the flanking chapels but
does not dominate the entire elevation. The pre-eminent feature is, of
course, the voluminous dome that crowns the composition. As revealed
in section (124), the dome is really the outer skin of a double-shelled
vault similar to those used much earlier at St. Peter's and the Duomo
of Florence. It differs from existing prototypes, however, in its proportion and articulation In comparison to the dome of St. Peter's, for example (18), that of S. Maria della Salute is taller with a more heavily
fenestrated drum. Its sculptural qualities are emphasized by massive
scroll-buttresses surmounted with statuary. In the zone above, Lon-

ghena followed the Veneto-Byzantine practice of using a simple hemi-spherical covering made of lead instead of a ribbed masonry vault as was customary elsewhere. Topped with a heavy lantern, the exterior constitutes a richly pictorial ensemble. Its use of light and shade, sculptural detail, and even color sustains the picturesque traditions of earlier Venetian architecture, while its sensuous massing and complex interrelationships reflect the drama of the true Baroque. Conceived in 1631, S. Maria della Salute can justifiably be called the first major Baroque church in Italy.

The originality of S. Maria della Salute unfortunately was not equalled by Longhena's other commissions in Venice. Facing only minor competition and serving an increasingly conservative and anachronistic nobility may have weakened his spirit of inventiveness. His works, on the whole, remain rather provincial and tend at times to rely on sculptural rather than architectural means to achieve their effect. Of the many secular buildings that he designed, the Palazzo Pesaro (127) is undoubtedly the finest and the most ambitious. Located about midway along the Grand Canal, it was begun around 1650 for the family of Giovanni Pesaro, who reigned briefly as Doge from 1658 to 1659. By 1679 the *piano nobile* was complete, but Longhena's design for the third story was not realized until 1710 by a student of his who incorporated changes of his own.

The broad facade of the Palazzo Pesaro exemplifies the insular nature of Venetian architecture, even of works conceived by as great a talent as Longhena's. Its inspiration is drawn from three Venetian buildings, each of which is located nearby on the Grand Canal. Sansovino's "Bramantesque" facade of the Palazzo Corner, built in the 1530s, was undoubtedly the principal model. To this prototype Longhena simply grafted the top floor of Sansovino's Library at St. Mark's (1537) and the diamond-pointed rustication of the Cà del Duca (1460–1464) on the upper and lower stories respectively.[11] The architect's own contribution was his use of boldly projecting structural and ornamental members to create a dramatic *chiaroscuro* effect. Unlike its Venetian forerunners, the Pesaro's columns are detached from the wall and its abundant sculpture is carved in the highest relief, assuring an active play of light over the entire surface. Longhena also accentuated the facade's vertical organization in the upper stories by framing the end bays and three central bays with paired columns *en ressaut*. Such ideas testify to his ability to harmonize a latent Baroque sensibility with a respect for the Grand Canal's legendary decorum and local architectural tradition.

9

Guarino Guarini

The most remarkable of all north Italian architects was Guarino Guarini, a man whose intellectual and creative energies surpassed even those of the better-known Borromini, Bernini, and Cortona. Born in 1624 in Modena, Guarini was a generation younger than the three great masters of the Roman Baroque and the one least bound by conventional practice. In 1647, after eight years of study in Rome, he took the vows of the Theatine order and subsequently taught philosophy, theology, and mathematics in Theatine seminaries in Modena, Messina, and Paris. His academic interests were further manifested in the publication of nine scholarly treatises on topics ranging from astronomy—he was among the last defenders of the geocentric concept of the universe—to philosophy, mathematics, and architecture. One of the culminating honors in his amazingly successful career was his appointment in 1680 as theologian to the Prince of Carignano in Turin. At that time he was praised by his new patron for the "ingenious and extraordinary principles" of his architecture, which were combined with "the most excellent knowledge of the philosophical, moral, and theological sciences as befits a zealous and worthy member of a religious order."[1]

Guarini profited from his dual role of priest–architect as few others have. During his career he was asked to design projects for Theatine churches in Lisbon, Munich, Nice, Paris, Prague, and in his native Italy, and his international reputation as an architect exceeded even that of Bernini. Yet few of his projects outside of Italy were executed according to plan; and not one survives to the present day.[2] Fortunately they are known through his engravings and text in two posthumously published books, *Disegni d'architettura civile ed ecclesiastica* (1686) and *Architettura civile* (1737).

In 1666 Guarini moved to Turin and soon after was appointed Engineer and Mathematician to Duke Carlo Emanuele II of Savoy. The dukes of Savoy had named Turin the capital of Piedmont a century earlier and had been strongly committed to rebuilding the city from the beginning. Until Guarini's arrival, however, they lacked a first-rate architect. From 1666 until his death in 1683, Guarini constructed for the duke and a few ecclesiastical patrons some extraordinarily interesting buildings in Turin that remain more or less intact and represent the best work of his mature years.

His earliest surviving building in Turin is the church of S. Lorenzo (128–131), built for the Theatines between 1666 and 1687 and the reason for his initial visit to the city in 1666. Its history began in 1634 with the laying of the foundation, but little more than the outside walls (indicated by lighter hatching in Guarini's own plan) had been built when he took over. Following a common north Italian tradition, the architect designed a sequential arrangement of independently vaulted spatial units, but treated the walls of these compartments as diaphanous and elastic boundaries rather than as impenetrable solids. The interior space of S. Lorenzo thus seems less the product of outward growth from a simple structural nucleus than the inward expansion of the outer enclosure. Guarini had no formal training in architecture, but as ducal engineer he understood the advantages of transferring the main support from the center to the periphery of the building. This allowed him to lighten the innermost structural members and to create for the first time an open, shell-like interior. It was a lesson that made a deep impression on the Rococo architects of central Europe in the eighteenth century.

An inner ring of sixteen free-standing columns effectively transforms the outer square of the building into an octagon, whose undulating and irregular sides are reminiscent of Borromini, an architect Guarini surely encountered during his stay in Rome from 1639–1647. Like Borromini and other Baroque architects, Guarini was fond of stressing vertical as well as longitudinal perspectives in his church interiors. In S. Lorenzo, a uniform arch-lintel sequence in the lower story unexpectedly gives way to an alternating series of pendentives and shallow barrel vaults in the section directly above. As at S. Carlo in Rome, this transitional zone supports a very unorthodox dome. In

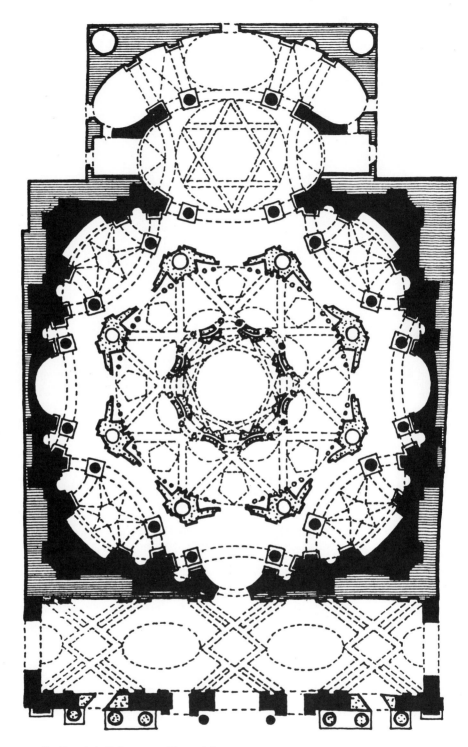

128. Guarini, S. Lorenzo, Turin, plan.

129. Guarini, S. Lorenzo, Turin, interior.

his treatise on architecture Guarini wrote that "vaults are the principal part of buildings," and the main dome of S. Lorenzo is certainly the most inspired and unconventional part of the building. Departing from traditional practice in almost every respect, it is testimony to Guarini's erudition and unbridled imagination.

The most novel feature of the dome is its skeletal use of intersecting ribs, a device unknown in the classical tradition of Renaissance and Baroque architecture, but not uncommon in Hispano-Moorish vaults of the later Middle Ages. Although there is no proof that Guarini ever went to Spain and saw the vaults at Burgos, Cordova, or Zaragoza, he could have seen similar cross-ribbed structures in southern France or even in the Piedmont.[3] Guarini's use of this device—regardless of its specific origin—shows that he was willing to explore and assimilate nonclassical sources of inspiration.[4] It is clear from his treatise, furthermore, that his interest in medieval construction was rigorously analyti-

cal and went beyond Hispano-Moorish tradition to the later, more
sophisticated practices of the Gothic period.

In the *Architettura civile* Guarini gives a technical analysis of
Gothic cross-vaults and concludes that "they are no longer in use but
might sometime come in handy." He is full of praise for Gothic
builders "who wanted their churches to appear weak so that it seemed
a miracle that they could stand at all" and for their arches, "which
seem to hang in the air," and their high windows and perforated towers.
His admiration for the technical virtuosity of Gothic architecture is
reflected in the diaphanous vault of S. Lorenzo, which is both taller
and better illuminated than any of its Moorish prototypes.

The design of the dome may reflect a blending of Moorish and
Gothic traditions, but its motivation undoubtedly sprang from the
common Baroque preoccupation with spatial illusionism. That the illusion of infinite space could evoke spiritual exaltation was an idea of

130. Guarini, S. Lorenzo, Turin, dome.

increasing popularity in the late seventeenth century. Ceiling paintings in Roman churches repeated the theme over and over, and for Guarini, the suggestion of infinity in the structure of the dome served as the very foundation of his architectural theology.

The mystical nature of Guarini's forms should not be viewed as deliberately anti-classical either. Like Borromini's creations, they may be complex, but they are never irrational and they never break entirely with the rules governing the use of the classical order. In fact, he vigorously rejected a contemporary theorist's proposal for an *architectura obliqua,* a bizarre method of counteracting "undesirable" perspectival effects by systematically distorting the offending architectural members.[5] A key element in this system was the use of oval columns which, when rotated on their axes, would increase or decrease in diameter without a corresponding alteration in height. In his treatise, Guarini called this device a "joke," and a "monstrous disposition that too boldly condemns ancient and modern architecture."

Guarini's architecture was not without one technical idiosyncracy however. To construct vaults of the height he desired, he based their design on conical rather than the customary spherical geometry. At S. Lorenzo this allowed him to dispense with a drum and still build a vault that was higher and more spectacular than those of contemporary churches. His practical adaptation of conic sections was based on his study of pure and applied mathematics. While teaching in Paris in 1662–1666 he probably became acquainted with the work of the French mathematicians Derand and Desargues, pioneers in stereotomy (the science of projective geometry applied to the cutting of solids).[6] Guarini's knowledge of modern French geometry is evident in his own mathematical treatise, the *Euclides Adauctus* (1671) as well as in his writings on architecture. In an early treatise on the measurement of buildings, for example, he wrote that "the parabola and the hyperbola are scarcely, if at all, known to architects" but "could very well serve in dome construction," while later, in the *Architettura civile* he proudly proclaimed that he was the first architect to do just that.

Guarini's use of conic sections was indicative of his entire approach to architecture, one in which he employed rational means to create mystifying expressive effects. The seventeenth century found no contradiction in the synthesis of rationalism and religious mysticism; indeed it was a typical atitude of the Baroque age, and can be seen in the paintings of Pietro da Cortona, the sculpture of Bernini, and in many of the more progressive buildings of the time.

131. Guarini,
S. Lorenzo, Turin,
exterior.

Beneath the unorthodox vaulting in S. Lorenzo, the elevation is otherwise unexceptional. Its wall surface is rich and pictorial, but its sequential arrangement of independently formed and illuminated spaces was, by the 1660s, a common feature in north Italian sacred architecture.

Of the exterior, only the dome (131) was executed according to Guarini's design. Like so many others in the region, the vault of S. Lorenzo is encased in a polygonal drum which, in turn, supports an oversize lantern. If the windows in this structure are counted—there are 48—it quickly becomes apparent why the interior vaulting seems to float so pellucidly overhead. In composition and embellishment, the dome reflects the boldness and exoticism of the author's imagination: walls undulate in different rhythms, windows are geometrically complex, and ornament traces the most unrestrained patterns. Outside and

215

in, S. Lorenzo is a structural and spiritual tour-de-force. Fittingly enough, the celebrant of the church's first mass in 1680 was Guarini himself.

The drama of S. Lorenzo was further heightened in Guarini's next commission, the nearby Chapel of the Holy Shroud, or *Santissima Sindone* (132–135).[7] It was built between 1667 and 1694 and was the architect's first assignment for the House of Savoy. The chapel is located between the Cathedral and the Royal Palace and is, as its name indicates, the permanent reliquary for the sepulchral shroud that bears the miraculous imprint of the body of Christ.

As at S. Lorenzo, Guarini had to adapt his design to the remains of an earlier building—an unimaginative circular chapel that was already one story high. In transforming this cylinder, he first spanned the three exits with convex, projecting portals and then surmounted the lower elevation with another of his extraordinary domes. The projecting portals disrupt the uneventful flow of the pre-existing elevation without changing its basic vocabulary or weakening its strength as a foundation. The three portals justify to some extent the shift from circular to triangular geometry in the zone directly above.

The presence of three pendentives at the second stage comes as a surprise. Normally pendentives were used in groups of four to reconcile a quadrilateral plan with a circular or elliptical dome, but the plan and the rim of the dome at the *Santissima Sindone* were already circular. Why then did Guarini use pendentives, and only three of them? His considerations may have been emblematic, structural, or even aesthetic. The triangle, of course, symbolizes the spirit of God the Father and the Trinity as a whole. The pendentives' placement between the relic of Christ below and the image of the Holy Spirit in the lantern above might mean that they were intended as part of the overall iconography of the chapel.

On the other hand, the pendentives do function structurally, both in raising the height of the dome and in adapting its circular rim to the larger diameter of the rotunda below. Since few alternatives would have worked as well, it could be argued that the irregularity of the lower story elevation made the adoption of only three pendentives practically inevitable. Finally, the pendentive zone prepares the way stylistically for the densely textured forms of the hexagonal vault in much the same way that the triad of portals below precede the pendentives themselves.

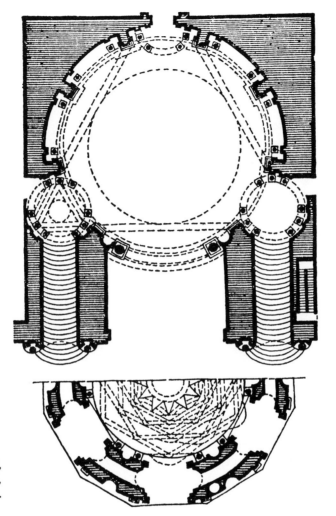

132. Guarini,
Chapel of the Holy Shroud,
Turin, plan.

The dome consists of a tall drum carrying a ribbed vault that is conical in profile. Thirty-six arched ribs, sprung horizontally rather than vertically, are stacked in six rows of six. With each rib framing a pair of windows, the solid supports virtually dissolve in a flood of indirect light, and the intricate structure seems all the more mystifying. No prototype has ever been found for this exotic construction, although Guarini may have been inspired by the skeletal, light-filled churches of the Gothic period, which so fascinated him.

The climax of the chapel's upward movement is a slender twelve-pointed star that bridges the base of the lantern and encircles the dove of the Holy Spirit. The complexity of the building thus culminates in the simplicity of a circle. A comparison of the cross-section with a view of the dome from below (134 and 135), reveals how much Guarini progressively diminished the size of the upper ribs in order to exaggerate the perspectival recession and to make the vault seem higher than it is. Surprisingly, it is not the vault but the drum that is really the major component of the dome.

In one's actual experience of the chapel, illusion and allusion are perfectly balanced. To enter, one ascends from the cathedral on either of two narrow and poorly fenestrated stairways. The dark, almost oppressive quality of these passages is only partially relieved on reaching the comparatively large rotunda that houses the sacred relic. Only in the better illuminated upper zones, where the ash-colored marble becomes silvery and translucent, does funereal gloom give way to spiritual exhilaration. The radiant star at the vault's apex is not only visually electrifying, it also illustrates a local theological argument that the "living rays of the Sun-Christ" were the true source of the shroud's miraculous imprint.[8]

The most important relic of Christ's existence on earth is thus linked with imagery suggestive of His celestial Being, and the contrast between the two states is further reinforced by the architecture itself. Guarini used nearly every available means, including color, light, and perspectival illusionism, to create a program in the chapel that expresses the distinctly Baroque notion of spiritual apotheosis. Seldom has the architectural contrast between terrestial and celestial, finite and infinite, been so sharply drawn. Even when seen from the exterior—and the dome is only partially visible from the ground—the spectral nature of its restless and ethereal forms is astonishing.

During his career, Guarini also drew plans for a number of longitudinal churches. Of those that were executed, only one modest example survives, but fortunately nearly all were reproduced in the engraved plates of the *Architettura civile*. Perhaps the most engaging of these designs is one for an unidentified and perhaps "ideal" church (136) reproduced on the final page of the treatise and datable on stylistic grounds to the later part of his career.[9]

Guarini held to the standard Latin Cross plan—a three-bay nave with side aisles, side chapels, and projecting transept—but transformed its traditional boxlike form into a remarkably graceful and unified whole. The nave, like those of many longitudinal churches in northern

133. Guarini, Chapel of the Holy Shroud, Turin, interior.

134. Guarini, Chapel of the Holy Shroud, Turin, dome.

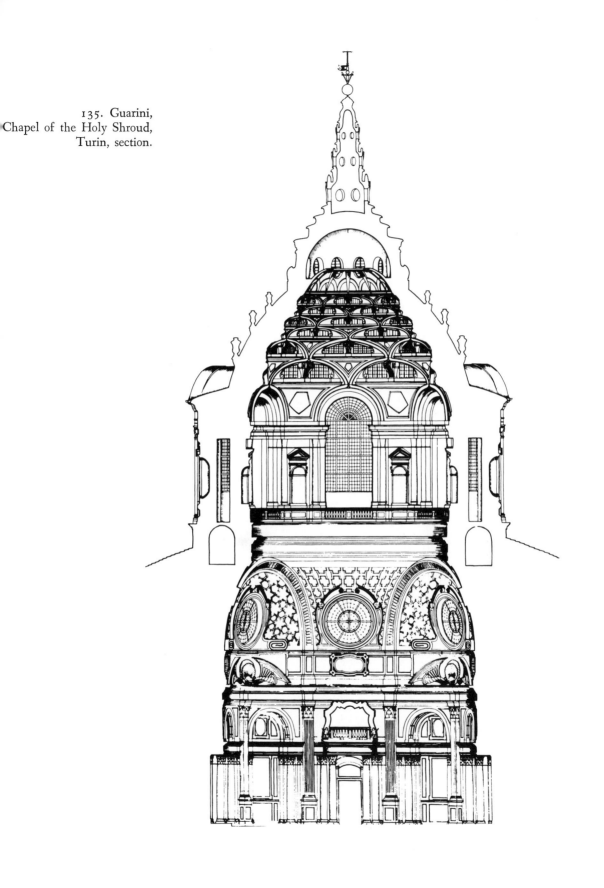

135. Guarini,
Chapel of the Holy Shroud,
Turin, section.

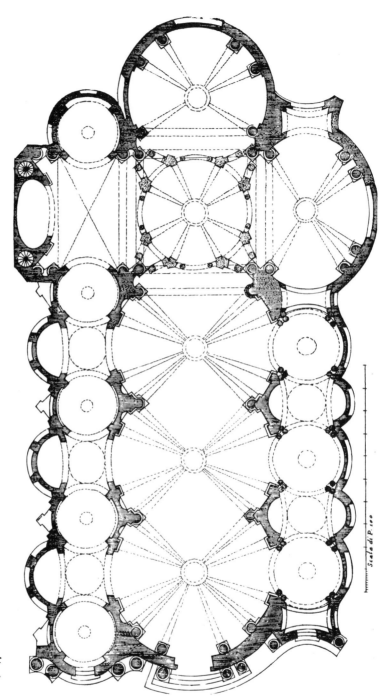

Scala di P. 100

136. Guarini, project for
an unidentified church.

Italy, is composed of a series of independently vaulted bays, but Guarini reinterpreted this regional custom in several ways. Unlike S. Salvatore in Bologna, for example (118), the transverse arches separating the bays have been eliminated and the individual vaults allowed to overlap. The circular vaults had to be quite large in order to do so, and Guarini solved the structural problem of supporting them through a simple innovation. By shaping the supporting piers to the curvature of the vaults, he eliminated the need for pendentives, which would have reduced the size of the vaults and interrupted the fluid contours of the whole structural system. The vertical linkages would have been effortless, smooth, and unexpectedly predictable, so unlike the discordant transitions at both S. Lorenzo and the Chapel of the Holy Shroud.

The ideal or experimental nature of the proposal is especially evident in Guarini's incongruous treatment of the side aisles. In both variations of the plan, a chain of alternately circular and hypocycloidal vaulted bays lead from the entrance to the transept, but there is no correspondence in either the number or the sequence of the aisle bays because of the optional reversals in the curvature of the facade. This had serious consequences for the symmetry of the side chapels, although both systems share the same pulsating rhythm of expanding and contracting spatial units.

The plan's major interest lies in the organic and complementary relationship of its two geometric components, the circle and the hypocycloid. Only in the main dome over the crossing—the spiritual and physical nucleus of the church—are the two forms finally reconciled and their origins suggested. The prototype for this intricate shape probably was Borromini's dome of S. Andrea della Fratte (34), just as the plan of the facade itself was evidently derived from S. Carlo alle Quattro Fontane (24). But far from being a mere tribute to Borromini's earlier work, the fluid spatial arrangement of the project offers a striking view of things to come in the eighteenth century. Certainly this and similar plates from the *Disegni d'architettura civile* profoundly influenced later Piedmontese and German architects such as Vittone, Neumann, and Hildebrandt.

In 1679, four years before he died, Guarini undertook the construction of a large palace for the Prince of Carignano, Emanuele Filiberto Amedeo, a cousin of Duke Carlo Emanuele II. Just a few blocks from S. Lorenzo and the Chapel of the Holy Shroud, in the center of Turin, this splendid palace (137–139) is without doubt the most unconventional secular building of the seventeenth century. The only

137. Guarini, Palazzo Carignano, Turin, exterior.

comparable designs—Cortona's Palazzo Chigi (73) and Bernini's Louvre (62)—were considerably less complex in sculptural embellishment. Nonetheless, it is very likely that Guarini saw and admired Bernini's projects in Paris, for several unusual features are common to both buildings, particularly the organization of the facade into a triptych with blocklike corners and an undulating center crowned by a low drum. But Guarini's unorthodox mind was not influenced by the logic and consistency of Bernini's plan, and some of the facade's more idiosyncratic features reflect their author's greater admiration for the architecture of Borromini. The projecting central window of the upper story, the shattered pediment above it, and the figurative nature of the ornamental vocabulary recall features on the facades of S. Carlo and the Oratory of S. Filippo Neri (28 and 38) in Rome. Typologically, the most significant aspect of the Palazzo Carignano, however, is the prominence of both a drum and a pediment on the exterior. Until then, Italian tradition restricted domes and pediments almost exclusively to sacred usage, but Guarini's exposure to the iconographically less rigid buildings of France may have caused him—as it had Bernini—to reconsider such matters.

Visually, the most engaging feature of the Palazzo Carignano is the warm color and soft texture of its brick facing. A dense network of pilasters and cornices subdivides the three principal masses into smaller and more intimate units, and richly worked window-surrounds and panelled and embossed pilasters create a lively relief over the entire surface. Despite the building's considerable size, much of the ornament was hand-crafted and deserves to be viewed at close hand. In the detail of a surround from the *piano nobile,* for example (138), the fanciful, almost painterly treatment of the facade's embellishment may

138. Guarini,
Palazzo Carignano, Turin,
detail of exterior.

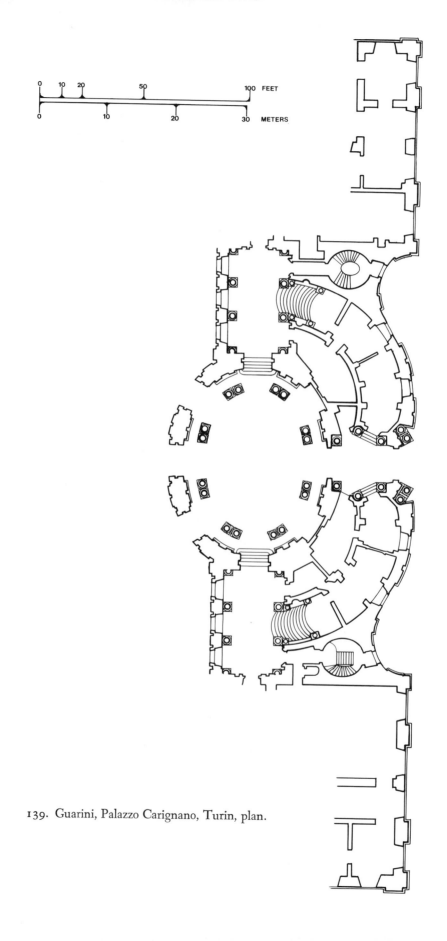

139. Guarini, Palazzo Carignano, Turin, plan.

be seen. Defying conventional practice, Guarini translated these forms from a tectonic into a sculptural vocabulary. On either side of the window, long strips of illusionistic drapery hang from a broken pediment whose own form seems distinctly anthropomorphic. The ultimate caprice is the stylized face at the apex of the motif, which surpasses even Borromini in iconographic license. With a feathered headdress, striped cheeks, and flowing cape, this figure seems to represent a North American Indian in full battle regalia. But why an American Indian on the facade of a Piedmontese prince's palace?

Guarini's motivation was not just whimsical. In 1665 the Regiment of Carignano—a forerunner of the French Foreign Legion—was sent to Canada to protect the country's 3,215 European inhabitants from attacks by the Iroquois and other tribes.[10] After forcing the Indians to surrender, the regiment's leader, Nicolis di Brandizzo, returned to Turin where he died in 1679—the year the Palazzo Carignano was begun. To Guarini it must have seemed only fitting that the longest and most adventurous campaign of the Regiment of Carignano should be commemorated on the facade of the Commander General's new palace.

Passing through the main entrance, one enters a large vestibule whose oval shape neatly echoes the curvature of the central section of the facade. The vestibule runs perpendicular to the main axis and opens directly into the courtyard and laterally into corridors leading to the main stairways. The organic nature of Guarini's planning is underlined by the natural way these stairways repeat the basic rhythms of the main block. Although he may have been inspired by one of Borromini's unexecuted designs, the cohesiveness and dynamism of the plan is Guarini's own.[11] In fact, both the narrow, convexly treaded stairways and the open columnar vestibule are reminiscent of his earlier work at the Chapel of the Holy Shroud and S. Lorenzo.

When Guarini died in 1683, all but the ornamentation of the palace was complete, and this continued intermittently until 1693 when the prince and his family finally moved in. To their contemporaries in other Italian cities, the ebullient Baroque style of the Carignano must have seemed rather out of date, but by the mid-eighteenth century, Guarini's work had become the stimulus for some of Europe's most inspired and progressive architecture.

10

Northern Italy in the Eighteenth Century

The eighteenth century in northern Italy witnessed a variety of architectural styles that were often quite independent of regional trends of the previous century. In Bologna, for example, there arose a dramatic and theatrical Late Baroque which compensated for an earlier conservatism, while in Milan and the province of Lombardy an unexpectedly suave version of the Rococo appeared. Florence remained a provincial backwater and Genoa even more so, but the Piedmont region and Turin its capital began to rival Rome in variety and quality of architectural expression. Venice moved from its own regional version of the Baroque to a stately and scholarly style that seems startlingly prophetic of Neo-Classicism. The architecture of northern Italy was as diversified, if not as well known, as that found anywhere in Europe at the time.

In Turin the familiar eighteenth-century dichotomy of Classicism and Rococo is readily apparent in the works of Filippo Juvarra (1678–1736) and Bernardo Vittone (1702–1770). Juvarra was born in Messina, Sicily and apprenticed as a silversmith in the family trade. In 1704 he went to Rome, where he received his architectural training in the studio of Carlo Fontana. Within a year of his arrival there, he had won first prize in the Concorso Clementino, an annual architectural competition at the Accademia di San Luca, and was on his way to an astonishingly successful career. In 1714 he became Royal Architect to Vittorio Amedeo II, Duke of Savoy and newly crowned king of Sicily. During the next two decades, Juvarra designed a number of fine buildings in Turin and in Sicily, Portugal, and Spain.

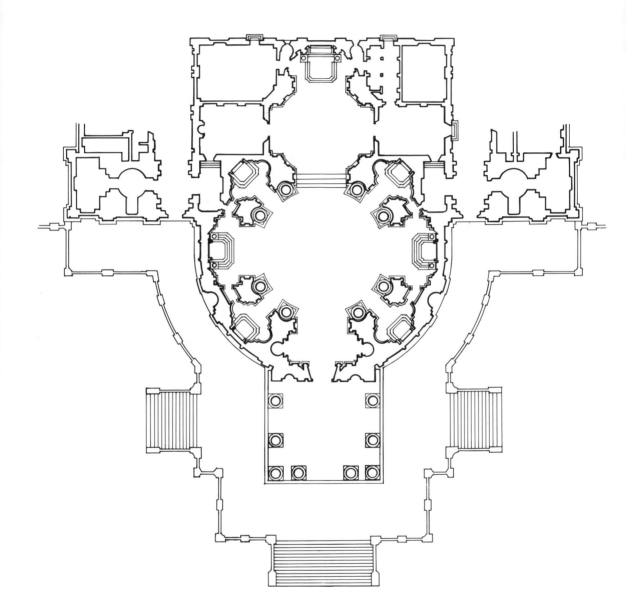

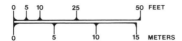

140. Filippo Juvarra, Church of the Superga, Turin, plan.

Juvarra's first major work was the Superga (140–142), a large monastic church built on a mountain peak overlooking Turin. Designed in 1715 as a votive offering after the city had resisted a French invasion, the Superga was constructed between 1717 and 1731.[1] Like Louis XIV's Church of the Invalids in Paris (1679–1691) and Charles VI's Karlskirche in Vienna (1716–1724), it expresses undisguised political ambition. The House of Savoy was particularly successful in realizing such ambitions, for in addition to their recent victory over the French, they had annexed the kingdom of Sicily in 1713 and, in 1720, Sardinia.

As might be expected of the work of a young architect fresh from a

141. Filippo Juvarra, Church of the Superga, Turin, exterior.

142. Filippo Juvarra,
Church of the Superga,
Turin, interior.

ten-year stay in Rome, the Superga is solidly grounded in Roman tradition. The domed rotunda with projecting portico is based on the Pantheon, but Juvarra modified the design in response to recently constructed variants that he had seen in Rome. The plan, for example, is similar to that of the twin churches in the Piazza del Popolo (87), especially the circular S. Maria dei Miracoli, which also contains a prominent cross-axis and an extended choir. It is no coincidence, perhaps, that the Miracoli was completed under the direction of his master Carlo Fontana, whose Jesuit complex in Loyola might have suggested the integration of a circular church within an oblong monastery.

232

Juvarra's dependence on Roman models is also apparent in the handling of the exterior elevation. Instead of basing his design on the low domes of the Piazza del Popolo churches, he planned a more prominent dome flanked by twin bell towers—inspired by S. Agnese in Piazza Navona (78) and ultimately St. Peter's itself (18). Despite its eclectic formation, the exterior is a unified ensemble whose massing and structural rhythms breathe new life into the traditional compositions from which they are derived. Juvarra's approach, moreover, was not so strictly doctrinaire or impersonal as that taken by Neo-Classical architects just a few decades later.

The inner rotunda of the Superga (142) is circumscribed by a ring of columns set directly beneath the main dome. Superficially, this arrangement recalls Longhena's church of the Salute in Venice (125), but by eliminating the ambulatory and varying the size and shape of the chapel openings, Juvarra weakened the diagonal axes and gave a greater sense of unity to the space as a whole. Even though the sanctuary is independently vaulted and illuminated, the dominant emphasis is on the rotunda, whose tall proportions are accentuated by the familiar Baroque devices of controlled light, structural linkage, and applied ornament. A final recollection of Rome occurs in the embellishment of the vault, where Bernini's idiosyncratic system of textured ribs superimposed on hexagonal coffers is employed.

While the Superga remained in the tradition of Bernini, Fontana, and the Roman Academy, its elegance and composure were typical of a new breed of international building in which regional identity gave way to a more cosmopolitan character. Political aspirations, naturally, played a major role in the commission of such buildings, which were meant to reflect the authority and the self-confidence of their patrons. For Vittorio Amedeo II, as for Louis XIV, Charles VI, and Phillip V (for whom Juvarra built the Royal Palace in Madrid), a whimsical style like the Rococo would have been unthinkable.

In 1718, one year after he began to build the Superga, Juvarra started the Palazzo Madama for the *Madame Royale,* the French-born mother of Vittorio Amedeo II and widow of Carlo Emanuele II. Situated in the Piazza del Castello, in the city's historic center, this gracious palace is attached to a medieval fortress that itself encases a Roman gateway. Juvarra originally intended to envelop the bulwarks within a much larger palace, but construction was halted in 1721 upon completion of the modest but well-proportioned centerpiece (143).[2]

The Palazzo Madama was the first important Italian building in

143. Filippo Juvarra, Palazzo Madama, Turin, facade.

centuries to be influenced by contemporary architecture outside the country. While its deepest roots are in the tradition of Bernini's Palazzo Chigi (61), its general similarity to the garden facade (144) of Versailles (1669–1685) is striking. Versailles was by then a universal symbol of political power that was as attractive an inspiration for state architecture as were the churches of Rome for sacred construction. Juvarra, who had just been to France, combined the grandeur of the Italian giant order with the elegance of French windows and a center loggia. For the Franco-Italian patron, the marriage of the two styles was particularly appropriate. Neither the Palazzo Madama nor Versailles is crowned with a pediment, and in this aspect, both buildings respect the iconographic conventions of earlier Italian architecture.

The exterior of the palace is uncompromisingly classical. Unlike Guarini's nearby Palazzo Carignano (137), there are no curved planes or complex ornamental rhythms. The tripartite arrangement of projecting and receding bays clearly emphasizes the entrance portal and gives the building a countenance that is proud but neither fatuous or pompous.

The chief function of the palace is to house a vestibule and open stairway that leads to the fortress behind (now used as the Town Hall and a museum of antiquities). The stairway (145) splits into a pair of double ramps that converge at the center of the *piano nobile*. The originality of this simple concept is enhanced by the brilliance of Juvarra's decorative vocabulary, which combined Roman-inspired ornament with motifs derived from his early experience in silver-smithing.[3] The result is a light but rich overlay of biomorphic and geometric carving that softens the sharp lines of the architectural framework. In late afternoon, the space is further animated by golden light that floods through the large French windows of the main facade. In its overall pictorial effect the Palazzo Madama reveals Juvarra as the eighteenth-century's principal heir to the legacy of Bernini.

144. Louis Le Vau and J. H. Mansart, Palace at Versailles, garden facade.

145. Filippo Juvarra, Palazzo Madama, Turin, stairway.

146. Filippo Juvarra, Church of the Carmine, Turin, interior.

A curious change occurred in Juvarra's work during the later years of his career. This change, which in part anticipated the later work of Vittone, was a turn from the classical severity of his early work to a lighter, more felicitous style, one that incorporated elements of the Rococo. The church of the Carmine in Turin (146) best exemplifies this late style. Built for the Carmelite Order in 1732–1736 (and skillfully reconstructed after being partially destroyed in World War II), the Carmine is a brilliant revision of the conventional longitudinal church. Juvarra dispensed with the usual transept and domed crossing, instead focusing attention on the high, open, and well-illuminated nave. His main innovation was a structural one. By raising the side chapels close to the full height of the nave, he completely transformed the character of the congregational space. The tall, skeletal piers counteract the horizontality of the axial plan while large gallery windows fill the interior with direct sunlight, alleviating the dimness so often found in longitudinal churches of the Gesù type. To give continuity to the row of chapels and to separate them visually if not struc-

237

turally from the galleries, Juvarra bridged the two zones with narrow, floating arches. The lavish, freely conceived ornamentation of these arches further contributes to the lively character of the interior space.

The inspiration for the light-filled, "open" structure of the Carmine has never been satisfactorily explained, although attempts have been made to relate its design to that of somewhat similar churches in southern Germany.[4] This church, more than the Superga or the Palazzo Madama, reflects Juvarra's complexity and independent creative spirit. His progression from a chilly academic formalism to a freer, more spirited style was virtually unprecedented among architects of the period. Although it is true that his career as a whole followed a somewhat unsteady course of development, this may in part have resulted from his sensitivity to both the needs of his patrons and the ideal demands of individual buildings.

Bernardo Vittone (1702–1770), the third great architect of the Piedmont, was the creator of one of the most dazzling and distinctive late Baroque styles. Vittone was born in the Piedmont and like Guarini and Juvarra, received his architectural training in Rome. During his stay in Rome (1731–1733), he won first prize in the 1732 Concorso Clementino at the Accademia di San Luca, and submitted an unsuccessful entry in the Lateran competition. It is likely that upon his return to Turin, Vittone worked in Juvarra's studio, gaining first-hand experience of the master's late works.[5] During these same years he also edited and oversaw the publication of Guarini's *Architettura civile* (1737). Thus in only six years, Vittone had been exposed to the methods of the Roman Academy, the late innovative work of Juvarra, and Guarini's famous treatise. Such diversity of background may explain why he advised architects, in a later treatise of his own, to study the "licentious and artful" work of Borromini and Guarini as well as the more orthodox examples of Bernini and Carlo Fontana.

In practice, Vittone adopted few academic principles, preferring to borrow from the seemingly irreconcilable styles of Guarini and Juvarra. This highly individual architect was at his best as the designer of small, centralized churches constructed for lesser parishes and religious orders. Some three dozen of these were built, most of them in small towns around Turin. The appeal of Vittone's rural churches was partly based on his ability to satisfy patrons who wanted, as one put it, "a church endowed with novelty and the most playful beauty, but without too much cost."

S. Chiara in the town of Brà, twenty-five miles south of Turin, is an exceedingly fine example of Vittone's work (147–149). Built in 1742–1748, the church was one of four he designed for the Poor Clares, a charitable order to which his three half-sisters belonged. The plan is a simple quatrefoil with a large circular crossing and shallow extensions for the presbytery and side chapels. Vittone chose this plan rather than the traditional north Italian sequential spatial arrangement in order to emphasize the central dome, rather than the high altar, as the spiritual center of the building. The dome, furthermore, is very high and is supported by narrow piers that rise through two stories. The tall piers and upper-story galleries recall the exuberant design of Juvarra's church of the Carmine, completed a decade earlier. Juvarra's influence was even more evident in S. Andrea in Chieri (1728–1733; destroyed in 1803), a church which anticipated S. Chiara in plan as well as elevation.[6]

147. Bernardo Vittone, S. Chiara, Brà, plan.

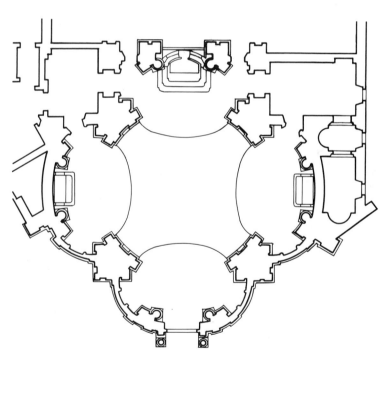

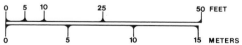

148. Bernardo Vittone, S. Chiara, Brà, dome.

149. Bernardo Vittone,
S. Chiara, Brà, exterior.

The real magic of S. Chiara lies in the ingenuity of its vaulting. Following the example of Guarini's ribbed, perforated domes at S. Lorenzo (130) and the Chapel of the Holy Shroud (134), Vittone created a singularly dramatic ascent from the floor of the church to the apex of the dome. He emphasized the ethereality of the space by fabricating the vault from two shells. Perforations in the inner shell reveal scenes of a celestial realm painted on the outer shell. The vault's link to the heavens is thus both vivid and symbolic. In creating this spectacular illusion, Vittone may have imitated methods first employed by the *quadraturisti,* or painters of architectural illusionism. Two years earlier, the dome of the Sanctuary of the Consolata in Turin had been frescoed in similar fashion on the design of the Bolognese scenographic artist Giuseppe Bibiena.[7] It is revealing of the eighteenth-century sensibility that the traditional hierarchy of the arts should now be reversed, with masonry construction imitating two-dimensional compositions originally devised for illusory purposes.

241

Color also plays a role in the expression of S. Chiara's interior. No longer monochromatic like most Baroque churches built from inexpensive materials, the plaster surfaces of the building are washed with pastel shades of green and ochre that further strengthen the Rococo effect created by the fragility of the structural membering. The interior of S. Chiara is, in the words of one author, as marvelous as a child's vision of a magical Easter egg.[8]

The exterior of the church is more modest, with no stucco or other ornamental sheathing on its plain brick surface. More than half of Vittone's churches were left unadorned. Certainly, a plain exterior would have reduced the cost of a building, but Vittone probably also appreciated the warm color and rustic texture of the brick. Most of the building's appeal rests in the full, sensuous shape of its exterior massing. The quatrefoil plan is directly revealed, with little effort made to differentiate the facade from the flanks, just as in the interior the high altar is not distinguished from those at the sides. The restrained exterior, of course, belies the flamboyance of the inner structure, but as in many Rococo buildings throughout Europe, the contrast makes the interior seem all the more exquisite.

In the mid-1740s Vittone began work on the parish church of S. Maria della Piazza in Turin (150, 151), a structure somewhat atypical of his work. Instead of using a central plan, the architect experimented with a compartmentalized axial plan consisting of a three-part nave and a square choir. In contrast to most north Italian churches of the composite type, its spatial development is fluid and continuous. The path from entrance to altar is regulated by a contrapuntal arrangement of four sequential vaults that rise and fall, expand and contract, before culminating in the tight, high confines of the sanctuary. A print from Vittone's treatise shows that this progression was once enlivened by light streaming in through windows that were later blocked up.[9]

In his concern for spatial orientation, Vittone abandoned the Juvarresque system of tall piers and open galleries that he used at Brà and S. Andrea in Chieri in favor of a more solid and unified structure that emphasized horizontal as well as vertical movement. There are two domes in the church, the grander and more innovative placed over the sanctuary. Its circular vault rests on pendentives, whose upper sections have been scooped out as if to deny the solidity of the support they provide. These sculpted pendentives, a drum filled with light, and a vault active with relief ornament infuse the upper elevation with an

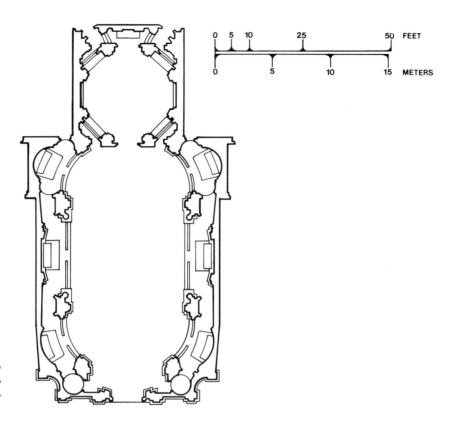

150. Bernardo Vittone,
S. Maria della Piazza,
Turin, plan.

0 5 10   25   50   FEET

0   5   10   15   METERS

explosive energy that echoes the miraculous transubstantiation taking place on the high altar below. Thus the presbytery and not the congregational space becomes the visual and spiritual focus, and the traditional Christian orientation is reaffirmed.

S. Maria della Piazza was among the last Rococo churches in Europe. As the trend toward Neo-Classicism gathered momentum in the Piedmont, even Vittone's work became rather staid at the end of his life. Just as Giambattista Tiepolo's paintings represented the end of an era, Vittone's late work was the swan song of a style that could be developed no further.

Milan and the surrounding province of Lombardy also was fertile territory for the growth of the early Rococo. Although the architects were not so prolific or so well known as in Piedmont, their work is sprightly and often quite charming. Marco Bianchi, who is said in his

151. Bernardo Vittone, S. Maria della Piazza, Turin, interior.

scant biography to have been born and trained in Rome, designed two churches in Milan that flowered from the same Rococo stem. In S. Francesco da Paola and S. Pietro Celestino, he created elegant designs, both draftsmanlike and suave. S. Francesco da Paola on the Via Mazzoni, built for the French order of the Minims from 1723–1735, is yet another variation of the composite plan. The interior (152) is composed of a violin-shaped nave and an extended but domeless choir. In some respects this unusual plan recalls that of the late Baroque church of the Maddalena in Rome (90), but Bianchi's plan is uncompromisingly Rococo. By constructing the nave walls from double reverse curves rather than from a polygonal configuration, he elasticized the interior space. Rejecting the more ponderous ornament of the Roman and Milanese Baroque, Bianchi used an extraordinarily light and delicate overlay of gilded stucco festoons, tendrils, and foliate clusters. This elegant detailing probably had its origins in France since it bears a striking resemblance to French Regency and Rococo interiors of the same period.[10] Unfortunately, however, we can only speculate how he acquired such a taste.

152. Marco Bianchi, S. Francesco da Paola, Milan, interior.

153. Marco Bianchi,
S. Francesco da Paola,
Milan, facade.

The facade of S. Francesco da Paola (153) harmonizes perfectly with the interior and is a work of the utmost refinement.[11] Like most facades of the Roman Rococo, it is strictly "wall" architecture that avoids the use of bold massing or columnar dynamics to achieve its effect. The wall undulates in a series of gentle reverse curves while the pilasters are part of an overall scheme of surface relief using delicate panels and moldings. The absence of a crowning pediment and of scrolls to connect the two stories indicates the extent to which

Bianchi was capable of revising traditional formulas for the triple entry facade.

Another fine example of the Milanese Rococo is the Palazzo Litta, commissioned by one of the city's most aristocratic families. It was begun in the seventeenth century by Francesco Maria Ricchino and reconstructed after 1745 by Bartolomeo Bolli (d. 1761). Bolli's facade (154) is eleven bays long, but its lively and well-regulated composition clearly emphasizes the triad of bays around the central doorway. A comparison with the Palazzo Doria-Pamphili in Rome (97), built in 1730–1735, discloses Bolli's innovations and his ultimate dependence on Roman and Lombard models. Like Valvassori, Bolli employed the Borrominesque vocabulary for the window pediments, but his handling of the orders is stronger and more coherent. Where there are rusticated wall strips on the Doria-Pamphili facade, the Litta deploys elegant composite pilasters whose 2/2/3/2/2 spacing is also more logical than the 1/3/4/1/4/3/1 of the Roman palace. In contrast to Valvassori's uniform and rather monotonous roofline, Bolli's typically Rococo crested pediment enlivens the building's profile and directs attention to the central bays. The upper and lower tiers of the central section are animated by sculpted atlantes which frame the pedimental cartouche and the main portal. These are the only features of the facade that are conspicuously north Italian, and they are clearly descendants of the caryatids on the facade of the Seminario Maggiore (115) just across town. Finally, Bolli gave a coloristic variety to his facade that is lacking in Valvassori's work. Playing the grey stone membering against pale stucco walling, he bestowed warmth and diversity on the palace's imposing front.

The facade of the Palazzo Litta is one of the most balanced secular designs of the eighteenth century. It achieves grandeur without gravity, and sophistication without yielding to cliché. The interior of the palace, which is now used for the offices of the Italian State Railway, was also ornamented under Bolli's supervision and contains some splendid Rococo stucco work, as well as a severe but fine imperial staircase designed by Carlo Merlo.[12]

The vitality of the Lombard Rococo also spread to smaller towns outside Milan. In Crema, Lodi, and Pavia, works of considerable interest were built by architects like Giovanni Ruggeri, Giovanni Antonio Veneroni, Lorenzo Cassani, and Andrea Nono. Nono's church of SS. Trinità in Crema (155), constructed in 1737–1739, is a good

154. Bartolomeo Bolli, Palazzo Litta, Milan, facade.

155. Andrea Nono,
SS. Trinità, Crema,
exterior.

example of this lively regional style. The only significant work of the
architect, the boxlike church is encased in a stucco shell as flamboyant
as any eighteenth-century exterior in Italy. Wrapped around two sides
of the building (the axial entrance is on the narrow side street), it embodies both the fantasy and the refinement of the Rococo sensibility.
While the entablature moldings and decorative panels are crisply in-
cised, the cornices and pediments are heavy and follow bold, extravagant curves. The lack of agreement between the front and side facades
might reflect Nono's lack of experience and provincial background,
but it detracts little from the exuberance of the exterior as a whole. In

249

the course of a recent restoration, the church was painted pale yellow, making it even more vivacious and true to its original appearance.

In eighteenth-century Venice, increasing political and economic insecurity produced an atmosphere of cultural orthodoxy and conservatism that was not conducive to the formation of a Rococo style in architecture.[13] The picturesque style of Baldassare Longhena (d. 1682) had barely survived the turn of the century when there emerged a nostalgic return to classicism based on Palladian and other early Venetian models. One of the architects of the transition to this more classical style was Domenico Rossi (1657–1737), a Lombard by birth who received part of his training in Longhena's studio.

In 1709, Rossi was one of seven entrants in a competition for the facade of the church of S. Stae on the Grand Canal. Most of the entries were Baroque in flavor, but Rossi's winning project (156) was unabashedly Palladian. It was inspired by the sixteenth-century master's Venetian churches of S. Francesco della Vigna and S. Giorgio Maggiore, both of which also have temple fronts of colossal half-columns on high pedestals that interlock with a lower secondary order. Rossi did not adopt the flanking half-pediments of his models and gave greater sculptural emphasis to the single doorway. These, of course, were minor revisions, and although the facade is harmoniously disposed, it is not a work of great imagination. Similarly, the severely classicizing front of S. Nicolo da Tolentino (1706–1714)—the work of Andrea Tirali, one of the unsuccessful entrants in the S. Stae competition—was little more than a posthumous reworking of Palladio's own project for the same church.

The colossal engaged temple front of S. Stae was only one of several neo-Palladian designs erected in Venice during the first half of the eighteenth century.[14] The most striking of these was Giovanni Antonio Scalfarotto's (c. 1690–1764) church of Ss. Simeone e Giuda (S. Simeone Piccolo), located at the head of the Grand Canal directly opposite the modern train station. This church, constructed in 1718–1738, synthesizes a number of models drawn from both Venetian and non-Venetian sources. The exterior (157) is generically related to Palladio's small chapel at Maser, and ultimately to the Roman Pantheon (58), but to this classical paradigm Scalfarotto ingeniously wedded a stilted Veneto-Byzantine dome like that of the medieval basilica of St. Mark's. Drawing from these sources, Scalfarotto created a unified whole which, compared to Juvarra's contemporary church of the Su-

156. Domenico Rossi, S. Stae, Venice, facade.

157. G. A. Scalfarotto, Ss. Simeone e Giuda, Venice, exterior.

perga or even the earlier Roman churches in the Piazza del Popolo, is refreshingly abstract and unportentous. This simplification of formal elements makes S. Simeone the building most prophetic of Neo-Classicism seen to date. With its picturesque setting on the Grand Canal, it must have made a powerful impression on English visitors like Lord Burlington and William Kent, who together soon designed a comparable if much smaller structure in the garden at Chiswick outside London.[15] Scalfarotto, however, was unaffected by the romantic sentiment and historical exactitude that one associates with true Neo-Classicism. In its synthetic formalism, S. Simeone was still closely aligned with the methods of Late Baroque Classicism.[16]

The interior (158) is also unmistakably based on the Pantheon. The principal space is circular, and its articulation is in many ways the same as that of the ancient rotunda as it appeared at the time. The fenestration of the upper sections of the elevation, the transverse placement of the attached presbytery, and the bichromatic membering, however, all depart from the Roman prototype, following instead the Venetian tradition of Longhena and Palladio. Palladio, in fact, was also fascinated by the Pantheon; he analyzed it at length in the fourth book

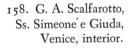

158. G. A. Scalfarotto,
Ss. Simeone e Giuda,
Venice, interior.

of his treatise and adapted several of its features in his own architecture.[17] It is possible that Scalfarotto, who never went to Rome, discovered even the Pantheon through the eyes of his Venetian predecessor.

In contrast to the classicizing, essentially provincial architecture of eighteenth-century Venice, that of Bologna was innovative, unorthodox, and only rarely based on local tradition. In fact, the city's most esteemed architect, Carlo Francesco Dotti (1670–1759) forswore both academic classicism and the Rococo in favor of an emboldened late Baroque whose only parallel at the time was found in southern Italy and Sicily. The magnificent Arco del Meloncello (159), spanning the Via Saragozza on the southwestern edge of the city, exemplifies the imaginative and even bizarre nature of his work.[18]

Built in 1718–1732, this gateway is connected by a long covered arcade to a hilltop sanctuary that Dotti rebuilt at about the same time. The plan of the arch traces an irregular double S-curve that violates every rule of architectonic symmetry. Because it is used by vehicles below and pedestrians above, the gateway is open on both stories, allowing scenographic effects to unfold both inside and out. The main drama is provided by a tall, vigorously composed frontispiece that satirizes the Porta Galliera, a fine seventeenth-century portal in the northern part of the city. The undeniable theatricality of the gateway is reminiscent of the flamboyant stage sets then being designed by various members of the Bibiena family. Francesco Bibiena, a prolific theatre architect, is even said to have been Dotti's collaborator. The effect of translating ephemeral compositions into solid stone was to create an alternative to the standard dialectic of Classical and Rococo. To give it a name of its own, this style may be called the Ultra-Baroque.[19]

After a strenuous climb from the gateway up a mile-long arcaded stair-corridor, one reaches the Sanctuary of the Madonna di San Luca. Dotti rebuilt the church from 1723 to 1752, designing the exterior (160) with a dramatically undulating, open-galleried elevation like that of the Arco. The plan, however, is symmetrical and the membering more restrained. The low, open wings of the facade recall the Vatican colonnade, but they are not particularly well adjusted to the ponderous upper body of the church. Undoubtedly an important element in Dotti's thinking was a desire to relate his architectural forms to the surrounding landscape while giving the church a striking profile that could be seen from a considerable distance. In both attempts he was entirely successful.

159. Carlo Francesco Dotti, Arco del Meloncello, Bologna.

160. Carlo Francesco Dotti, Madonna di S. Luca, Bologna, exterior.

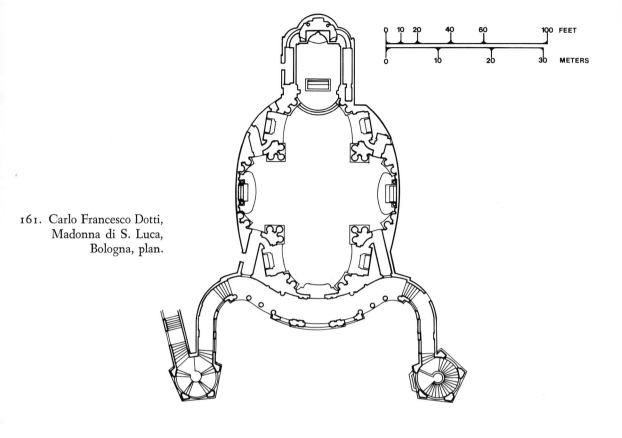

0 10 20 40 60 100 FEET

0 10 20 30 METERS

161. Carlo Francesco Dotti, Madonna di S. Luca, Bologna, plan.

As early as 1758, visitors noted a resemblance between the Madonna di San Luca and the Superga in Turin (141). Both sanctuaries occupy magnificent hilltop sites near major cities and share the Baroque conceit of Christian triumph over nature, but they also reflect the special needs of their individual patrons. For the ambitious and politically motivated House of Savoy, the Superga symbolized the majesty of their aspiration; the Madonna di San Luca, on the other hand, expressed the religious zeal of a small city that remained a papal possession. Financed by the Order of Servites with the help of Pope Benedict XIV, it performed the more traditional role of meeting the spiritual needs of its community. Inspired by the natural forms of the surrounding hilly landscape, the Madonna di San Luca is about as far in spirit from Juvarra's academic thinking as can be imagined.

The freely conceived architecture of the sanctuary does not extend beyond the exterior, however. Inside (161, 162) is a regular Greek Cross with rounded arms and an appended sanctuary, a scheme that probably was derived from Pietro da Cortona's church of Ss. Martina e Luca in Rome (64, 65). The choice of model is understandable, given Bologna's strong ties to Rome, the sanctuary's dedication to the Madonna di San Luca, and Dotti's predilection for powerful Baroque compositions. Dotti even traveled to Rome in 1726 to confer with members of the Accademia di San Luca about the placement within the church of an icon believed to have been painted by Saint Luke. The architect's reliance on Roman prototypes should not be overestimated, however. The sequence of stately columns is akin to earlier Bolognese elevations like that of S. Salvatore (118), while the attached presbytery was long a standard feature of north Italian sacred architecture. Moreover, Dotti altered the proportions and orientation of Cortona's church by expanding the crossing and strengthening the longitudinal axis. Despite its predominantly modern decoration, the interior is less idiosyncratic and considerably blander than its formidable exterior.[20]

162. Carlo Francesco Dotti, Madonna di S. Luca, Bologna, interior.

163. Francesco Maria Angellini, Palazzo Aldrovandi-Montanari, Bologna, staircase.

The work of Dotti's Bolognese contemporaries tended more toward the Rococo than the impassioned Ultra-Baroque of the buildings just discussed. In Alfonso Torreggiani (1682–1764) and Francesco Maria Angelini (1680–1731), the city had two designers of considerable talent. Examples of their work can be seen in the Palazzo Aldrovandi (now Montanari) on the Via Galliera in the center of town. Angelini's stairway of about 1725 (163) and Torreggiani's facade of 1744–1752 are in many respects comparable to the Bolli-Merlo scheme for the Palazzo Litta in Milan, although it is the Aldrovandi stairway, not the exterior, that is the more felicitous Rococo feature. A reduced version of the "imperial" type, there are just two parallel flights leading to the lofty upper vestibule.[21] This upper zone is a model of eighteenth-century elegance with a rose and white color scheme and some rather

164. Giovanni Carlo Bibiena, Palazzo Fantuzzi-Garagnani, Bologna, staircase.

extravagant stuccowork that includes zoomorphic devices perched at the four corners of the cornice. The ceiling is pierced by an oval oculus with a *quadratura* or illusionistic architectural scheme painted on the vault of its lantern.

Angelini's stairway is but one of several imaginative examples constructed in Bologna at this time. Many, like that which Dotti added to the earlier Palazzo Davia-Bargellini, are quite grand, but certainly the most charming and unusual was designed by Giovanni Carlo Bibiena for the Palazzo Fantuzzi-Garagnani on the Strada Maggiore (164). Giovanni Carlo (1717–1760) was the son of Francesco Bibiena, and like other members of this remarkable family, was primarily active as a stage designer.[22] The Fantuzzi-Garagnani stairway, which was designed in 1750, is his most important surviving work in Bologna. As might be expected, its design has more in common with the theatrical Ultra-Baroque of Dotti than with the Rococo refinement of Angelini.

Turning a cramped site to his advantage, Bibiena constructed a serpentine ramp that twists upward along a steep and irregular course. The bizarre space is more than matched by the decoration which adorns it. Figural and zoomorphic sculptures, executed by the sculptor Filippo Scandellari, are rich with heraldic, allegorical, and even satiric associations. Anyone familiar with the architecture of the Strada Maggiore will recognize that the pivotal atlantid carrying a boulder is, in fact, a parody of a figure from Provaglia's nearby portal of the Palazzo Davia-Bargellini (120). The oppressive feeling this struggling figure conveys is partly alleviated by a gradual increase in illumination as one ascends the tortuous ramp. To achieve this effect, Bibiena followed the example of the Aldrovandi staircase and perforated the ceiling to capture additional light from a lantern that, in turn, is decorated with a resplendent illusionistic fresco. Of all the structures conceived in the permissive atmosphere of eighteenth-century Bologna, this is one of the most witty and informal.

11

Southern Italy

Some of the most fanciful and regionally distinctive buildings of the later Baroque period are found in southern Italy, especially in Naples, the province of Apulia, and Sicily. Historical factors undoubtedly played a part in isolating this region from the rest of Italy. The lands south of Rome remained under foreign control throughout the seventeenth and eighteenth centuries, passing in 1713 from the Spanish to the Austrian Hapsburgs, and then to the Bourbons before the short-lived Napoleonic conquest in 1806. Only in the south did the feudal system of land ownership still hold sway, concentrating great wealth in the hands of a few barons while most of the people lived in miserable poverty. The Church, while offering spiritual succor to the poor, itself retained vast tracts of land—for example, it is estimated that the Church owned one half of the total acreage of the city of Naples. Such unique economic and social conditions were important factors in the commissioning of architecture.

The earliest south Italian buildings that can be called Baroque date from the mid-seventeenth century in Naples, then the largest city in Italy and the fourth largest in Europe. The exoticism of this bustling port has been described by travellers from Goethe to Mark Twain. Dickens called it the city of "buffoons and pickpockets, opera singers and beggars, rags, puppets, flowers, brightness, dirt, and universal degradation." The religious ardor of Neapolitans is legendary. Out of a population of around 300,000, there were some 20,000 clerics, a ratio that exceeded even that of Rome.[1] Backed by the substantial wealth of the religious institutions, more than 170 churches and dependent

261

buildings were built in Naples in the seventeenth century alone, and commissions hardly abated in the following century. In fact, Naples in the Baroque era became so rewarding a place for artists and architects that established Roman painters like Domenichino and Lanfranco and architects like Domenico Fontana and Ferdinando Fuga left Rome to settle there permanently.

Cosimo Fanzago (1591–1678) is the best known architect of seventeenth-century Naples.[2] A Lombard by birth, he came to the city to study sculpture when he was seventeen, and except for brief trips to Rome and Venice, remained there until his death. His works include magnificent inlaid marble and sculpted decoration, more than a dozen churches, and several palaces. The collective style of these architectural works is not easy to characterize, however, for Fanzago was a versatile designer and few of his buildings remain wholly intact today. One of his earliest and most successful works is at the Certosa, or Charterhouse, of S. Martino, on a scenic hill overlooking the city. In 1623, Fanzago began renovating a Gothic church on the site while he completed a cloister that the Florentine architect Giovanni Antonio Dosio had begun earlier in the century.

In each of the cloister's four corners, Fanzago placed a pair of elaborately worked doorways (165) that exemplify his taste for rich and profuse ornament. These doorways, completed except for the busts by 1631, are delightfully ornamental if somewhat weak and illogical structurally. The linkage between the upper and lower tiers is inexact, and there is little concern for the propriety of the classical components. One senses from this early work that Fanzago had a natural talent for designing decorative ensembles rather than architectonic structures, and this continues to be apparent in his later works. It is interesting that the origin of much of the ornament is Florentine.[3] Like Pietro da Cortona, Fanzago adopted some of the Mannerist devices of Michelangelo's followers and infused them with the exuberance of the Baroque.

In Fanzago's more ambitious designs for ecclesiastical patrons, a split between rich decoration and sober structure can often be detected. His church interiors are, for the most part, unremarkable; most use Greek Cross plans, which were somewhat unfashionable at the time elsewhere in Italy. S. Maria degli Angeli alle Croci is an exception, for it has a Latin Cross plan, but there is reason to suppose that in this case Fanzago was simply remodelling an existing building.[4] The facade (166), begun in 1639, is more interesting. As is often found in

165. Cosimo Fanzago, Certosa di S. Martino, Naples, courtyard doorways.

166. Cosimo Fanzago, S. Maria degli Angeli alle Croce, Naples, exterior.

Naples, the facade is integrated with a broad stairway—albeit one that dates from the eighteenth century—and is topped by a flat, unpedimented roofline. Fanzago occasionally experimented with an internal rather than external stairway, but in either instance he usually combined it with an open narthex or vestibule. The flat, unpedimented roofline is not uncommon among Neapolitan churches, and is one of the distinguishing features of this region's architecture.

The exterior of S. Maria degli Angeli masks monastic quarters as well as the church proper. Despite the fact that the right side of the elevation was never completed, and the open portico was later blocked up, it is one of Fanzago's best-preserved works. The dichotomy between structure and ornament is apparent in the contrast between the colossal pilasters and the window surrounds of the upper story. The

264

order is flat and austere, but the ornament is more extravagantly conceived, using devices reminiscent of sixteenth-century Mannerism. Even more than at the Certosa, the overall composition is diffuse, with little effort made to organize individual features into a coherent design. Although the disjunctive nature of the facade would have been less pronounced before the lower sections were filled in, this is hardly the only instance in Fanzago's architecture of what by Roman standards would be considered formal disarray.

It was really in the eighteenth century that Neapolitan architecture came conspicuously into its own. The name of Ferdinando Sanfelice is reasonably well known, but other talented architects have yet to receive the recognition they deserve outside of their native city. Of the several commissions attributed to the shadowy figures Arcangelo Guglielmelli and his son Marcello, the reconstruction of the small church of S. Angelo a Nilo in the Piazza S. Domenico may be taken as a particularly fine example. The exterior elevation (167), attributable to

167. Marcello Guglielmelli, S. Angelo a Nilo, Naples, exterior.

Marcello Guglielmelli ca. 1725, is a paragon of Rococo refinement with its neatly creased wall vibrating in shallow relief.[5] The activity of the wall is complemented by the flow of color and ornament that spreads evenly across its surface. While the ornament is light and sparingly applied, the color—burnt orange painted to imitate brick, contrasted with grey *piperno* stone—is disposed so as to emphasize the uniformity of the total scheme. Unlike the strongly contrasting relationship between order and wall that is customarily found in bichromatic compositions of the Baroque period, Guglielmelli deliberately blurred the structural distinctions on S. Angelo's exterior. Grey stone is used for some panelling and walling as well as for the adjacent pilasters. The resulting dissolution of the building's tectonic character is fully in keeping with the spirit of the Rococo that existed elsewhere in Italy during this period. The buildings in Rome designed by Filippo Raguzzini are the closest parallel.[6]

The refurbishing of the interior of S. Angelo a Nilo (168), which seems to pre-date that of the exterior, remained more faithful to the character of the pre-existing church. Its simple plan has neither side aisles nor regularly spaced chapels, and while the choir is domed, the nave is covered with a modest coved ceiling (which was subsequently rebuilt in the nineteenth century). Despite its uneventful spatial arrangement, the presence of robust half-columns in the nave and freestanding columns in the choir give the interior a certain brio. Above the nave entablature, Guglielmelli has taken the unusual step of placing sequences of broken pediments topped with putti, an inventive and welcome addition to an otherwise bland part of the church. The total effect of the interior is thus somewhat more forceful—and Baroque—than that of the Rococo exterior, which probably was built more than a decade later.[7]

We are on firmer ground when examining the work of Domenico Antonio Vaccaro (1678–1745), a more prolific, and better studied figure than the Guglielmelli. The son of a sculptor and grandson of an even more successful painter, Vaccaro ignored his family's inducements to become a lawyer and at an early age began his career as a decorator and architect. The church of the Concezione a Montecalvario stands out as the finest example of his many ecclesiastical commissions in and around Naples. Constructed from 1718 to 1724, the church is also something of a rarity in that the architect both designed it and sculpted its decoration himself.

168. Arcangelo Guglielmelli (?), S. Angelo a Nilo, Naples, interior.

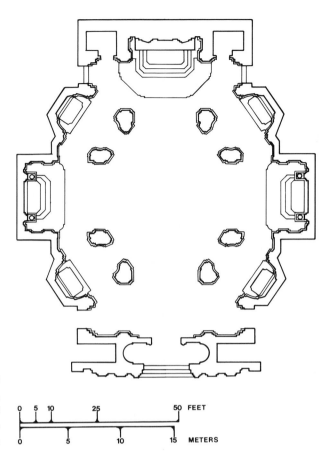

169. Domenico
Antonio Vaccaro,
Concezione
a Montecalvario,
Naples, plan.

As with the four other churches that Vaccaro designed, the plan of
the Concezione (169) is centralized. Like all but one of them, it de-
velops an elongated axis from an octagonal core, a practice similar to
Fanzago's own habit of extending the longitudinal axis of a Greek
Cross. Here Vaccaro adjusted the angles and alternated the length of
the octagon's sides to emphasize the ritual direction without upsetting
the plan's basic symmetry. By so doing, he provided a new and ingenious solution to an age-old problem in Italian architecture. Because
the octagon also contains diagonal apertures, the interior (170) was
opened up and the perceptual experiences of walking through the
church were increased. In the middle zone of the elevation, Vaccaro
transformed the diagonal piers into pendentives, which, along with
small choir niches suspended below, are thickly ornamented in stucco.
The confectionery quality of the ornament, the lightness of the orders,
and the unrelieved whiteness of the whole ensemble are hallmarks of
Vaccaro's style.

268

170. Domenico Antonio Vaccaro, Concezione a Montecalvario, Naples, interior.

171. Domenico Antonio Vaccaro, Concezione a Montecalvario, Naples, exterior.

The facade of the Concezione (171) is perfectly attuned to the interior. Located on a narrow, sloping street of the same name, it rises from a tall plinth, and the single doorway is framed by paired pilasters. The elevation is a virtual repetition of that of the interior cross-arms but for the shape of the window and the presence of the crested pediment. The oddly shaped window, of course, matches that over the high altar, and both, in fact, may have been influenced by an engraving in Guarino Guarini's treatise, published several decades earlier. The crested pediment is a more indigenous Neapolitan feature, which Vaccaro has skillfully blended with scrolls that also are borrowed from the interior.

One of Vaccaro's few non-religious commissions was the Palazzo Abbaziale di Loreto near the town of Avellino, in the hills some thirty miles east of Naples. From 1734 to 1749 Vaccaro built a summer residence there for the monks of Montevergine, a Neapolitan order that had a sanctuary nearby. The plan of this palace is too irregular to be easily described, but the shape of its grand courtyard suggests an elongated octagon with alternately straight and curved sides.

The entrance facade (172) is appropriately simple, given its rustic location. Away from the formality of the city, Vaccaro eliminated the classical order altogether in favor of light, predominantly atectonic stucco decoration concentrated about the windows and under the roof-line. This decoration is as free and frothy as any created during the eighteenth century in Italy. The fanciful and undoctrinaire approach is typical of the permissive atmosphere that existed in Naples, and the whole of the South, at this time.

Among all the architects of the Neapolitan Rococo, Ferdinando Sanfelice was probably the most strikingly original. Like Vaccaro, Sanfelice (1675–1748) began as a painter, but later turned to architecture, achieving his greatest fame for his design of residential buildings.

172. Domenico Antonio Vaccaro, Palazzo Abbaziale di Loreto, Avellino, exterior.

173. Ferdinando Sanfelice,
Palazzo Sanfelice,
Naples, stairway.

Taking advantage of the unusual height of contemporary Neapolitan palaces—a result of the city's overcrowded living conditions—Sanfelice made the staircase the focus of his creative thinking. His facades, by comparison, tend to be more conventional, with heavily ornamented portals often derived from earlier models by Fanzago.

Sanfelice's staircases can be divided between those that open onto a courtyard and those that are enclosed within the fabric of the building. Among the open stairways, the larger of two in his own palace on the Via Arena della Sanità (173) is his most magnificent creation. Open stairways had been known since the fifteenth century in Naples, but only at this time—the palace was built ca. 1725—did they become so tall. The majesty of this example depends on both its height and on its extensive perforation which permits scenographic views of the courtyard on one side and the garden on the other. Moreover, Sanfe-lice varied the size and shape of the openings to suggest the motion of soaring flight (an allusion not lost on his contemporary biographer who compared the staircase to a bird with outstretched wings). Rather than being strenuous to climb, the stairs themselves are uplifting and even exhilarating.

Of the many stairways attributed to Sanfelice, that of the nearby Palazzo Di Maio (Discesa della Sanità, 69) is the most intriguing example of the enclosed type (174). Sanfelice's biographer called it "the most capricious in all of Naples," and happily, it was not destroyed when the palace was partially demolished in the nineteenth century to make way for a new street. The plan of the stairway is lozenge-shaped with the ramps coiled loosely about an open well. Instead of being buttressed by a solid newel as was customary, the steps are supported only by the outside walls. This concept of a "flying staircase" can be traced back to Palladio, but never before had it been used so whimsically.[8] Because the triangular landings between the slanted flights of steps do not correspond to the actual floor levels, additional steps were required to gain entry into the individual apartments. Looking up from below, one marvels at the array of sail vaults that make this improbable structure possible. The Di Maio stairway was recently restored and is now the best-preserved example of Sanfelice's work, much of which has fallen into appalling disrepair.

By the end of Vaccaro's and Sanfelice's lives, in the 1740s, Neapolitan taste had begun to change. This was a local development, brought about in part by the influential patronage of the young Bourbon King Charles III, who had come to power in 1734 at the age of eighteen. With his French blood, Spanish upbringing, and pragmatic nature, Charles III introduced some long-needed changes into Neapolitan life. He restricted the privileges of the clergy and reformed the feudal system by giving peasants greater individual rights. In architecture, he supplanted the spicy but essentially provincial Neapolitan style with a more international and classical one. He did so, simply enough, by importing two architects from Rome, Ferdinando Fuga and Luigi Vanvitelli, for his most important commissions.

Fuga (1699–1782) and Vanvitelli (1700–1773) both arrived in Naples in 1751. Although Fuga was the more experienced and better-known architect (see chapter 7), his most ambitious Neapolitan commissions were for relatively utilitarian buildings; Charles gave the less renowned Vanvitelli the task of building his fabulous new palace

174. Ferdinando Sanfelice, Palazzo Di Maio, Naples, stairway.

at Caserta and a few other interesting projects. The work of both men, however, was as strongly predisposed toward academic classicism as it was devoid of Neapolitan reference.

The palace at Caserta (175), fifteen miles north of Naples, is a perfect case in point.[9] Built from 1752 to 1774, it is one of the largest buildings in Europe and contains some 1200 rooms. Vanvitelli's elevation for the main facade—which is almost 800 feet long—is predictably cosmopolitan. Its sources spring from the tradition of such stately buildings as Versailles (144), the Palazzo Madama in Turin (143), and the Royal Palace in Madrid, designed by Juvarra in 1735 for Charles' father, Phillip V. A significant departure from these models, however, is the use of a pediment over the central pavilion, an odd breach of etiquette in an Italian building, but one that is wholly characteristic of the eighteenth-century tendency to secularize forms that previously had been used only for sacred architecture.

Another remarkable feature of the palace at Caserta is its main vestibule and stairway (176). Located at the intersection of two inner wings that cross in the courtyard, the vestibule is a spacious octagon whose plan is strikingly similar to that of the church of S. Maria della Salute in Venice (124). The scenographic possibilities of Longhena's

175. Luigi Vanvitelli, Royal Palace at Caserta, exterior.

176. Luigi Vanvitelli, Royal Palace at Caserta, staircase.

plan were not wasted on Vanvitelli. He joined the open octagon with an imperial staircase to create an ensemble of unparalleled grandeur and scenic variety. This dramatic space is unexpectedly complemented by some suave relief decoration fashioned on French classical models. A French model was also followed in the design of the chapel located off the stairway on the *piano nobile*. For this, Vanvitelli turned again to Versailles, and J. H. Mansart's chapel of half a century earlier. Throughout the palace, one fails, in fact, to find any purely Neapolitan characteristics.

The work of Mario Gioffredo (1718–1785) shows to what extent local architects also came to abandon the Rococo for the classical style. In the church of the Spirito Santo in Via Roma (177) of 1757–1774, Gioffredo built a starkly handsome structure that is similar to Vanvitelli's own SS. Annunziata of 1760–1782. Both churches have longi-

276

tudinal plans with barrel vaulted naves and domed crossings, but more important, both substitute a straight entablature for the conventional nave arcade. In the Spirito Santo, the classical severity of this system is reinforced by the cool monochromatic color scheme and the sparse use of applied ornament. The author of a dogmatic architectural treatise and the first recorded architect to study the ruins of the Greek temples at Paestum, Gioffredo brought Neapolitan architecture very close to the formal advent of Neo-Classicism.

Lecce, the provincial capital of Apulia, is the most beautiful and architecturally distinctive city on the south Italian mainland. Nineteenth-century writers described it as "seductive, a precious jewel of a town" and "the Florence of Apulia." Despite its remoteness in the heel of the Italian boot, Lecce and its environs was a prosperous center of agriculture and trade with the East. Culturally, it remained more or less independent of both Naples and Spain, and one searches in vain

177. Mario Gioffredo, Church of the Spirito Santo, Naples, interior.

for any easy explanation of its idiosyncratic architectural personality.[10] Lecce, moreover, is an ancient city whose origins can be traced back to the Messapian, Greek, and Roman periods.

The Apulian Baroque began in the last quarter of the sixteenth century and continued unabated, with only modest changes, until the mid-eighteenth century. An early example is the small building in the center of town known as Il Sedile (178). This curious structure, which stands adjacent to a Roman ampitheatre, was built in 1592 to serve various public functions. It is thought that its author was Giuseppe Riccardi, Lecce's most accomplished sixteenth-century architect. The Sedile embodies three characteristics common to its city's architecture: the unorthodox handling of the classical orders; the adoption of outdated elements like the Gothic pointed arch; and the love of sculptural ornament. Here, the treatment of the corner pilasters is the building's most eccentric and memorable feature. Gouged out to reveal round columns within, these pilasters are as bizarre and redundant a combination of structural elements as can be found anywhere. The pilasters' abbreviated Corinthian capitals are a final "mannerist" touch. With a Gothic arch below, and a Renaissance loggia above, the building has a whimsical, delightfully imaginative character. Given its early date, it is also one of the first Baroque buildings in Italy, if by the term Baroque we mean spirited and self-assured.

As a rule, the interior of most Apulian buildings is not as interesting or complex as the exterior. The contrast is typified by the church of S. Matteo by Achille Carducci (ca. 1644 to ca. 1712). Its interior, begun in 1667, consists of a single oblong nave with rounded ends and shallow side chapels. The blandness of this scheme is alleviated not by the pilaster order or routine vaulting, but by the lavish use of sculpture on the altars and projecting pilaster pedestals. Other churches in Lecce experiment with different plans, but the result is seldom very compelling architecturally.

The facade (179), by contrast, is more dramatic. It is more complex spatially and uses a more diverse repertory of architectural devices. Completed in 1700, its robust elevation is based on the Baroque tradition of curved planes and three-dimensional structural members. Like Borromini's facade of S. Carlino in Rome (28), the upper story of S. Matteo reverses the curvature of the one below. The linkage here is more inexact, however, for Carducci failed to suggest any real correspondence between either the structural or decorative elements. It is

178. Giuseppe Riccardi,
Il Sedile, Lecce,
exterior.

with the work of Guarini, in fact, that S. Matteo is most closely associated. In the *Disegni d'architettura civile* there are plates of facades with similar reversals in curvature and flattened Palladian windows.[11] Whatever its sources, S. Matteo is an amazingly free and unself-conscious structure whose temperament is purely Leccese. This is especially obvious in the surface decoration. Nowhere but in this isolated coastal province could one find an entrance bay carved with fish scales,

279

179. Achille Carducci, S. Matteo, Lecce, facade.

or cornice brackets covered with a dense carpet of tiny suckers.

The local stone, one of the most beautiful in Italy, was itself important in the development of Apulian architecture. It is soft enough when quarried to be easily cut, but it hardens with time, and its warm ochre color and rough texture actively respond to the strong southern sun. Baroque architects were not the first to recognize its virtues: Romanesque builders also had taken advantage of its potential for smooth dressing and intricate detailing. In fact, it was probably the nature of the local stone that caused most architects in the region to foreswear facades with complex plans, like that of S. Matteo, for ones with flatter but highly activated surfaces.

The church of the Rosary by Giuseppe Zimbalo (1620–1710) is in that respect more characteristically Leccese. Constructed from 1691 to 1728, it was partially paid for by Zimbalo himself, who, despite his sobriquet "lo zingarello" (the little gypsy), was one of Lecce's most successful and prolific architects. The Rosario's huge interior is in the shape of a Greek Cross, but like S. Matteo, there is nothing remarkable about its dry elevation or flat timber roofing. The exterior, however, warrants close study (180). Here, as in his other commissions, Zimbalo constructed an essentially flat facade, with a pair of detached columns flanking the doorway. The columns display an unusual motif which is the architect's virtual trademark: a thick foliate band that marks the juncture of the cabling and fluting. Above the columns on the second story rest vases carved with massive fruit bushes and plump birds. Elsewhere on the densely worked facade are embellishments that seem to spring from a different, more delicate sensibility. Over the doorway is a squarish relief carved in flat arabesque patterns that recall Islamic art. How Zimbalo could have been familiar with such exotica is not known, but, most likely, he had seen small importable items such as miniatures, ceramics, or textiles. Instances of such early borrowings from the East were rare in architecture, despite their relatively frequent occurrence in European painting and decorative arts of the period.[12]

One of Lecce's most attractive features is the Piazza del Duomo (181).[13] This square, which contains a cathedral, a seminary, and a bishop's palace, is unusual among piazzas of its type in that it is only open at one end and contains no shops or businesses. In reality, it is more a courtyard than a true piazza, and part of its charm is its unhurried atmosphere and lack of congestion. The history of its construc-

180. Giuseppe Zimbalo, Church of the Rosary, Lecce, facade.

tion is complicated. In the 1420s the courtyard was laid out around a medieval basilica and the bishop's palace was begun. During the seventeenth and early eighteenth centuries, the bishop's palace was completed (1632–1761); the cathedral was rebuilt (1658–1670); and the campanile (1661–1682) and seminary (1694–1709) were constructed. In 1761 the entrance gate was designed. The main sponsor of the seventeenth-century campaign was Bishop Luigi Pappacoda, whose favorite architect, Zimbalo, rebuilt the Duomo and the campanile. The most interesting structures in the piazza, however, are the episcopal and seminary palaces.

The *Episcopio*, or bishop's palace, at the far end of the square, consists of an open arcaded loggia raised on a rusticated base. Despite its long and complicated building history, it is a distinctive and ruggedly handsome structure that blends easily with its surroundings. The Seminario (182), by Zimbalo's follower Giuseppe Cino (1644–1722), is an equally impressive building that takes up the theme of Zimbalo's own monastery for the Celestini (now Museo Provinciale) of 1659–

181. Piazza del Duomo, Lecce.

182. Giuseppe Cino, Seminary Palace, Lecce, facade.

1695. Both facades are embellished with rustication that spreads over the pilasters as well as the actual wall. Cino tightened the organization of the earlier facade by substituting a giant order for Zimbalo's two-tiered system and giving greater emphasis to the central doorway, surmounting it with a heavy balcony and a triple-arched Renaissance loggia. This loggia is, of course, even more anachronistic than that of the Sedile (178) from which it may derive. Cino's design of the windows, on the other hand, is more in the spirit of Lecce's own florid late Baroque. That this building—and the entire Piazza del Duomo—was the product of so many architects, working over such a long period of time, testifies to the continuity and stylistic conviction of Lecce's architecture. Indeed, few other urban complexes in Italy are so harmoniously composed.

Goethe wrote during a visit in 1787 that "to have seen Italy without having seen Sicily is not to have seen Italy at all, for Sicily is the clue to everything." Although he was not speaking of architecture, his observation could apply. Sicilian buildings are almost archetypally Baroque in their stark columnar membering and elastic conceptions of space—characteristics that distinguish them from the kind of building we have just seen in Lecce, and that, in a larger context, exemplify the so-called Ultra-Baroque style of the eighteenth century.

As in Naples, it was during the eighteenth century that architecture in Sicily flourished.[14] Much of the eastern part of the island had to be rebuilt after a major earthquake in 1693, which claimed 60,000 lives and destroyed hundreds of churches. In its aftermath, towns and cities like Noto, Ragusa, Syracuse, and Catania were transformed by the vast array of Baroque buildings that went up in place of the ruins. In the western part of the island, only the capital city of Palermo rivals them in architectural grandeur.

The most ingenious architecture in Palermo is found in the marvelous villas built for the nobility in the nearby towns of Piana dei Colli and Bagheria. The Villa Palagonia in Bagheria (183), begun by Tommaso Napoli in 1705, is justifiably the most celebrated, if not for its true architectural qualities, for its strange assortment of sculpted monstrosities that were commissioned by the original owner's eccentric grandson. The plan of the villa is crown-shaped, with a concave front and a convex rear. As in most of these villas, the rustic simplicity of the exterior elevation acts as a backdrop for an intricate and impressively large staircase. Here, the double staircase consists of four flights on each side that change direction and play vivaciously against the facade's own irregular geometry. Even in its present neglected condition, the villa is one of the most striking in all of Italy. Ironically, much of the bizarre decoration that for years distracted visitors from the building's real merits has disappeared and we are again free to concentrate on the architecture itself.

Only in the southeast do we find ecclesiastical architecture of comparable interest. Andrea Palma's facade of the Cathedral of Syracuse (184), built in 1728–1754, typifies the region's stylistic independence from the Rococo and Classical options then in vogue elsewhere in Italy.[15] Palma (1664–1730) was born in Trapani on the west coast of Sicily and worked in Palermo before receiving this commission at the end of his career. The facade, which replaced one destroyed in the earthquake, bears a curious resemblance to such earlier Roman works as S. Maria in Campitelli (84), begun sixty-five years earlier. Although Palma apparently never left his native island, it is not unlikely

183. Tommaso Napoli,
Villa Palagonia,
Bagheria, exterior.

that his inspiration for the dramatically projecting columns and broken pediments came from Rainaldi's facade. Because it faces west, Palma's facade is bathed in chiaroscuro by the late afternoon sun, an advantage its Roman prototype, which is oriented towards the northeast, does not share. Despite its strong visual impact, the Syracusan front has none of the subtlety that is characteristic of the architecture of mid-seventeenth-century Rome. Certainly it lacks S. Maria in Campitelli's intricate interplay of columnar sequences (having a dozen fewer members) even though its sculptural program does fulfill Rainaldi's unrealized intention of similarly embellishing the Roman facade.

286

184. Andrea Palma, Syracuse Cathedral, facade.

185. G. B. Vaccarini, Catania Cathedral, facade.

Catania, the second largest Sicilian city, employed Giovanni Battista Vaccarini (1702–1769) to direct its reconstruction. Born in Palermo, Vaccarini was trained in Rome at the Accademia di San Luca, then returned to Sicily and settled in Catania ca. 1730. In 1736, a year after he was appointed City Architect, he began the new facade of Catania Cathedral (185), the last part of the eleventh-century structure to be rebuilt.

Despite his Roman training, the style of Vaccarini's facade is recognizably Sicilian, especially its use of a third story to house the belfry.[16] Equally notable is the dynamic, integrated arrangement of its freestanding columns. While the background wall is straight and firm, the column bases are canted so as to stir the facade with a gently undulating movement. In this, Vaccarini reversed the usual relationship between wall and order by relying on the columns to give the facade both its chiaroscuro and its shifting planarity. Furthermore, he kept the rhythm from becoming predictable by alternating pilasters with columns on the lower story, and by varying the size and shape of the window and door surrounds. It might be argued that he was too purposeful in these efforts, for the facade's overall effect is somewhat diffuse and lacking in concentration.

Vaccarini's other works in Catania are occasionally more revealing of his Roman training. One of his most celebrated commissions, the church of S. Agata (1735–1767), is an adaptation of the interior of S. Agnese in Piazza Navona, with an imaginative Borrominesque facade. Similarly, in the Palazzo del Municipio (186), situated across the square from the Cathedral, Vaccarini blended a pre-existing, typically south Italian lower story with an upper elevation based on Roman models. A comparison of this facade of 1732–1750 with Ferdinando Fuga's slightly later Palazzo Cenci-Bolognetti (107), suggests their common ancestry. Only the detailing of Vaccarini's elevation gives any hint of its stylistic independence. The licentious Michelan-

186. G. B. Vaccarini, Palazzo del Municipio, Catania, exterior.

gelesque capitals, the broken, obliquely projecting window aedicules, and the elliptical balustrade openings of the *piano nobile* all betray Vaccarini's impatience with academic orthodoxy.

The boldest, most flamboyant examples of Sicilian eighteenth-century architecture are the creations of Rosario Gagliardi, who was active from 1721–1770 in the smaller southeastern towns of Noto, Modica, and Ragusa-Ibla. The church of S. Giorgio in Ragusa-Ibla (187) is one of his most impressive commissions and the one in which his participation is most thoroughly documented. It was begun in 1744 and was completed by 1775, except for the uncomplementary Neo-Classical cupola that was added in 1820.

Rising above a tall flight of steps, the church looms majestically over a long, narrow piazza. The grandeur of the setting is matched by the lofty proportions and tectonic exuberance of the exterior elevation. The facade's forceful upward thrust ends in a very Sicilian third-story belfry, topped by an onion dome. As Vaccarini did at Catania Cathedral, Gagliardi grouped clusters of columns around the central bay of the two lower stories. Here, however, they are placed closer together, and arranged in parallel rather than radial planes, making the composition seem tighter and more concentrated. The slight curvature of the central bay—a Gagliardi trademark—gives the composition movement without upsetting its stability. The relief sculpture around the portal and on the scroll-buttresses at the sides is nearly as dense, although not nearly as profuse, as that commonly seen on the facades of Apulian churches. It is typical of Sicilian architecture that the ornament never competes with the tectonic membering for expressive primacy.

Equally Sicilian is Gagliardi's grandiloquent use of the classical language. Like Andrea Palma, he exaggerated the rhetoric of the Roman Baroque while simplifying its grammar for a provincial taste. The change is apparent in a comparison of S. Giorgio with Ss. Vincenzo ed Anastasio (77), the Roman church that it most closely resembles. Martino Longhi's facade, begun a century earlier, represents an effort to create, but then minimalize, a functional disparity between two pairs of superimposed columnar triads. One instinctively questions the logic of its structure, and anything more than a cursory examination becomes a rigorous visual exercise. The church at Ragusa-Ibla also uses a system of superimposed triads, but the link between columnar tiers is exact and predictable. There is little more to the elevation than first meets the eye.

187. Rosario Gagliardi, S. Giorgio, Ragusa-Ibla, facade.

188. Rosario Gagliardi, S. Chiara, Noto, interior.

Gagliardi's interiors usually complement the architecture of his exteriors, but at Ragusa-Ibla, the church was built on a traditional Latin Cross plan with a rather flat, pedestrian elevation. A group of small centralized churches that he built in the town of Noto are more interesting. Their plans include the basic alternatives of the oval, Greek Cross, and elongated octagon. At S. Domenico, built on a Greek Cross plan, Gagliardi proved his ability to handle stucco ornament with unexpected Rococo delicacy. His more characteristic robust, mature style is best seen, however, in the oval church of S. Chiara (188), completed in 1758.

Here Gagliardi introduced the geometric innovation of constructing the church not from a regular, "rounded" oval as was generally done elsewhere, but from a narrower, more pointed ellipse.[17] In effect he made the church more "longitudinal," strengthening the axis leading from the rectangular narthex to the attached chancel. The interior of S. Chiara is also unusual in that Gagliardi placed sixteen free-standing columns inside the elliptical shell. Like those on his facade at Ragusa-Ibla, these smooth-shafted columns give an impression of forceful

292

strength that contrasts with the more festive and relaxed elevation above. Here again, he emphasized verticality by inserting a tall attic, which houses a nun's gallery, between the main story and the vault. Because the nave's only figural sculpture is placed above this attic zone, the interior appears even taller than it actually is. By stretching both the vertical and horizontal axes, Gagliardi cleverly varied the traditional, if now somewhat outdated, configuration of the oval church. In this respect, the architect's vivacious style—which at S. Chiara originally included a warmer color scheme and a fine maiolica pavement—was a sort of sunset of the true Baroque.

The town of Noto is also interesting for its urban planning.[18] After the original town was demolished by the earthquake, a completely new settlement was begun on another site a few miles closer to the sea. The master plan, attributed to a Jesuit named Fra Angelo Italia, called for an integrated, gridlike layout of streets, squares, and major buildings, which is thought to be based on Scamozzi's design for an ideal city published in Venice in 1615.[19] Despite its modest size and

189. Vincenzo Sinatra, Palazzo del Municipio, Noto, exterior.

sparse population—at the time of the earthquake, there were 12,000 inhabitants—Noto soon became one of Italy's finest, most thoroughly Baroque towns. The planner's design was realized by talented architects like Rosario Gagliardi, who used a local pale yellow stone that is exceptionally beautiful.

During the three-quarters of a century it took to rebuild Noto, local architects were gradually turning away from the flamboyance of the Sicilian Baroque style. The most prominent buildings in its main square, the Piazza del Municipio, which were finished toward the end of the town's reconstruction, are more sober and restrained. The facade of the cathedral on the north side of the square seems unusually cosmopolitan for its provincial location. Its sources can even be traced to Mansart's church of Notre-Dame at Versailles, a reminder of France's widespread cultural influence in Sicily around this time.[20] A new conservatism can also be seen in the Palazzo del Municipio, or Town Hall (189), directly across the square. It was begun in 1742 by Gagliardi's nephew and pupil, Vincenzo Sinatra, but the second story was not added until the twentieth century. The original plan called for the lower elevation to be domed in the manner of a French garden palace, a building type that was then becoming fashionable all over Europe.

Like the Bishop's Palace in Lecce (181), which it perhaps only coincidentally resembles, the lower story of the Town Hall consists of an arcaded loggia rising from a low rusticated base. Sinatra's chief innovation was to integrate curved segments at the center and corners of the long straight facade. The concave corners are especially successful in orienting the building to the diagonal perspectives of those entering the piazza from the east or west. Beneath the ever-present Sicilian charm, however, the sparseness of ornament and the discipline of the design's organization betray the important change that was taking place.

By Sicilian standards the cathedral and the Town Hall seem restrained, yet both reflect the same change in artistic sensibility that was occurring throughout Italy at this time. In fact, several architects of Sinatra's generation had begun to take a nationalistic interest in the Greek antiquities of Sicily, a foretaste of the antiquarianism that was soon to captivate all of Europe. Before long, such blatantly Neo-Classic buildings as Dufourny's Entrance Pavilion of the Palermo Botanical Gardens of 1789 would issue in the new age.[21] But nowhere in Italy did the Baroque die so graceful and dignified a death.

Notes

Chapter 1

1. See, for example, O. Kurz, "Barocco, storia di una parola," *Lettere italiane* XII (1960), 414–44, and B. Migliorini, "Etimologia e storia del termine 'barocco'" in *Manierismo, barocco, rococo: concetti e termini,* Convegno internazionale, Rome, 1960 [1962], 39–49.

2. The opposition between Classicism and the Baroque is central to the organization of the standard reference book for Italian Baroque art, R. Wittkower's *Art and Architecture in Italy 1600–1750,* 1st ed. (Baltimore: 1958). The limitations of this viewpoint are discussed by J. R. Martin, *Baroque* (New York: 1977), 33–34. In painting and sculpture, the issues are further clouded by the existence of strong naturalistic currents as well.

3. M. Lyttleton, *Baroque Architecture in Classical Antiquity* (Ithaca: 1974). On D'Ors and other aspects of the terminological problem, see A. Blunt, *Some Uses and Misuses of the Terms Baroque and Rococo as Applied to Architecture* (London: 1973).

4. On rhetorical theory and the arts, see H. J. Jensen, *The Muses' Concord: Literature, Music, and the Visual Arts in the Baroque Age* (Bloomington: 1976), esp. chapter 6. B. Contardi has written on the subject in his little book *La retorica e l'architettura del barocco* (Rome: 1978), as have G. C. Argan and G. Dorfles in *Retorica e barocco* (Rome: 1955).

5. Bernini's remark was part of a longer memorandum on the construction of the Piazza of St. Peter's, transcribed by T. Kitao, *Circle and Oval in the Square of St. Peter's* (New York: 1974), 98 note 40.

6. Such was the view, for example, of Mark Twain, in *The Innocents Abroad* (New York: 1869), chapter 25.

7. Anthony Blunt, in *Uses and Misuses of the Terms Baroque and Rococo,* p. 28, incomprehensibly denied the existence of a Rococo architecture in Italy by insisting that only buildings inspired by French prototypes can be called by that name. The term is usefully adopted by N. A. Mallory in *Roman Rococo Architecture from Clement XI to Benedict XIV* (New York and London: 1977). The term Ultra-Baroque seems to have been first used by B. Bevan in *History of Spanish Architecture* (London: 1938), 165, and was adopted by E. Kaufmann, *Architecture in the Age of Reason* (Cambridge: 1955), 86. It has not met with universal acceptance, however.

8. P. Mezzanotte, "L'architettura da F. M. Ricchino al Ruggeri," in *Storia di Milano*, vol. XI, part VIII (Milan: 1958), 441.

9. On the earlier history of the Academy, see H. Hager's introduction to the exhibition catalogue *Architectural Fantasy and Reality, Drawings from the Accademia Nazionale di San Luca in Rome* (University Park: 1982).

10. On the formation of the academies and professional practice, see N. Pevsner, *Academies of Art, Past and Present* (Cambridge: 1940), esp. chapter 3.

11. Andrea Palladio's *Four Books of Architecture* (Venice: 1570), and Vincenzo Scamozzi's *L'idea della architettura universale* (Venice: 1615), are, of course, exceptions, but their influence was generally confined outside the Italian peninsula. On fifteenth- through eighteenth-century architectural theory in general, see D. Wiebenson, ed., *Architectural Theory and Practice from Alberti to Ledoux* (Chicago: 1982).

12. The most recent treatment, albeit with greater emphasis on the immediately preceding period, is C. Wilkinson, "The New Professionalism in the Renaissance," in *The Architect* (New York: 1977), chapter 5. Informative too is P. Waddy, "The Design and Designers of Palazzo Barberini," *Journal of the Society of Architectural Historians* 35 (1976), 151–85. The fundamental study, however, remains O. Pollak, "Der Architekt in XVII Jahrhundert in Rom," *Zeitschrift für Geschichte der Architektur* III (1909–10), 201–210.

13. The best source of information on the tools and methods of early construction is N. Zabaglia, *Castelli e ponti di Niccola Zabaglia con alcune ingegnose pratiche e con la descrizione del trasporto dell'obelisco Vaticano coll' aggiunta di macchine posteriori e premesse le notizie storiche dello stesso Zabaglia*, 3d ed. (Rome: 1824). Zabaglia, who lived from 1664 to 1750, was head of the carpentry workshop at the Basilica of St. Peter's.

14. See G. Bauer, "From Architecture to Scenography: The Full-Scale Model in the Baroque Tradition," in *La scenografia barocca*, A. Schnapper, ed. (Bologna: 1982), 141–150.

15. In the diary of Pope Alexander VII, Carlo Rainaldi and Pietro da Cortona are cited as having shown models of prospective buildings to the pontiff. R. Krautheimer and R. Jones, "The Diary of Alexander VII," *Römisches Jahrbuch für Kunstgeschichte* 15 (1975), 199–233, entries 334 and 564.

16. *Le lettere di Luigi Vanvitelli della Biblioteca Palatina di Caserta*, 3 vols. (Galatina: 1976–77). A good synopsis of his views of the architectural scene is given in J. Pinto's review in *The Burlington Magazine* 120 (1978), 170. For Italian artistic patronage in general, see F. Haskell, *Patrons and Painters: Art and Society in Baroque Italy* (New York: 1963).

17. The importance of stucco is discussed by N. A. Mallory, *Roman Rococo Architecture*, and P. Portoghesi, *Roma barocca* (Cambridge: 1970), 371, who says that "the pontificate of Benedict XIII might be defined as the pontificate of stucco." This is not to suggest that stucco was unknown in earlier periods; it occasionally was used in antiquity and in the Renaissance as well.

18. On color in eighteenth-century architecture, see E. Lavagnino, "Il colore di Roma nel settecento," *Palladio* 14 (1964), 83–84.

19. A fine analysis of Vatican finances during this period is J. Delumeau's "Rome: Political and Administrative Centralization in the Papal State in the Sixteenth Century," in *The Late Italian Renaissance 1525–1630*, E. Cochran, ed. (London: 1970), 287–304.

20. The situation is discussed in C. Cipolla, "The Decline of Italy: The Case

of a Fully Matured Economy," *Economic History Review* 5–6 (1952–53), 178–87.

21. The effects on artistic patronage are treated by F. Haskell, *Patrons and Painters*, 149f.

22. J. Delumeau, *Vie économique et sociale de Rome dans la seconde moitié du XVI siècle*, vol. I (Paris: 1957), 359.

23. On this notion, see D. Sella, "European Industries, 1500–1700," in *The Fontana Economic History of Europe: The Sixteenth and Seventeenth Centuries*, C. Cipolla ed. (Glasgow: 1974), 354–426, esp. 369–372.

24. The statistic is cited by Delumeau in *The Late Italian Renaissance*, 298f.

25. On the Council of Trent and religious art, see A. Blunt, *Artistic Theory in Italy 1450–1600* (Oxford: 1940), chapter 5.

26. The churches are described in a guidebook published for the Jubilee of 1725. O. Panciroli–F. Posterla, *Roma sacra e moderna* (Rome: 1725). For population statistics, see F. Cerasoli, *Censimento della populazione di Roma dall'anno 1600 al 1739* (Rome: 1891).

27. A discussion of "the passions of the soul" in seventeenth-century Europe is found in Martin, *Baroque*, chapter 3.

28. On bible study in Italy, see E. Eisenstein, *The Printing Press as an Agent of Change* (Cambridge: 1982), 347–349, 411–412, and K. Foster, "Italian Versions," in *The Cambridge History of the Bible*, vol. III (Cambridge: 1963), 110–113, 358–360.

29. The low rate of literacy among laymen of the period is discussed by C. Cipolla, *Literacy and Development in the West* (London: 1969).

30. The propagandistic use of papal medals during the Baroque period was the theme of the exhibition catalogue by N. Whitman with J. Varriano, *Roma Resurgens: Papal Medals from the Age of the Baroque* (Ann Arbor: 1983).

Chapter 2

1. Vignola's two earlier churches were S. Andrea in Via Flaminia and S. Anna dei Palafreneri. For a general survey of Roman church planning at this time, see M. J. Lewine, "The Roman Church Interior, 1527–1580," unpublished Ph.D. thesis, Columbia University, 1960. For Il Gesù, see J. Ackerman, "The Gesù in the Light of Contemporary Church Design," in *Baroque Art: The Jesuit Contribution* (New York: 1972).

2. A detailed study of the text is provided by E. C. Voelker, "Charles Borromeo's *Instructiones Fabricae et Supellectilis Ecclesiasticae*, 1577," Ph.D. dissertation, Syracuse University, 1977.

3. The derivations from the two designs are the subject of an analysis by N. Whitman, "Roman Tradition and the Aedicular Facade," *Journal of the Society of Architectural Historians* 29 (1970), 108–23.

4. A survey of the architecture of this period is given by L. Heydenreich and W. Lotz, *Architecture in Italy 1400–1600* (Baltimore: 1974), chapter 23, and by H. Hibbard, *Carlo Maderno and Roman Architecture 1580–1630* (University Park: 1971), chapter 2.

5. The most thorough treatment of Sixtus' planning remains S. Gideon, *Space, Time and Architecture*, 4th ed. (Cambridge: 1963), 75–106.

6. The basic study of Mascarino is J. Wasserman, *Ottaviano Mascarino and his Drawings in the Accademia Nazionale di S. Luca* (Rome: 1966).

7. See H. Hibbard, "The Early History of S. Andrea della Valle," *The Art Bulletin* 63 (1961), 289–318.

8. Hibbard, *Carlo Maderno,* is the standard monograph on the architect.

9. On villas as an architectural type, see C. Franck, *The Villas of Frascati* (London: 1966), and D. Coffin, *The Villa in the Life of Renaissance Rome* (Princeton: 1979). For the program here, see R. Steinberg, "The Iconography of the teatro dell'acqua at the Villa Aldobrandini," *The Art Bulletin* 47 (1965), 453–463.

10. On matters of attribution pertaining to the palace, see Hibbard, *Carlo Maderno,* and Waddy, "The Design and Designers."

Chapter 3

1. Hibbard, *Carlo Maderno,* 88.

2. On Borromini's personality, see R. Wittkower, "Francesco Borromini, his Character and Life," in *Studies in the Italian Baroque* (London: 1975), chapter 8. For general studies of Borromini's architecture, see P. Portoghesi, *Borromini* (London: 1968); A. Blunt, *Borromini* (Cambridge: 1979); and J. Connors, "Francesco Borromini," in the *Macmillan Encyclopedia of Architects,* vol. I (London: 1982), 248–260.

3. The basic study of the church remains the Ph.D. dissertation of Leo Steinberg written in 1958–59 and recently revised and reprinted: *Borromini's San Carlo alle Quattro Fontane: A Study in Multiple Form and Architectural Symbolism* (New York and London: 1977). See also the review by J. Connors in *Journal of the Society of Architectural Historians* 38 (1979), 283–85. Further documentation of the church's construction has recently been published by M. Bonavia et al., "San Carlo alle Quattro Fontane: le fasi della costruzione, le techniche caratteristiche, i prezzi del cantiere," in *Conoscenza dell'architettura barocca* (Ricerca di storia dell'arte, no. 20, 1983, 11–38).

4. Steinberg, in *Borromini's San Carlo,* sees the symbolism evolving from the more complex geometric figures of the cross, the octagon, and the oval.

5. An appendix in Steinberg's *Borromini's San Carlo,* 252–260, gives a history of the use of the motif in the periods from antiquity through the Renaissance, citing some 22 examples of its occurrence before Borromini.

6. Contemporary evidence for the symbolism of the bee is given in J. Scott, "S. Ivo alla Sapienza and Borromini's Symbolic Language," *Journal of the Society of Architectural Historians* 41 (1982), 294–317, esp. 298–302.

7. Sebastiano Serlio, for example, published a woodcut plan of a Roman temple just outside Rome that has a similarly shaped apsidal projection. *Tutte l'opere d'architettura et prospettiva* (Venice: 1619), 62. During the later Middle Ages, the shape also appears in the right doorway of the south transept of Chartres Cathedral, and in the spandrels of the Loggia dei Lanzi in Florence.

8. The fullest and most recent discussion of the stucco reliefs is Scott, "S. Ivo," 313–316.

9. In an allusion that apparently was directed towards Borromini, Bernini is said to have remarked that "it is better to be a bad Catholic than a good heretic." F. Baldinucci, *The life of Bernini,* 1st ed., 1682; trans. C. Enggass (University Park: 1966), 82. Filippo Juvarra later called Borromini "the Calvin of architecture."

10. This is the view of J. Scott, "S. Ivo," 302–312, who also provides a summary of the earlier interpretations of the lantern.

11. The first to suggest that Borromini's spire may have been derived from a conch shell was P. Portoghesi, "Borromini decoratore," *Bolletino d'arte* 40 (1955), 28–29, and the idea has been revived by Scott, "S. Ivo," 307–308.

12. L. Neppi, *Palazzo Spada* (Rome: 1975), 147, 175–82, and 271f. Neppi's second thoughts on Bitonto's role are given in "Punti di vista sulla prospettiva Spada," *Bolletino d'arte,* serie VI (1983), no. 22, 105–118, esp. 110f.

13. G. B. Montano, *Scelta di vari tempietti antichi* (Rome: 1624), plate 3. See also G. Zander, "Le invenzione architettoniche di G. B. Montano," *Quaderni,* 30 (1958), 1–21 (part I); 49–50 (1962), 1–32 (part II).

14. For this commission, see J. Connors, *Borromini and the Roman Oratory* (Cambridge: 1980).

15. The top story was added in 1704. The building's original appearance is recorded in a print by G. B. Falda made in 1665. G. Antonazzi, *Il palazzo di Propaganda* (Rome: 1979), figure 41.

16. On the chapel by Bernini, see F. Borsi, *Bernini architetto* (Milan: 1980), 63–64, 301–302.

17. Connors, *Borromini,* 137, has observed that Borromini derived his elevation from Palladio's Palazzo Valmarana in Vicenza, and his plan from the same architect's church of the Redentore in Venice.

18. Borromini's geometry has been the subject of studies by Steinberg, *Borromini's San Carlo,* and R. Wittkower, *Gothic vs. Classic* (New York: 1974), chapter 5. J. Connors, "Bernini's S. Andrea al Quirinale: Payments and Planning," *Journal of the Society of Architectural Historians* 41 (1982), 25, has further contrasted Borromini's geometry with that of Bernini by saying "If Bernini's plans are generated from centers, Borromini's are generated both from centers and epicenters, or points on the periphery of one geometrical figure that generate another figure further out."

Chapter 4

1. The basic study of Bernini's sculpture remains R. Wittkower, *Gian Lorenzo Bernini, The Sculptor of the Roman Baroque,* 1st ed. (London: 1955), 3rd ed. (1981). For Bernini's activity as a whole, see H. Hibbard, *Bernini* (New York: 1965), and H. Brauer and R. Wittkower, *Die Zeichnungen des Gianlorenzo Bernini,* 2 vols. (Berlin: 1931). For his architecture, see F. Borsi, *Bernini architetto* (Milan: 1980).

2. G. Bauer, "Gian Lorenzo Bernini: The Development of an Architectural Iconography," Ph.D. dissertation, Princeton University, 1974, 13, has demonstrated that the upper aedicule was originally much deeper than it presently appears. See also the recent article by C. Baggio et al., "Considerazioni sulla facciata di S. Bibiana in Roma," *Quaderni,* serie XXVII, fasc. 169–74 (1982), 61–68.

3. The form and iconography of the baldachin have been studied by I. Lavin, *Bernini and the Crossing of St. Peter's* (New York: 1968) and H. Thelen, *Zur Entstehungsgeschichte der Hochaltar-Architektur von St. Peter in Rom* (Berlin: 1967). The relative merits of these two books are discussed by H.

Hibbard, "Recent Books on Earlier Baroque Architecture," *The Art Bulletin* 55 (1973), 127–135.

4. The fullest study of the piazza and colonnade is T. Kitao, *Circle and Oval in the Square of Saint Peter's* (New York: 1974).

5. The most likely source for the colonnades is the Roman Sanctuary of Fortune at Palestrina whose ruins were reconstructed by Pietro da Cortona in 1636 and were illustrated in a scholarly study of the site published in 1655. For the plan of the piazza, H. W. Kruft, "The Origin of the Oval in Bernini's Piazza S. Pietro," *The Burlington Magazine* 121 (1979), 796–801, argues that the source was a recent hypothetical reconstruction of the Circus of Nero which stood behind St. Peter's.

6. The fountain on the right was designed by Carlo Maderno for a nearby location and that on the left was only added during the pontificate of Clement X (1670–76) who had to enlarge the aqueduct from Lago di Bracciano to supply the fountains with sufficient water.

7. See chapter 1, p. 14. Haskell, *Patrons and Painters,* 149ff gives further evidence on popular opinion of the time.

8. The most recent discussion of the Scala Regia is in I. Lavin et al., *Drawings by Gianlorenzo Bernini from the Museum der Bildenden Künste, Leipzig* (Princeton: 1981), 241–246.

9. Baldinucci, *The Life of Bernini,* 80.

10. On S. Andrea, see J. Connors, "Bernini's S. Andrea al Quirinale," and C. Frommel, "S. Andrea al Quirinale: genesi e struttura," in *Gian Lorenzo Bernini architetto e l'architettura europea del Sei-Settecento,* M. Fagiolo and G. Spagnesi eds., vol. 1 (Rome: 1983), 211–253.

11. Haskell, *Patrons and Painters,* 86–88, provides some interesting background on the patronage.

12. Serlio's woodcut illustration of an oval temple (*Tutte l'opere d'architettura,* folio 204r) seems to have been especially important in Bernini's formulation of the plan.

13. The photograph illustrated here minimizes the contrast in actual light levels. On the role of hidden lighting in Bernini's architectural ensembles, see I. Lavin, *Bernini and the Unity of the Visual Arts,* vol. 1 (New York: 1980), 33–36.

14. See chapter 5, note 2.

15. As, for instance, Carlo Lombardi's two facades of S. Prisca and S. Francesca Romana, built ca. 1600 and 1608–1615, respectively.

16. Bernini's use of this compositional type is the subject of T. Kitao's article "Bernini's Church Facades: Methods of Design and the *Contrapposti,*" *Journal of the Society of Architectural Historians* 24 (1965), 263–84.

17. Connors, "Bernini's S. Andrea," figure 11. The wall appears on the papal chirograph of October 26, 1658, which authorized the church's construction. It was designed in response to Alexander VII's request that the Jesuit novices be guarded from street-life outside.

18. In his biography of Bernini, *The Life of Bernini,* 78–79, Baldinucci quotes the artist as saying that the most important painter of all time was Raphael, whom he called "a bottomless vessel that collected waters from all the springs." On Bernini and the Renaissance, see P. Askew, "The Relation of Bernini's Architecture to the Architecture of the High Renaissance and of Michelangelo," *Marsyas* 5 (1950), 39–61, and C. Thoenes, "Bernini architetto

tra Palladio e Michelangelo," in *Gian Lorenzo Bernini architetto,* 105–134.

19. On the problem of orientation in centralized churches of the Renaissance, see R. Wittkower, *Architectural Principles in the Age of Humanism,* part I (New York: 1965).

20. Bernini's efforts to restore the Pantheon are discussed in Borsi, *Bernini architetto,* esp. 96–101.

21. The most recent study of the church is T. Marder, "La chiesa del Bernini ad Ariccia," in *Gian Lorenzo Bernini architetto,* 255–277.

22. See preceding note 16 for further reference.

23. Bernini's projects for the Louvre are reproduced and discussed in Borsi, *Bernini architetto,* 132–38 and 334–335. The projects of Cortona and Rainaldi are discussed in K. Noehles, "Die Louvre-Projecte von Pietro da Cortona und Carlo Rainaldi," *Zeitschrift für Kunstgeschichte* 24 (1961), 40–74.

24. Two articles by R. Berger treat the question of French influence in greater depth: "Antoine Le Pautre and the Motif of the Drum-Without-Dome," *Journal of the Society of Architectural Historians* 25 (1966), 165–180 and "Louis Le Vau's Chateau du Raincy," *Architectura* 6 (1976), 36–46. Wittkower, *Art and Architecture,* 3rd rev. ed. (1982), 527, note 90 does not agree that Bernini was so indebted to French sources.

25. Wittkower, *Art and Architecture,* 189.

26. See E. Kieven, "Revival del Berninismo durante il Pontificato di Clemente XII," and H. Hager, "Gian Lorenzo Bernini e la ripresa dell'alto barocco nell'Architettura del Settecento romano," in *Gian Lorenzo Bernini architetto,* vol. II, 459–468; 469–496.

Chapter 5

1. An extremely thorough study of the church is K. Noehles, *La chiesa di Ss. Luca e Martina nell'opera di Pietro da Cortona* (Rome: 1970).

2. It is not certain from the drawings published by Noehles, *ibid.,* figures 61, 84a, 91, that Cortona intended from the beginning to stucco the vaults and dome with both ribs and coffers. Documents published by the same author (docs. 94, 123a) indicate that the stuccowork only began in 1652 and was finished in 1679. In any event, Cortona had employed a very similar scheme as early as ca. 1640 in the Chapel of S. Filippo Neri in S. Maria in Vallicella (Noehles, *ibid.,* figure 217 and p. 156 note 307). J. Connors, in "Pietro da Cortona," the *Macmillan Encyclopedia of Architects,* vol. I, 459, claims that "the rib system of the half-domes of the apses . . . is based on Michelangelo's famous motif in the apses of St. Peter's, studied and used by all Baroque architects."

3. For Buontalenti and Florentine Mannerism, see L. Heydenreich and W. Lotz, *Architecture in Italy 1400–1600* (Baltimore: 1974), chapter 27.

4. See C. Coffey, "Pietro da Cortona's Project for the Church of San Firenze in Florence," *Mitteilungen des Kunsthistorischen Institutes in Florenz* 22 (1978), 85–118.

5. See R. Krautheimer, *The Rome of Alexander VII (1655–1667)* (Princeton: 1985).

6. The most extensive study of the complex is H. Ost, "Studien zu Pietro da Cortonas Umbau von S. Maria della Pace," *Römisches Jahrbuch für Kunstgeschichte* 13 (1971), 231–285.

7. Cortona was not unfamiliar with theatre and set design for earlier he had built the theatre at the Palazzo Barberini, and throughout his career he was engaged in the construction of temporary stage and festival designs.

8. Dúperac's reconstruction of the caldarium of Diocletian's Bath includes such a feature (Ost, "Studien," figure 45). Ost's article includes a section on the iconography of the rounded portico (*ibid.*, 269–279).

9. See R. Krautheimer, "Alexander VII and Piazza Colonna," *Römisches Jahrbuch für Kunstgeschichte* 20 (1982), 193–208.

10. See the discussion of S. Agnese in Piazza Navona in chapter 6.

11. There is also a resemblance to Cortona's reconstruction of the ancient Sanctuary of Fortune at Palestrina, reproduced in Noehles, *La chiesa*, figure 26.

12. See chapter 4, note 23.

13. On the attribution of the small domes of St. Peter's, see Heydenreich/ Lotz, *Architecture in Italy*, 256–257.

Chapter 6

1. For a discussion of the more conservative architects active in Rome, see A. Blunt, "Roman Baroque Architecture: The Other Side of the Medal," *Art History* 3 (1980), 61–80.

2. Other facades of two equal stories include S. Luigi dei Francesi by Giacomo Della Porta and Domenico Fontana and the directly adjacent front of Ss. Domenico e Sisto by Nicola Torriani.

3. For a discussion of some of Soria's lesser contemporaries, see P. Portoghesi, *Roma barocca* (Cambridge: 1970), 539–53.

4. For Longhi, see J. Varriano, "The Architecture of Martino Longhi the Younger," *Journal of the Society of Architectural Historians* 30 (1971), 101–118.

5. Sculpted reliefs were originally intended on the panels of the lower story side bays.

6. See the exhaustive monograph on the church by G. Eimer, *La fabbrica di S. Agnese in Navona*, 2 vols. (Innsbruck: 1970–71).

7. And there are recollections of the antique as well. Two imaginative reconstructions in G. B. Montano's *Scelta di vari tempietti antichi* (Rome: 1624), plates 73 and 92, are prototypical of the facade.

8. On Baroque attitudes towards the transcendental, see R. Assunto, *Infinita contemplazione* (Naples: 1979).

9. See R. Wittkower, "Carlo Rainaldi and Roman Architecture of the Full Baroque," *The Art Bulletin* 19 (1937), 278–293.

10. A. Del Bufalo, *G. B. Contini e la tradizione del tardomanierismo tra '600 e '700* (Rome: 1982), plates LXVIII and LXIX, compares Rainaldi's plan with those of S. Carlo ai Catinari and S. Francesco da Paola in Rome, but that of S. Maria in Campitelli is more forcefully longitudinal.

11. The Glory of angels was only added in 1727 and the fresco above in 1925. The coloristic contrast is greater than it appears in the black and white photograph.

12. Wittkower, *Art and Architecture*, p. 282, sees this type of facade as originating in northern Italy, a view opposed by N. Whitman, "Roman Tradition and the Aedicular Facade," *Journal of the Society of Architectural Historians* 29 (1970), 108–123, who considers the examples of northern Italy as

only "a catalyst to the vigorous, continually evolving tradition in Rome that went back at least to Vignola and Della Porta."

13. The drawing is illustrated in Eimer, *La fabbrica*, vol. 2, figure 307.

14. The most exhaustive study of the churches is H. Hager, "Zur Planung und Baugeschichte der Zwillingskirchen auf der Piazza del Popolo," *Römisches Jahrbuch für Kunstgeschichte* 11 (1967–68), 191–306. An abbreviated version is given in A. Braham and H. Hager, *Carlo Fontana: The Drawings at Windsor Castle* (London: 1977), 64–65.

15. F. Trevisani, "Carlo Rainaldi nella chiesa di Gesù e Maria," *Storia dell'arte* 11 (1971), 163–171.

16. On De Rossi, see G. Spagnesi, *Giovanni Antonio De Rossi, architetto romano* (Rome: 1964). Blunt, "Roman Baroque Architecture," 71, calls De Rossi "the chief protagonist of the anti-Baroque movement."

17. Fontana's students included Fischer von Erlach, Lukas von Hildebrandt, the Asam Brothers, Matthaeus Pöppelmann, James Gibbs, and Thomas Archer.

18. He assisted in the construction of S. Maria della Pace, the Palazzo Chigi, and the twin churches in the Piazza del Popolo.

19. H. Hager, "Le facciate dei Ss. Faustino e Giovita e di S. Biagio in Campitelli a Roma," *Commentari* 23 (1972), 261–271 points to the upper story of the Palazzo Barberini and the portal of the Ospedale di S. Spirito as probable sources for the motif.

20. For Doge Giovanni Cornaro. Reproduced in Wittkower, *Bernini*, figure 63.

21. See H. Hager, "La facciata di San Marcello al Corso," *Commentari* 24 (1973), 58–73. In 1644, Martino Longhi the Younger designed a concave facade, that remained unexecuted, for S. Giovanni Calibita in Rome. J. Varriano, "Martino Longhi the Younger and the Facade of S. Giovanni Calibita in Rome," *The Art Bulletin* 52 (1970), 71–74.

22. This is the view of C. Elling, *Rome: The Biography of her Architecture from Bernini to Thorwaldsen*, English trans. (Boulder: 1975), 273–274.

23. See Braham and Hager, *Carlo Fontana*, pp. 112–125.

24. The project is discussed in greater detail by H. Hager, "Carlo Fontana's Project for a Church in Honour of the 'Ecclesia Triumphans' in the Colosseum, Rome," *Journal of the Warburg and Courtauld Institutes* 36 (1973), 319–337.

Chapter 7

1. On the use of the term Rococo, see chapter 1, note 7. For further information on eighteenth-century architecture, see N. A. Mallory, *Roman Rococo Architecture from Clement XI to Benedict XIV* (New York and London, 1977); P. Portoghesi, *Roma barocca*, English trans. (Cambridge, 1970); and C. Elling, *Rome*.

2. See two studies by M. Rotili, *Filippo Raguzzini e il rococo romano* (Rome: 1951) and *Filippo Raguzzini nel terzo centenario della nascita* (Naples: 1982).

3. The commission is fully discussed by D. M. Habel, "Piazza S. Ignazio, Rome, in the 17th and 18th Centuries," *Architectura* 11 (1981), 31–65.

4. The composition is derived from the larger facade of S. Croce in Gerusalemme (104).

5. See W. Lotz, "Die Spanische Treppe," *Römisches Jahrbuch für Kunstgeschichte* 12 (1969), 39–94.

6. One thinks of the now destroyed Porto di Ripetta on the banks of the

Tiber in Rome. T. Marder, "The Porto di Ripetta in Rome," *Journal of the Society of Architectural Historians* 39 (1980), 28–56.

7. Galilei's facade has been related to Henry Aldrich's Church of All Saints, Oxford (1706–1710), to Hawksmoor's Blenheim Palace (1705–1724), and to unspecified works by Christopher Wren. The most recent study of the architect is E. Kieven, "Alessandro Galilei," in the *Macmillan Encyclopedia of Architects,* vol. II, 145–149.

8. The facade is often jointly attributed to Passalacqua and Gregorini, but in a recent study, E. A. Plummer, "Santa Croce in Gerusalemme, Rome: A Drawing and an Attribution," *Journal of the Society of Architectural Historians* 43 (1984), 356–363, minimizes the role played by Passalacqua.

9. This is the observation of C. Elling, *Rome,* 309–310, who, in general, is quite effective in interpreting late Baroque buildings in their urban context.

10. On the Trevi Fountain, see J. Pinto, *The Trevi Fountain* (New Haven: 1985).

11. The foundations for Bernini's project are known from a drawing made in 1685 by Lieven Cruyl. M. and M. Fagiolo dell'Arco, *Bernini* (Rome: 1967) cat. 106.

12. In a comparable fountain of the late sixteenth century, Sixtus V's Acqua Felice in Piazza S. Bernardo, the figure of Moses stands in the central niche of a three-bay triumphal arch.

13. On the Villa Albani and Roman architecture in the second half of the eighteenth century, see C. Meeks, *Italian Architecture 1750–1914* (New Haven: 1966), esp. 56f.

Chapter 8

1. It is noteworthy that Borromeo does not specify the use of a Latin Cross, but rather "una croce allungata." Milanese Early Christian architecture was more often centralized than were comparable churches in Rome. A detailed study of Borromeo's text is cited in chapter 2, note 2.

2. See S. Colombo, *Profilo della architettura religiosa del Seicento: Varese e il suo territorio* (Milan: 1970).

3. See E. Poleggi, *Strada Nuova, una lottizzazione del Cinquecento a Genova* (Genoa: 1968), and for the architecture of Bianco, A. De Raimondo, and L. Müller Profumo, *Bartolomeo Bianco e Genova* (Genoa: 1982).

4. This motif, which can be thought of as a continuous "Palladian motif" or "Serliana," is found in the nave of several Genoese churches as well as in Alessi's courtyard of the Palazzo Marino in Milan (begun 1558) and Tibaldi's courtyard of the Collegio Borromeo in Pavia (begun 1564). In Rome, it appears as something of an oddity in the late sixteenth-century courtyard of the Palazzo Borghese.

5. It is a variation on what is often called an Imperial Staircase. For definitions and precedents in Italy and Spain, see C. Wilkinson, "The Escorial and the Invention of the Imperial Staircase," *The Art Bulletin* 57 (1975), 65–90.

6. The best example is the rejection of Cortona's project of the 1640s for the modernization of the Palazzo Pitti in favor of an unaltered enlargement of the extant building. In 1633, the Grand Duke of Tuscany still planned to adopt G. A. Dosio's project of 1587 for the facade of the Florence Cathedral. It was finally rejected in response to criticism that is was not sufficiently in accord with the medieval portions of the cathedral.

7. The main cornice and the coat of arms over the doorway are nineteenth-century additions. The original appearance of the palace is known from an early eighteenth-century drawing by Ferdinando Ruggieri. L. Ginori Lisci, *I palazzi di Firenze* (Florence: 1972), figure 290.

8. See R. Wittkower, "S. Maria Salute," in *Studies in the Italian Baroque*, 125–152. For the career of Longhena in general, see G. Cristenelli, *Baldassare Longhena*, 2d ed. (Padua: 1978).

9. For the tradition of centralized churches dedicated to the Virgin, see S. Sinding Larsen, "Some Functional and Iconographical Aspects of the Centralized Church in the Italian Renaissance," *Acta ad archaeologiam et artium historiam pertinentia* 2 (1965), 203f.

10. Illustrated in Heydenreich/Lotz, *Architecture in Italy*, figures 103 and 104 and plates 330 and 331.

11. Illustrated in Heydenreich/Lotz, *Architecture in Italy*, plates 242, 239, and 79.

Chapter 9

1. See R. Wittkower, "Guarini the Man," in *Studies in the Italian Baroque*, 177–186, for the architect's biography. The most thorough study of his work is *Guarino Guarini e l'internazionalità del barocco. Atti del convegno internazionale*, 2 vols. (Turin: 1970).

2. Only the churches in Lisbon and Paris were ever built and these were destroyed in 1755 and 1823 respectively.

3. In France, there are Hispano-Moorish vaults at St. Pé-de-Bigorre, St. Croix d'Oloron, and the Hospital-St. Blaise. In the 1660s Guarini designed a project for S. Filippo in Casale Monferrato, a town in Piedmont which has a cross-ribbed vault in the narthex of S. Evasio. However, recently a critic has suggested that Guarini derived his vaults from examples he saw in Spain. J. Ramirez, "Guarino Guarini, Fray Juan Ricci and the 'Complete Salomonic Order,' " *Art History* 4 (1981), 175–181.

4. See R. Wittkower, *Gothic vs. Classic*, chapter 5.

5. The theorist was Juan Caramuel de Lobkowitz, a Spaniard of wide-ranging interests and talents. See W. Oechslin, "Osservazioni su Guarini e Lobkowitz," *Guarino Guarini . . . . Atti*, vol. 1, 573–595.

6. See W. Müller, "The Authenticity of Guarini's Stereotomy in his *Architettura civile*," *Journal of the Society of Architectural Historians* 27 (1968), 202–208, and Wittlower, "Guarini the Man."

7. The scientific literature on the Shroud itself is immense. Of the more than 75 books published on the subject, one of the most interesting is the *Proceedings of the United States Conference of Research on the Shroud of Turin* (Albuquerque: 1977).

8. M. Fagiolo, "La Sindone e l'enigma dell' eclisse," *Guarino Guarini . . . . Atti*, 205–227, figures 10 and 11.

9. R. Pommer, *Eighteenth-Century Architecture in Piedmont* (New York: 1967), 91, note 15, noted that since the scale is measured in *palmi* or *piedi* and not in *trabucchi*, it was probably intended for a site outside the Piedmont region.

10. On this and other matters related to the palace, see A. Lange, Disegni e documenti di Guarino Guarini," *Guarino Guarini . . . . Atti*, vol. 1, 91–344, esp. 166–202.

11. One thinks of Borromini's unexecuted plans for the Palazzo Carpegna in Rome, illustrated in A. Blunt, *Borromini,* 161–169.

Chapter 10

1. See the recent monograph on the church by N. Carboneri, *La Superga* (Turin: 1979). On Juvarra's career in general, see H. Millon, "Filippo Juvarra," in the *Macmillan Encyclopedia of Architects,* vol. II, 519–533.

2. There is some question about the palace's appearance before Juvarra came on the scene. L. Mallé, *Palazzo Madama,* vol. 1 (Turin: 1970), 120–121, reproduces a print of the palace during the funeral of Carlo Emanuele II in 1676 which shows what is probably a temporary facade erected for that occasion that is somewhat prototypical of Juvarra's design.

3. Whether or not the plan of the stairway is derived from Fischer von Erlach's Schloss Klesheim of ca. 1700 is a matter of some debate. H. Aurenhammer, *J.B. Fischer von Erlach* (Cambridge: 1973), 110. Although both Fischer and Juvarra had been students of Carlo Fontana in Rome, they could not have met there, for Fischer left Italy in 1687 when Juvarra was nine years old.

4. Wittkower, *Art and Architecture,* 565, note 46, relates it to the late seventeenth-century Cistercian church of Waldsassen, while Pommer, *Eighteenth-Century Architecture,* 87, prefers to see it springing from more indigenous architectural currents in the Piedmont.

5. There is no documentary evidence for his association with Juvarra except for a reference in his own treatise, *Istruzioni elementari* of 1760, where he refers to Juvarra as his teacher. In 1735, Juvarra left Turin for Spain where he made plans for the Royal Palace in Madrid.

6. See Pommer, *Eighteenth-Century Architecture,* 113 and figures 51–53.

7. Noted by Wittkower, *Art and Architecture,* 565, note 64.

8. Pommer, *Eighteenth-Century Architecture,* 111.

9. Vittone's written analysis of the church in his second treatise, the *Istruzioni diverse* of 1766 is, in fact, preoccupied with the matter of illumination in the interior. See P. Portoghesi, *Bernardo Vittone* (Rome: 1966), 225, cat. 29.

10. But it should be noted that the gilding of the interior was only done in 1769. On the Regency style, see M. Levey and W. Kalnein, *Art and Architecture in Eighteenth-Century France* (Baltimore: 1972), 259–264.

11. The third story of the facade is said not to have been finished until 1891, but since it harmonizes so well with the lower elevation, there is little reason to doubt that it was executed according to Bianchi's original project.

12. For Merlo and a discussion of Milanese eighteenth-century architecture in general, see M. Gatti Perer, *Carlo Giuseppe Merlo architetto* (Milan: 1966) and L. Grassi, *Province del barocco e del rococo* (Milan: 1966).

13. For an excellent profile of life in eighteenth-century Venice, see F. Haskell, *Patrons and Painters,* part III. Wittkower, *Art and Architecture,* 372–373, proposes that it was the intellectual rationalism of Lodoli and others that sealed the fate of the Rococo in Venice. Lodoli, however, rejected classicism in favor of pure functionalism. The best survey of architecture in this period is E. Bassi, *Architettura del Sei e Settecento a Venezia* (Naples: 1962).

14. See R. Wittkower, "Palladio's Influence on Venetian Religious Architecture," in *Palladio and Palladianism* (New York: 1974), 9–22.

15. But they would have known it mainly from plans since they were last in Venice in 1719, just one year after the church was begun.

16. For an assessment of his position in the development of Neo-Classic architecture in Italy, see C. Meeks, *Italian Architecture 1750–1914*, 166–190.

17. The free-standing portico appears in his project for S. Nicolo da Tolentino and the chapel at Maser while the secondary pediment of the attic inspired that of Il Redentore. The interior screen wall is employed at both S. Giorgio Maggiore and Il Redentore.

18. For the architecture of Dotti and the Bolognese eighteenth century in general, see A.M. Matteucci, *Carlo Francesco Dotti* (Bologna: 1969).

19. On the use of the term Ultra-Baroque, see chapter 1, note 7.

20. Matteucci, *Dotti*, 96–97, indicates that the marble revetment of the sanctuary and column bases was done in 1869, while the cupola fresco, gilding, and ochre paint were only added in 1932. The exterior forecourt was, in turn, begun in 1938.

21. See chapter 8, note 5.

22. For his biography, see A.M. Matteucci, D. Lenzi et al., *Architettura, scenografia, pittura di paesaggio: l'arte del Settecento emiliano* (Bologna: 1980), 266.

Chapter 11

1. In 1600, Rome had 5,989 clerics in a population of 110,000. The numbers, however, fluctuate in Naples where there was a clerical population of 11,000 in 1606, 33,000 in 1619, 20,000 in 1685 and 50,000 in 1765. For the effect this had on Neapolitan architecture, see F. Strazzullo, *Edilizia e urbanistica a Napoli dal '500 al '700* (Naples: 1968).

2. The classic study by P. Fogaccia, *Cosimo Fanzago* (Bergamo: 1942), has been largely superseded by A. Blunt, *Neapolitan Baroque and Rococo Architecture* (London: 1975), chapter 3.

3. In this connection it should be noted that Fanzago's early partner and father-in-law was the Florentine sculptor Angelo Landi and that, artistically, Naples was closely tied to Florence during the Renaissance.

4. For S. Maria degli Angeli, see the review by R. Bösel of Blunt's *Neapolitan Baroque and Rococo Architecture* in *Zeitschrift für Kunstgeschichte* 40 (1977), 81–87, esp. 84.

5. Blunt, *Neapolitan Baroque and Rococo Architecture*, 104, attributes the reconstruction to Arcangelo ca. 1709, but this date is certainly too early for the very Rococo exterior, which is dated by contemporary sources ca. 1725. R. Di Stefano, "La chiesa di S. Angelo a Nilo e il Seggio di Nido," *Napoli nobilissima* 4 (1964), 12–21, esp. 18, note 42. On the Guglielmelli, see G. Amirante, "Arcangelo Guglielmelli e l'architettura a Napoli tra la fine del '600 e l'inizio del '700," *Napoli nobilissima* 18 (1979), 88–104. Amirante records no activity by Arcangelo after December 1722 and presumes that he died in 1723.

6. For example, the Ospedale di San Gallicano of 1724–26 where similar bi-chromatic effects appear. M. Rotili, *Filippo Raguzzini e il rococo Romano* (Rome: 1951), plate VII.

7. An inscription referring to a restoration of 1709 is found in the interior, but sources recorded in the article by Di Stefano, cited in note 5 above, make

it clear that the exterior is to be dated in the mid or late 1720s.

8. Palladio constructed an elliptical spiral stairway of this type in the monastery of S. Maria della Carità in Venice. The Di Maio stairway has recently been discussed by C. Thoenes, "A Special Feeling for Stairs: Eighteenth-Century Staircases in Naples," *Daidalos* no. 9 (1983), 77–85. Blunt, *Neapolitan Baroque and Rococo Architecture*, figure 22, mistakenly identifies the plan of the Palazzo De Sinno in Via Roma as that of the Palazzo Di Maio.

9. See R. de Fusco et al., *Luigi Vanvitelli*, Naples, 1973, and G. Hersey, *Architecture, Poetry and Number in the Royal Palace at Caserta* (Cambridge: 1983).

10. Not long ago it was thought that the relationship with Spain was much stronger than we now know it to have been. This is the chief shortcoming of the pioneer study of M.S. Briggs, *In the Heel of Italy* (New York: 1911). The recent study by M. Calvesi and M. Manieri-Elia, *Architettura barocca a Lecce e in terra di Puglia* (Rome: 1971), is the most useful source for all aspects of Apulian architecture. See also M. Paone, *Chiese di Lecce* (Lecce: 1979).

11. Calvesi/Manieri-Elia, *Architettura barocca*, 96, rightly point to Guarini's engravings of the Porta del Po and the churches of S. Lorenzo and S. Filippo Neri in Turin (*Disegni d'architettura*, plates 1, 6, and 15). Carducci's background unfortunately is unknown, and S. Matteo is the only building attributed to him.

12. As, for example, in the work of Rubens and Van Dyck. On the concept of orientalism in the seventeenth century, see J.R. Martin, *Baroque*, 181–185. One should probably not discount the possible influence of Spanish Moorish and Churrigueresque architecture either.

13. For further study, see T. Pellegrino, *Piazza del Duomo a Lecce* (Bari: 1972).

14. The most readily available study in English is A. Blunt, *Sicilian Baroque* (New York: 1968). S. Boscarino, *Sicilia barocca, architettura e città 1610–1760* (Rome: 1981), is especially useful for its treatment of urbanistic developments on the island.

15. The Cathedral has a history almost as long as that of the city itself, which was founded in 733 B.C. Incorporated in the present structure are the remains of a fifth-century B.C. Doric temple which was adapted to Christian usage in the seventh century A.D. The previous facade dated from the Norman period of the eleventh and twelfth centuries.

16. Wittkower, *Art and Architecture*, 560, note 104, has understandably pointed to Austrian prototypes for this feature while Blunt, *Sicilian Baroque*, 18, sees it as an indigenous carry-over from medieval times.

17. An explanation of oval geometry in sixteenth and seventeenth century Italian architecture is given by T. Kitao, *Circle and Oval in the Square of St. Peter's*, 31–35 and 71–73.

18. See S. Tobriner, *The Genesis of Noto, an Eighteenth-Century Sicilian City* (London: 1982).

19. V. Scamozzi, *L'idea della architettura universale* (Venice: 1615).

20. On the Cathedral, whose architect is unknown, see Blunt, *Sicilian Baroque*, 149, note 62. It was begun sometime after 1693 and completed only in 1770. French influence is only to be expected after the Bourbon takeover of Sicily in 1734.

21. See Meeks, *Italian Architecture 1750–1914*, 91–97.

Glossary

Aedicule	A window, door, or niche framed by two columns or pilasters and topped by a pediment.
Apse	A vaulted, semicircular, or polygonal end of a church or chapel.
Arcuation	Construction using arches and vaults (as opposed to posts and lintels).
Atlantes	Sculpted human figures that are used in place of columns. Male figures are called *atlantes* or *telamones;* females, *caryatids.*
Bay	The spatial unit between windows, columns, pilasters, etc., in a building or wall.
Caryatids	Columnar supports sculpted as female figures. See *atlantes.*
Castello	Castle or fortress.
Centralized plan	A symmetrical ground plan such as a circle, octagon, or Greek cross.
Centro	The center of an Italian city.
Chancel	The part of a church containing the principal altar which is reserved for the clergy and choir.
Chiaroscuro	The arrangement or treatment of light and dark in painting and architecture.
Choir	The section of a church, usually the west part of the chancel, where the choir sits.
Crossing	The part of a church where the nave and transept intersect in a cruciform plan.
Dome	A vault, which in seventeenth-century architecture usually consists of a drum, an attic, the vault proper, and a lantern.
Duomo	The principal cathedral of an Italian city or town.
Elevation	The vertical face, or plane, of a building.
Encased pediment	See *pediment.*
Entablature	The upper section of a columnar order, consisting of three horizontal parts: the architrave, frieze, and cornice.
Fabbrica	The office that supervised construction.
Giant order	A classical order that extends through two or more stories.
Greek cross	A cross with four arms of equal length.
Herm	A decorative form that consists of a human half-figure above and a pilaster below.

Hypocycloid	The curve traced by a point on the circumference of a small circle rolling within a larger circle.
Intercolumniation	The distance between columns.
Latin cross	A cross with one arm longer than the other.
Loggia	A roofed gallery open on one or both sides.
Longitudinal plan	A plan that runs longitudinally along an axis.
Martyrium	A commemorative building erected over the grave of a martyr.
Merlon	The solid part of a parapet, alternating with depressed openings.
Narthex	The transverse vestibule of a church.
Nave	The central and principal aisle in a longitudinal church.
Order	The column and its entablature proportioned and decorated in the Doric, Tuscan, Ionic, Corinthian, or Composite modes.
Palazzo	A palace or large city residence.
Palladian motive	An arrangement popularized by Palladio that consists of an arch supported by columns flanked by lower, narrower, trabeated openings.
Pediment	The ornamental gable that crowns a classical building. It is usually triangular, but it may be curved, broken, or set within another, in which case it is called a compound or encased pediment.
Pendentive	A curving triangular surface used as a transition between a square base and a circular dome.
Piano nobile	The main floor of an Italian residence, one flight above the ground floor.
Piedroit	A pier or small pillar which has no base or capital.
Pier	A solid masonry support in an architectural system.
Pilaster	A flattened column projecting slightly from a wall.
Plinth	The base of a column pedestal.
Presbytery	The part of a church reserved for the clergy.
Putto	A cherub. (The plural is *putti*.)
Quadratura	Illusionistic or *trompe l'oeil* renderings of architecture painted on walls or ceilings.
Quoin	A vertical strip of rusticated stones placed at the corners of a building.
Ressaut	The projection and recession of an entablature as it runs above a colonnade.
Roman arch order	A structural system that combines arcuation with trabeation.
Rustication	Masonry in which the joints between blocks are deeply cut and the stone surfaces are rough-hewn.
Sanctuary	The part of a church around the main altar.
Scenographic	A term used to describe a type of architecture which consists of a series of independent spatial units.
Scudo	The standard monetary unit in Baroque Rome. Its equivalent modern value would be a few dollars.
Surround	An ornamental frame, usually of a window or door.
Tabernacle	The receptacle or recess that contains the eucharist.
Tectonic	Structural.

Telamon	A sculpted columnar support in the shape of a male figure. See *atlantes*.
Tholos	A small circular building.
Trabeation	Construction using vertical posts and horizontal lintels (column and entablature) as opposed to arches and vaults.
Transept	The transverse arm of a Latin cross church which runs perpendicular to the nave.
Trompe l'oeil	An artistic rendering that fools the eye.
Villa	A country residence.

Illustration Credits

Abbreviations

A/AR   Alinari/Art Resource, New York
KW   Kevin Wilson
ICCD   Istituto Centrale per il Catalogo e la Documentazione, Rome (formerly Gabinetto Fotografico Nazionale)

1. Nicola Michetti, drawing of Ss. Apostoli under construction, 1708. Royal Library, Windsor Castle (Courtesy H.M. the Queen)
2. Giacomo da Vignola, Il Gesù, Rome, plan (KW)
3. Leon Battista Alberti, S. Andrea, Mantua, interior (Rotalfoto)
4. Giacomo da Vignola, Il Gesù, Rome, interior (ICCD)
5. Giacomo da Vignola, project for the facade of Il Gesù, Rome. Engraving by M. Cartari (from Hibbard, *Maderno*)
6. Giacomo della Porta, Il Gesù, Rome, facade (ICCD)
7. Ottaviano Mascarino, S. Maria in Traspontina, Rome, facade (author)
8. Domenico Fontana, Lateran Palace, Rome, exterior (author)
9. Sangallo and Michelangelo, Farnese Palace, Rome, exterior (A/AR)
10. Domenico Fontana, Sixtine Chapel, S. Maria Maggiore, Rome (A/AR)
11. Rome, Sixtus V's Town Planning (from Gideon, *Space, Time, and Architecture*)
12. Ottaviano Mascarino, S. Salvatore in Lauro, Rome, interior (ICCD)
13. Grimaldi and Della Porta, S. Andrea della Valle, Rome, interior (A/AR)
14. Carlo Maderno, S. Susanna, Rome, facade (ICCD)
15. Maderno and others, St. Peter's, Rome, plan (KW)
16. Carlo Maderno, St. Peter's, Rome, nave (A/AR)
17. Carlo Maderno, St. Peter's Rome, facade (author)
18. Carlo Maderno, project for facade of St. Peter's, Rome. Engraving by M. Greuter (Courtesy Metropolitan Museum of Art, H. B. Dick Fund)
19. Carlo Maderno, facade project for S. Andrea della Valle, Rome. Engraving by V. Regniert (Courtesy Metropolitan Museum of Art, H. B. Dick Fund)
20. Carlo Maderno, Palazzo Mattei, Rome, courtyard (ICCD)
21. Carlo Maderno, Villa Aldobrandini, Frascati, water theatre (A/AR)
22. Maderno and others, Palazzo Barberini, Rome, exterior (ICCD)

23. Borromini, S. Carlo alle Quattro Fontane, Rome, courtyard (ICCD)
24. Borromini, S. Carlo alle Quattro Fontane, Rome, plan (KW)
25. Borromini, S. Carlo alle Quattro Fontane, Rome, interior (A/AR)
26. Borromini, S. Carlo alle Quattro Fontane, engraving of interior (From D. De Rossi, *Studio;* courtesy British Library)
27. Borromini, S. Carlo alle Quattro Fontane, Rome, cupola (author)
28. Borromini, S. Carlo alle Quattro Fontane, Rome, facade (A/AR)
29. Borromini, S. Ivo alla Sapienza, Rome, exterior (ICCD)
30. Borromini, S. Ivo alla Sapienza, Rome, plan (KW)
31. Borromini, S. Ivo alla Sapienza, Rome, interior (author)
32. Borromini, S. Ivo alla Sapienza, Rome, cupola (Witt Library)
33. Borromini, S. Ivo alla Sapienza, Rome, lantern (author), Temple of Venus, Baalbek (From D. S. Robertson, *Greek and Roman Architecture,* 2d ed., Cambridge University Press, 1969, pl. 19a)
34. Borromini, S. Andrea della Fratte, Rome, dome and campanile (A/AR)
35. La Conocchia at Capua Vetere (Bibliotheca Hertziana)
36. Borromini with Giovanni Maria da Bitonto, Palazzo Spada, Rome, perspective colonnade (A/AR)
37. Borromini, Oratory of St. Phillip Neri, Rome, interior (ICCD)
38. Borromini, Oratory of St. Phillip Neri, Rome, exterior (author)
39. Borromini, Collegio di Propaganda Fide, Rome, exterior (author)
40. Borromini, Collegio di Propaganda Fide, Rome, detail of exterior (author)
41. Borromini, Collegio di Propaganda Fide, Rome, interior (ICCD)
42. Bernini, S. Bibiana, Rome, facade (author)
43. Bernini, baldachin in St. Peter's, Rome (A/AR)
44. St. Peter's, Rome, facade with Bernini's tower as it appeared in 1641–46 (From Fontana/Specchi, *Templum Vaticanum;* courtesy British Library)
45. Bernini, St. Peter's Square, Rome, engraving (From G. B. Falda, *Il nuovo teatro;* courtesy New York Public Library)
46. Bernini, St. Peter's Square, Rome, elevation (author)
47. Bernini, St. Peter's Square, Rome, view from colonnade (author)
48. Bernini, Scala Regia, Vatican, section and plan (From Fontana/Specchi, *Templum Vaticanum;* courtesy British Library)
49. Bernini, Scala Regia, Vatican, elevation (A/AR)
50. Bernini, S. Andrea al Quirinale, Rome, plan (KW)
51. Bernini, S. Andrea al Quirinale, Rome, interior (A/AR)
52. Bernini, S. Andrea al Quirinale, Rome, cupola (author)
53. Bernini, S. Andrea al Quirinale, Rome, facade (A/AR)
54. Bernini, S. Tommaso di Villanova, Castel Gandolfo, plan (KW)
55. Bernini, S. Tommaso di Villanova, Castel Gandolfo, interior (From Borsi, *Bernini architetto)*
56. Bernini, S. Tommaso di Villanova, Castel Gandolfo, exterior (Cucco and Carteny)
57. Bernini, S. Maria dell'Assunzione, Ariccia, exterior (author)
58. Pantheon, Rome, exterior (author)
59. Bernini, S. Maria dell'Assunzione, Ariccia, plan (KW)
60. Bernini, S. Maria dell'Assunzione, Ariccia, interior (Fototeca unione)
61. Bernini, Palazzo Chigi, Rome, engraving of exterior (From G. B. Falda, *Il nuovo teatro;* courtesy Bibliotheca Hertziana)
62. Bernini, three projects for the East Facade of the Louvre (From Dell'Arco, *Bernini)*
63. Cortona, Villa Pigneto, Rome, engraving of exterior (From G. Vasi, *Delle magnificenze;* courtesy New York Public Library)

64. Cortona, Ss. Martina e Luca, Rome, plan (KW)
65. Cortona, Ss. Martina e Luca, Rome, interior (ICCD)
66. Cortona, Ss. Martina e Luca, Rome, interior vaulting (ICCD)
67. Cortona, Ss. Martina e Luca, Rome, facade (ICCD)
68. Cortona, S. Maria della Pace, Rome, engraving of piazza (From G Vasi, *Delle magnificenze;* courtesy New York Public Library)
69. Cortona, S. Maria della Pace, Rome, plan (KW)
70. Cortona, S. Maria della Pace, Rome, exterior (A/AR)
71. Cortona, S. Maria della Pace, Rome, corner and palace fronts (author)
72. Cortona, S. Maria in Via Lata, Rome, facade (ICCD)
73. Cortona, project for the Palazzo Chigi in Piazza Colonna, Rome (From Noehles, *Ss. Luca e Martina*)
74. Cortona, dome of S. Carlo al Corso, Rome (author)
75. G. B. Soria, S. Caterina a Magnapoli, Rome, facade (ICCD)
76. Martino Longhi the Younger, S. Antonio dei Portoghesi, Rome, facade (ICCD)
77. Martino Longhi the Younger, Ss. Vincenzo ed Anastasio, Rome, facade (A/AR)
78. Carlo Rainaldi and others, S. Agnese in Piazza Navona, Rome, facade (A/AR)
79. Carlo Rainaldi and others, S. Agnese in Piazza Navona, Rome, plan (KW)
80. Carlo Rainaldi and others, S. Agnese in Piazza Navona, Rome, interior (ICCD)
81. Carlo Rainaldi, S. Maria in Campitelli, Rome, project (From Eimer, *La fabbrica di S. Agnese*)
82. Carlo Rainaldi, S. Maria in Campitelli, Rome, plan (KW)
83. Carlo Rainaldi, S. Maria in Campitelli, Rome, interior (A/AR)
84. Carlo Rainaldi, S. Maria in Campitelli, Rome, facade (A/AR)
85. Reconstruction of Roman Theatre, Aspendus (From Robertson, *Greek and Roman Architecture*)
86. Carlo Rainaldi and others, S. Maria in Montesanto and S. Maria dei Miracoli, Rome, exterior (A/AR)
87. Carlo Rainaldi and others, S. Maria in Montesanto and S. Maria dei Miracoli, Rome, plan (KW)
88. Carlo Rainaldi, Gesù e Maria, Rome, facade (Soprintendente dei Monumenti di Lazio)
89. G. A. De Rossi, Palazzo D'Aste, Rome, facade (author)
90. G. A. De Rossi, S. Maria Maddalena, Rome, plan (KW)
91. Carlo Fontana, S. Rita, Rome, exterior (author)
92. Carlo Fontana, S. Marcello al Corso, Rome, facade (A/AR)
93. Carlo Fontana, Palazzo Bigazzini, Rome, engraving of facade (From Coudenhove-Erthal, *Carlo Fontana*)
94. Carlo Fontana, project for a church in the Colosseum, Rome (From Carlo Fontana, *L'Anfiteatro Flavio;* courtesy Bibliotheca Hertziana)
95. G. O. Recalcati, S. Agata in Trastevere, Rome, facade (author)
96. Giuseppe Sardi, S. Maria del Rosario, Marino, interior (author)
97. Gabriele Valvassori, Palazzo Doria-Pamphili, Rome, Corso facade (author)
98. Filippo Raguzzini, Piazza di S. Ignazio, Rome, isometric view (From Portoghesi, *Roma barocca*)
99. Filippo Raguzzini, Piazza di S. Ignazio, Rome, view (author)
100. Filippo Raguzzini, S. Maria della Quercia, Rome, facade (author)
101. Pietro Passalacqua, Oratory of SS. Annunziata, Rome, facade (author)
102. Francesco de Sanctis, Spanish Staircase, Rome, plan (KW)

103. Francesco de Sanctis, Spanish Staircase, Rome (author)
104. Alessandro Galilei, S. Giovanni in Laterano, Rome, facade (author)
105. Domenico Gregorini assisted by Pietro Passalacqua, S. Croce in Gerusalemme, Rome, facade (author)
106. Ferdinando Fuga, S. Maria Maggiore, Rome, facade (A/AR)
107. Ferdinando Fuga, Palazzo Cenci-Bolognetti, Rome, facade (A/AR)
108. Nicola Salvi, Trevi Fountain, Rome (author)
109. Carlo Marchionni, Villa Albani, Rome, garden facade (ICCD)
110. Lorenzo Binago, S. Alessandro, Milan, plan (KW)
111. Lorenzo Binago, S. Alessandro, Milan, interior (ICCD)
112. Francesco Maria Ricchino, S. Giuseppe, Milan, plan (KW)
113. Francesco Maria Ricchino, S. Giuseppe, Milan, interior (ICCD)
114. Francesco Maria Ricchino, S. Giuseppe, Milan, facade (author)
115. Francesco Maria Ricchino, Seminario Maggiore, Milan, portal (author)
116. Giuseppe Bernasconi, Sanctuary at Varese, fourth chapel (author)
117. Giovanni Ambrogio Mazenta, S. Salvatore, Bologna, plan (KW)
118. Giovanni Ambrogio Mazenta, S. Salvatore, Bologna, interior (author)
119. Giovanni Ambrogio Mazenta, S. Salvatore, Bologna, facade (Villani)
120. Bartolomeo Provaglia, Palazzo Davia-Bargellini, Bologna, facade (A/AR)
121. Bartolomeo Bianco, University of Genoa, courtyard (author)
122. Matteo Nigetti, Church of the Ognissanti, Florence, facade (author)
123. Gherardo Silvani, Palazzo Fenzi, Florence, facade (A/AR)
124. Baldassare Longhena, S. Maria della Salute, Venice, plan and section (From Wittkower, *Art and Architecture in Italy: 1600–1750*)
125. Baldassare Longhena, S. Maria della Salute, Venice, interior (Böhm)
126. Baldassare Longhena, S. Maria della Salute, Venice, exterior (A/AR)
127. Baldassare Longhena, Palazzo Pesaro, Venice, facade (A/AR)
128. Guarini, S. Lorenzo, Turin, plan (From Guarini, *Architettura civile*)
129. Guarini, S. Lorenzo, Turin, interior (author)
130. Guarini, S. Lorenzo, Turin, dome (Rotalcalco Dagnino)
131. Guarini, S. Lorenzo, Turin, exterior (author)
132. Guarini, Chapel of the Holy Shroud, Turin, plan (From Guarini, *Architettura civile*)
133. Guarini, Chapel of the Holy Shroud, Turin, interior (A/AR)
134. Guarini, Chapel of the Holy Shroud, Turin, dome (author)
135. Guarini, Chapel of the Holy Shroud, Turin, section (From Passanti, *Nel mondo magico di Guarino Guarini*)
136. Guarini, project for an unidentified church (From Guarini, *Architettura civile*)
137. Guarini, Palazzo Carignano, Turin, exterior (A/AR)
138. Guarini, Palazzo Carignano, Turin, detail of exterior (Thomas Kren)
139. Guarini, Palazzo Carignano, Turin, plan (KW)
140. Filippo Juvarra, Church of the Superga, Turin, plan (KW)
141. Filippo Juvarra, Church of the Superga, Turin, exterior (A/AR)
142. Filippo Juvarra, Church of the Superga, Turin, interior (author)
143. Filippo Juvarra, Palazzo Madama, Turin, facade (A/AR)
144. Louis Le Vau and J. H. Mansart, Palace at Versailles, garden facade (author)
145. Filippo Juvarra, Palazzo Madama, Turin, stairway (A/AR)
146. Filippo Juvarra, Church of the Carmine, Turin, interior (author)
147. Bernardo Vittone, S. Chiara, Brà, plan (KW)

148. Bernardo Vittone, S. Chiara, Brà, dome (author)
149. Bernardo Vittone, S. Chiara, Brà, exterior (author)
150. Bernardo Vittone, S. Maria della Piazza, Turin, plan (KW)
151. Bernardo Vittone, S. Maria della Piazza, Turin, interior (author)
152. Marco Bianchi, S. Francesco da Paola, Milan, interior (ICCD)
153. Marco Bianchi, S. Francesco da Paola, Milan, facade (author)
154. Bartolomeo Bolli, Palazzo Litta, Milan, facade (A/AR)
155. Andrea Nono, Ss. Trinità, Crema, exterior (A/AR)
156. Domenico Rossi, S. Stae, Venice, facade (Giacomelli)
157. G. A. Scalfarotto, Ss. Simeone e Giuda, Venice, exterior (author)
158. G. A. Scalfarotto, Ss. Simeone e Giuda, Venice, interior (Böhm)
159. Carlo Francesco Dotti, Arco del Meloncello, Bologna (author)
160. Carlo Francesco Dotti, Madonna di S. Luca, Bologna, exterior (author)
161. Carlo Francesco Dotti, Madonna di S. Luca, Bologna, plan (KW)
162. Carlo Francesco Dotti, Madonna di S. Luca, Bologna, interior (author)
163. Francesco Maria Angellini, Palazzo Aldrovandi-Montanari, Bologna, staircase (author)
164. Giovanni Carlo Bibiena, Palazzo Fantuzzi-Garagnani, Bologna, staircase (author)
165. Cosimo Fanzago, Certosa di S. Martino, Naples, courtyard doorways (A/AR)
166. Cosimo Fanzago, S. Maria degli Angeli alle Croce, Naples, exterior (author)
167. Marcello Guglielmelli, S. Angelo a Nilo, Naples, exterior (author)
168. Arcangelo Guglielmelli (?), S. Angelo a Nilo, Naples, interior (Witt Library)
169. Domenico Antonio Vaccaro, Concezione a Montecalvario, Naples, plan (KW)
170. Domenico Antonio Vaccaro, Concezione a Montecalvario, Naples, interior (author)
171. Domenico Antonio Vaccaro, Concezione a Montecalvario, Naples, exterior (author)
172. Domenico Antonio Vaccaro, Palazzo Abbaziale di Loreto, Avellino, exterior (A/AR)
173. Ferdinando Sanfelice, Palazzo Sanfelice, Naples, stairway (author)
174. Ferdinando Sanfelice, Palazzo Di Maio, Naples, stairway (author)
175. Luigi Vanvitelli, Royal Palace at Caserta, exterior (A/AR)
176. Luigi Vanvitelli, Royal Palace at Caserta, staircase (A/AR)
177. Mario Gioffredo, Church of the Spirito Santo, Naples, interior (author)
178. Giuseppe Riccardi, Il Sedile, Lecce, exterior (author)
179. Achille Carducci, S. Matteo, Lecce, facade (author)
180. Giuseppe Zimbalo, Church of the Rosary, Lecce, facade (author)
181. Piazza del Duomo, Lecce (author)
182. Giuseppe Cino, Seminary Palace, Lecce, facade (A/AR)
183. Tommaso Napoli, Villa Palagonia, Bagheria, exterior (author)
184. Andrea Palma, Syracuse Cathedral, facade (A/AR)
185. G. B. Vaccarini, Catania Cathedral, facade (author)
186. G. B. Vaccarini, Palazzo del Municipio, Catania, exterior (author)
187. Rosario Gagliardi, S. Giorgio, Ragusa-Ibla, facade (author)
188. Rosario Gagliardi, S. Chiara, Noto, interior (author)
189. Vincenzo Sinatra, Palazzo del Municipio, Noto, facade (author)

Index